CLASSICAL MONOLOGUES

FROM
AESCHYLUS
TO
BERNARD SHAW

Volume Two: **Older Men's Roles**

COPYRIGHT INFORMATION

CLASSICAL MONOLOGUES

FROM
AESCHYLUS
TO
BERNARD SHAW

Volume Two: **Older Men's Roles**

edited with introductions by **Leon Katz**
with the assistance of **Georgi Iliev**

APPLAUSE
THEATRE & CINEMA BOOKS

Classical Monologues
From Aeschylus to Bernard Shaw
Edited with Introductions by Leon Katz

3 1257 01470 3002

ISBN: 1-55783-576-4

Library of Congress Cataloging in Publication Data
Classical monologues from Aeschylus to Bernard Shaw / edited with introductions by Leon Katz with the assistance of Georgi Iliev.
   p. cm.
   ISBN 1-55783-575-6
1. Monologues.
2. Drama—Collections.
3. Young men—Drama.
I. Katz, Leon, 1919-
   PN2080 .C58 2002
   808.82'45—dc21
   2002004863

British Library Cataloging in Publication Data
A catalogue record for this book is available from the British Library.

Applause Theatre & Cinema
151 West 46th Street
New York, NY 10036
Phone: 212-575-9265
Fax: 646-562-5852
Email: info@applausepub.com

Sales and Distribution

in North America:
HAL LEONARD CORP.
7777 West Bluemound Road
P.O. Box 13819
Milwaukee, WI 53213
Phone: 1-414-774-3630
Fax: 1-414-774-3259
Email: halinfo@halleonard.com
Internet: www.halleonard.com

in the United Kingdom:
COMBINED BOOK SERVICES LTD.
Units I/K, Paddock Wood Distribution Centre
Paddock Wood, Tonbridge, Kent TN12 6UU
Phone: (44) 01892 837171
Fax: (44) 01892 837272
United Kingdom

CONTENTS

ELIZABETHAN/JACOBEAN

XVII CENTURY FRENCH

XIX CENTURY FRENCH/GERMAN

XIX/XX CENTURY ENGLISH

COMEDY

GREEK

XIX CENTURY GERMAN/SCANDINAVIAN

XIX/XX CENTURY ENGLISH

This anthology consists of more than five hundred entries in four volumes, the first two of men's monologues (v.I, for younger, v.II, for older men's roles), the other two for women (v.III for younger, v.IV for older women's roles)[1].

The initial question is of course: what is "classic" and what is "classical"? "Classic" is more easily defined: every movie more than a year old. "Classical" as it pertains to plays is necessarily more difficult to pin down. For practical purposes, it involves some sort of separation from "modern," and the guidelines for that separation might be these: 1) texts that are "classical" are restricted by date to those that are roughly a century away (with a few exceptions which conscience did not permit to be excluded), and 2) texts that are recognizably at a distance from contemporary speech, and that demand a reasonable, sometimes considerable, stretch from an actor's normal rhetorical habits. Under these guidelines, it seems reasonable to include, for example, some 19th century texts from farce and melodrama that have currently unfamiliar dialectal twists (see, for example, Sailor William in *Black-Ey'd Susan*, I, #70)[2], as well as translations that though friendly to contemporary ears are still sufficiently distant from current speech to qualify. These demarcations, like the Mexican border, may be a bit porous, but for practical purposes of audition and workshop, they should hold.

Similarly, the division between "younger" and "older" is also porous. What's young? Before our own age of lengthening longevity, it was more or less the rule, right through the 19th century, that "young" hardly extended beyond the twenties — men possibly to very early thirties, women at the very best to early twenties. But not to be too harsh or doctrinaire, there is added here another, more malleable criterion: the weight of authority, the weight of experience, the dignity of title. Between the two the decision regarding the age of characters remains of course subjective, but the harm to characters' standing or reputation, in whatever category or anthology volume they find themselves, is at most slight.

* * *

Emotion is the beginning, the wellspring, from which we naively suppose actors channel and shape their performances and bring them to life. Well, in a way, yes. But consider: a sequence of thoughts can, conceivably, be expressed with no particular emotion, be understood and accepted as rational communication. Try it the other way around — expressing emotion

---

1 Volumes III and IV to be published in the Fall of 2003
2 Cross-references are cited by Volume and Monologue Number, e.g., "(See II,#45)."

with no particular thought — and you'd be certifiable. Emotion is the ephemera of thought. And the actor's performance begins inside the line of logical connections — not emotional connections — of a text's moment to moment.

This anthology is devoted to the proposition that the intelligence of textual analysis is the first, the primary instrument of performance, and it gives the occasion, in a large number of its instances, for the actor to draw significantly on intellectual acuity preceding any emotional urges. To put it another way, a speech's emotional progression is its logical progression at a second remove. And the particularity and finesse of emotional performance corresponds precisely to the particularity and finesse of its intellectual perception.

With that proposition in mind, the headnotes preceding each of the monologues are of three kinds — sometimes featured singly, sometimes all in one: a description of the speech's strategy; a breakdown of its logical progression; a description of its context. Let's go over them one at a time:

Strategy: (1) The speaker's strategy (his/her intention.) Sometimes it's uniform throughout the speech, and in the labor of defining it, I've seen many, many actors stuck trying to articulate what that uniform intention might be. ("I want love" — no, says the mentor, that's not specific. Alright, "I want to get her into bed" — no, says the mentor, that's not the motive behind the motive. OK, "I want to dominate" — Well, let's talk further about this.) But articulated precisely or not, as likely as not that initial intent may not stay fixed throughout the speech. When it doesn't, the vagaries of the character's mind may dance through a jungle of intents (have a look at Lorenzaccio's remarkable speech when he's getting ready to murder de Medici (see I, #76)) or the speaker taking cues from his listener's silent or spoken reaction, or his own, may alter its direction, or qualify it, or change it altogether. The tendency in classically structured soliloquy is of course to stay doggedly on track, since the soliloquy's private conference with the self is usually working toward the resolution of a dilemma, or working through the likely obstacles to a plan of action, or — and these are the most interesting ones — are governed by battles of conscience whose fixed ideals and unspoken beliefs overwhelm practical intent. Whatever the case may be, the tracking of the "intent's" progress is one task assumed in these headnotes.

(2) The playwright's strategies: They're not formulas but habits. Major speeches tend to fall into distinguishable kinds, and tend to be shaped, by both habit and tradition, into certain formal patterns that remain fairly

fixed throughout the course of Western drama. Some of the most powerful speeches — in, for example, Euripides, Seneca, Schiller, Buchner, and Shaw — are almost identical in their rhetorical structure. Some examples of the most usual ones (it might be helpful if we give them names): the Speech of Justification (among the greatest, the Emperor Augustus in Corneille's *Cinna*); the Speech of Persuasion (among the most moving, Jocasta in Seneca's *Phoenician Women*); the Speech of Denunciation (in which the decibels run from wrath — Theseus in Euripides' *Hippolytus* — to barely audible contempt — Mr. O'Connell's great speech in Granville-Barker's *Waste*); the Formal Narrative Speech (Messengers' recitations of off-stage catastrophes in Greek tragedy, or Rodrigue's recounting of his battlefield triumph in *Le Cid*). All of these formally shaped addresses in which, over and above their dramatic function and emotional investment (which is sometimes enormous and sometimes nil), the actor has also to catch the sheer display involved in the music and the epic scaling of their rhetoric. The playwright's strategy in these passages usually comes as close to aria as it does to flat speech, and not to honor that dimension is like muttering under your breath instead of singing the lyrics of a song.

Logical (sometimes alogical) Progression: Whether rational or deranged, the mind is moving from one notion to the next in a chain of changing assertions that link. Figuring out the exact continuity of those links can be easy — in narratives or in expositions which merely detail a sequence of ordered events. But when the connections are either muffled or random, the work of the actor begins. The headnotes try particularly hard to be helpful in this respect: at the risk of being accused of childishness, they sometimes enumerate unashamedly and naively the steps of these progressions; sometimes — can you believe it? — by the numbers. Why such silliness? Because it is precisely these progressions of linked-but-difficult-to-grasp sense that provide the basis for the emotional progressions which become, only then, the sustaining life of soliloquies.

Context: Obviously, there's the plot, the character, the situation just before, and the surrounding situation that provide the immediate context for individual monologues. The headnotes of course provide necessary information concerning these facts. But there's the larger, enormously significant perspective — the mindset, the contexts of beliefs and assumptions which the plays and their texts inevitably reflect — that the headnotes dwell on too. It's within these structures of belief that plays and speeches harbor their ultimate meanings, and their exploration, certainly in the greatest performances I've been privileged to see, give the ultimate richness of meaning and effect to actors' interpretations.

* * *

On the question of translation, Voltaire still, I think, has the last word. It's discouraging. How close can translation get — to meaning, to tone, to deftness of statement — in translatorese? Voltaire in the 18th century had this to say, and nobody has yet spoken the bad news better:

> It is impossible to convey through any modern language, all the power of Greek expressions; they describe, with one stroke, what costs us a whole sentence…That language had not only the advantage of filling the imagination with a word, but every word, we know, had its peculiar melody, which charmed the ear while it displayed the finest pictures to the mind; and for this reason all our translations from the Greek poets are weak, dry, and poor; it is imitating palaces of porphyry with bricks and pebbles.

What's true for Greek remains as true for modern language translation as well: no language can give up its peculiar music/sense to equivalents in another language. What Molière, for example, suffers in transit from French to English is possibly an exceptionally grim instance of bricks and pebbles making believe they're porphyry. His clarity, his ease, his perfect accommodation of plain sense to the straitjacket of hexameter couplets, when imitated precisely in English, converts into deadly banality, insufferable in expression and plainly laughable in sense. (Goethe, another victim, this editor felt it best to sidestep altogether. Faust in English sometimes marches to the tune and sense of Jack and Jill.)

What to do? Without hoping for true equivalence, for the purposes of actors speaking texts intended to stand in for some of the greatest dramatic passages in other languages, the uneasy solution is simply to avoid the unspeakable, in both senses. No rigid policy was followed: for example, of using only up-to-date, "relevant" (and sometimes hopelessly removed from the original) translations on the one hand, or scrupulously "faithful" (and sometimes hopelessly unspeakable) versions on the other. Compromises, of course, abound — some for reasons of availability, others in the interest of sampling different tacks to a single author's texts when multiple selections from the same author are included. The criterion was, roughly, this: how comfortably can the text sit on the actor's tongue, and how far can it reach toward the overall effect, admittedly very approximate, of the original? And admittedly, you can't win.

1

PROMETHEUS CRIES OUT AGAINST HIS SUFFERINGS WILLED BY ZEUS

(468+ BC) AESCHYLUS, Prometheus Bound, *tr. D. Grene*

Zeus rebelled against his father Cronus, who, with the Titans, had ruled the universe. The Titan Prometheus deserted his brothers in support of Zeus, lending his intelligence to aid Zeus in his victory. Zeus in turn became the ruling despot, and when he desired to destroy mankind, Prometheus, their champion, defended them, and stole for them forbidden fire to advance their struggle toward civilized life. For this transgression, Zeus ordered him chained to a rock in desolate Scythia, where compassionate creatures, the Oceanids (the Chorus), offer him their tears and sympathy.

But Prometheus' lamentation for his punishment is also a cry of defiance against the despotic Zeus, and further, bears the proud certainty of his secret knowledge: that in time, Zeus must be suppliant to *him* if the secret event Prometheus foresees, the event which would bring about Zeus' destruction, is not forestalled by Zeus' learning of it, from Prometheus, in time.

Aeschylus' portrayal of Prometheus' defiance against cruel and omnipotent godhead has become the ultimate symbol of incorruptible moral rebellion against tyranny in Western culture.

> **PROMETHEUS**
> Bright light, swift-winged winds, springs of the rivers, numberless
> laughter of the sea's waves, earth, mother of all, and the all-seeing
> circle of the sun: I call upon you to see what I, a God, suffer
> at the hands of Gods—
> see with what kind of torture
> worn down I shall wrestle ten thousand

years of time—
such is the despiteful bond that the Prince
has devised against me, the new Prince
of the Blessed Ones. Oh woe is me!
I groan for the present sorrow,
I groan for the sorrow to come, I groan
questioning when there shall come a time
when He shall ordain a limit to my sufferings.
What am I saying? I have known all before,
all that shall be, and clearly known; to me,
nothing that hurts shall come with a new face.
So must I bear, as lightly as I can,
the destiny that fate has given me;
for I know well against necessity,
against its strength, no one can fight and win.

I cannot speak about my fortune, cannot
hold my tongue either. It was mortal man
to whom I gave great privileges and
for that was yoked in this unyielding harness.
I hunted out the secret spring of fire,
that filled the narthex stem, which when revealed
became the teacher of each craft to men,
a great resource. This is the sin committed
for which I stand accountant, and I pay
nailed in my chains under the open sky.
Would that he had hurled me
underneath the earth and underneath
the House of Hades, host to the dead—
yes, down to the limitless Tartarus,
yes, though he bound me cruelly
in chains unbreakable,
so neither God nor any other being
might have found joy in gloating over me.
Now as I hang, the plaything of the winds,
my enemies can laugh at what I suffer.

Yes, there shall come a day for me
when he shall need me, me that now am tortured
in bonds and fetters—he shall need me then,
this president of the Blessed—
to show the new plot whereby he may be spoiled
of his throne and his power.
Then not with honeyed tongues
of persuasion shall he enchant me;
he shall not cow me with his threats
to tell him what I know,
until he free me from my cruel chains
and pay me recompense for what I suffer.
I know that he is savage: and his justice
a thing he keeps by his own standard: still
that will of his shall melt to softness yet
when he is broken in the way I know,
and though his temper now is oaken hard
it shall be softened: hastily he'll come
to meet my haste, to join in amity
and union with me—one day he shall come.

new Prince of the Blessed Ones: Zeus **"that filled the narthex-stem"**: the forbidden fire Prometheus stole inside the hollow stem of a narthex plant **house of Hades... Tartarus**: the distance of it from the earth was equal to the distance of the earth from the heavens **"to show... power."** Prometheus, able to foresee the future, is talking about the Titans' rebellion against Zeus

2

THE CHORUS REMEMBERS THE DEAD BROUGHT HOME FROM TROY

(458 BC) AESCHYLUS, Agamemnon, *tr. L. Katz*

The Chorus is a character. In Greek Tragedy, especially in Aeschylus, it has, to be sure, multiple functions, but primary among them is its functional relation, *as a character,* to the central event. In *Agamemnon,* so integral is its characterization to the tragedy's structure that even in the choral odes between dramatic episodes, it sings—and is an actor—in the context of its specific relation to the concurrent event.

But to what aspect of the event? Within the dramatic episodes themselves, the chorus will advise, dissent, worry, hope, etc., as a person would in the circumstance, as a character in a scene. But in the odes between episodes, it responds not merely to the moment, but to the overriding and deepest implications of the drama—in the widest sense, to its moral and religious context. And to these, it speaks from specific character motive, specific character perspective: the old men who did not go to war but sent their sons, the old men too weak to do more than mutter at the anomaly of Clytemnestra's rule with her paramour; the old men of the city who are as much disaffected from their King who went off to a war without moral value or meaning, as they are loyal to him out of habit and custom; the old men who have lived during the years of the war in anger and fear, suffering the horror of their sons being returned to them in ash-filled urns, and living with the dread of what is in store for them and for their king on his return. "The voice of the people is fierce," they sing, "charged with anger and hate." Small wonder that Marx returned to Aeschylus and reread him every year: "Their muffled curse is a promise/ Of doom for the mighty in guilt." There's more than a sliver of difference though between the yearning of Marx and the old men's yearning to stay low, out of the way of the thunderbolt when the "mighty" are toppled by fate. Impotent though the old men are, and insist they are, they imply in this ode a warning against what is later to find open expression in their address to Agamemnon on his return.

The chorus, then, is a collective character, and so can be appropriately voiced by one.

> **CHORUS**
> Many and many the griefs
> That cut to the very heart,
> The saying goodbye to a son,
> A husband, a living man,
> And welcoming back in his place
> A pinch of dust in an urn.
>
> For the God of War, gold-changer
> Of the bodies of the dead,
> Weighs them in scales after battle,
> Transmuting in his flames
> Once-living gold into ashes,
> And the heavy ashes of heroes,
> Back from the wars, at home,
> Are bitterly mourned and remembered.
> One praised for his skill in battle,
> Another, how nobly he died,
> But secretly muttered under
> The breath is the memory:
> "For the sake of a criminal woman!"
> And grief crammed with resentment
> Secretly spreads against
> The twin champions of justice,
> The sons of Atreus,

While others who never returned,
Remaining far from home,
Rest, in the bloom of their youth,
Below the city walls
In the kingdom of Ilium,
Wrapped in the soil they won.

The voice of the people is fierce,
Charged with anger and hate.
Their muffled curse is a promise
Of doom for the mighty in guilt.
What is it I wait for and fear
That is hidden in shadow, in mist?
For those who have spilled the blood
Of many are watched by the gods.
The black Eryinys, the Furies,
Blacken the fates of men
Great, but fattened on evil,
And wither their fortunes to nothing,
Then toss them below among
Multitudes vanished in shadow,
Nothingness, comfortless, lost.

Mocked is the greatness of man
Swollen with glory and praise.
The highest peak is the first
In the path of the thunderbolt.
Let me be lower in luck,
Eyed and envied by none,
No great sacker of cities,
No victim of city's ruin,
Wearing out life as a captive,
Slave to another man's whim.

sons of Atreus: Agamemnon and Menelaos, leaders of the Greek army against
Troy

3

THE CHORUS CONDEMNS HELEN FOR THE RUIN OF TROY

(458 BC) AESCHYLUS, *Agamemnon,* tr. L. Katz

When Clytemnestra learned from beacon signals that Troy had fallen and the war was over, the chorus was skeptical, but soon after, a Herald arrived to confirm the news and to announce the imminent arrival of the victorious Agamemnon. Clytemnestra, overjoyed, sent what were apparently messages of welcome and love to her husband, but the chorus, in its responsive ode, sings only of the inevitability of retribution, expressing no joy at Agamemnon's homecoming but only the inevitability of retributive justice over the pride and arrogance of the great.

They offer two examples: the adulterous Helen's festive welcome into Troy, but out of that feast was born its opposite:"a sudden shift" to vengeful fury; and a lion cub nurtured by a kindly man, but out of that cub, the 'lion-seed' grew to vengeful fury. The chorus is warning of the future—most particularly concerning the still-to-arrive Agamemnon—that the seed of ill implanted at the beginning of an action may remain invisible even through the high moment of its victory, but if it was evil at the start, what will follow is inevitable.

Two notes: their hatred of Helen's act which provoked the war, and their grim assurance of the future's punishing inevitability.

> **CHORUS**
> A story is told of a kindly man
> Who brought to his house a lion's cub
> Robbed of its mother's milk and yet
> Longing to suckle at the breast.

Gently the cub, in infant life
Dear to the young, delight to the old,
Nestled in arms like a nursing child
Bright eye turned to the one who fed,
Licking the hand of the kindly man
Who stilled its belly's growl.

But brought by time to its body's strength,
The lion-seed within it grew
And in recompense for its nurturing
Set for itself a hideous feast,
Slaughtering cattle and flocks of sheep
Defiling the house with corpse and blood.
And they who had fondled and reared the cub
Suffered the anguish of all their store
Leveled in carnage and death,
In anguish learned that they had reared
Destruction's priest, by will of god,
A votary of Ate, Ruin.

So at first there came to Troy
A delectable a windless calm.
The ease of luxury,
The softest glance of the eye,
The flower of love that melts
And breaks the tender heart.
But after the marriage vows
A sudden shift, and she
Who presided over the feast
Managing secretly
Under the eye of Zeus.
Protector of guest and host
Struck down Priam's sons.
Blasted the marriage bed
She who secretly managed the feast,
The Fury, Erinyes.

An ancient proverb has it that
A man's prosperity,
When it has fattened and reached its term,
Breeds evil progeny
So that after his full and happy life
He leaves misery for his sons.
Not so; from those who hold to this,
I stand apart alone:
It is the deed, the crime, that breeds
Crime and evil like itself.
The just, the honored house is blessed
With honorable seed.

Old deeds of sacrilege breed new,
And soon or late, the hour of birth arrives
When he, the young, the new transgressor,
Reckless, irresistible, defiled,
Brings black destruction on his house,
Echoing his father.

Justice walks in huts
And smoke-filled cottages,
And honors dwellers there
Who live in righteousness.
From great, from gilded palaces
Where men's hands are unclean,
Averting eyes, she turns away,
And goes to what is holy.
Bowing before no wealth
Made counterfeit with praise,
She walks, and moves all things
To just, to fated ends.

4

AEGISTHUS REJOICES IN THE DEATH OF AGAMEMNON

(458 BC) AESCHYLUS, Agamemnon, *tr. L. Katz*

After the double murder of Agamemnon and Cassandra, and Clytemnestra's joyful display of their bodies to the citizens (the Chorus), with the certainty of that accomplished fact behind him and in the company of armed bodyguards, Aegisthus feels it safe to appear before the citizens of Argos, triumphant. Gloating over the murder of Agamemnon, with unabashed glee he evokes the name of justice. A savagely inhuman crime had been committed against his father Thyestes by Atreus, the father of Agamemenon: he slaughtered Thyestes' sons and fed their flesh to him. In revenge, Thyestes killed Atreus, and, revenging in turn, his son Agamemnon killed Thyestes. Aegisthus from childhood waited for *his* revenge, "working subtly and with cunning for Agamemnon's ruin." For Aegisthus, it is double revenge: adultery with Agamemnon's wife and the murder which, he claims, he planned.

His life-purpose, Aegisthus claims, is now fulfilled—"Were I to die now, death were sweet to me." There is another intention operating in his speech, which emerges overtly later, but in this first assault against the citizenry's estimate of him, it is only in his tone. It is, though, an important part of his message: that he has total authority over the citizenry now, and it is from now on to be so understood. He holds the reins of power, he genuinely supposes.

(Aegisthus enters with armed retainers)

AEGISTHUS
Done! All hail to justice! It is done!
The gods this moment suffer us to know
That they see well the crimes of men
And claim their vengeance! Here, their victim,
Slaughtered, sprawling in the net they spun,
The loathsome butchery of his father's hand
Paid for in full. Sweet and joyful sight!
It is Atreus, this man's father,
When challenged by Thyestes for his throne,
Who drove Thyestes from his city and his home,
His brother and my father.
When he returned, a suppliant, a beggar,
To his hearth, my broken father found himself
In safety, seeming safety.
He did not suffer death,
Nor stain his native soil with blood,
For he, the godless father of this corpse,
Brother in blood, this Atreus,
Welcomed him with arms thrown wide,
Eager, hearty, but not kind,
And set a feast to celebrate the festive day
When brother met with brother, reconciled.
Ah, but the feast,
The hospitable feast was made of meat,
As banquet for my father's coming home,
Of his own children's flesh.
Toes, fingers of the children were lopped off,
Set in dishes that my father ate,
Unwittingly, not recognizing at the first
How precious was the flesh his brother served.
My father, when he saw, reeled back,
Vomited the slaughtered flesh,
Invoked a curse upon the race of Atreus:
'May all so fall to ruin, all this house's seed!'

Out of this cause, you see the man ruined here.
I it was who planned this murder,
Planned and done with justice.
Together with my ruined, my wretched father,
He drove me out, I, a third born, still in swaddling clothes.
But grown to manhood, justice brought me back.
An exile, distant from the murder's place,
Still I laid my hands upon this enemy,
Worked subtly and with cunning for his ruin.
Were I to die now, death were sweet to me
Now that I see him ruined, justly slain.

I, a third born...: Aegisthus was the third son of Thyestes after the two slaughtered by Atreus

5

AJAX PRETENDS TO BE RECONCILED TO HIS SHAME

(450-440 BC) SOPHOCLES, Ajax, *tr. J. Moore*

Between Ajax and Odysseus, one was to be awarded the arms of the dead Achilles, a tribute to the most honored of Greek warriors. The chieftains, Agamemnon and Menelaus, chose Odysseus. Ajax, mortified by the dishonor, set out in the dead of night to kill the two leaders, but the Goddess Athena, outraged at his pride and violence, caused madness to possess him. Imagining the army's cattle to be warriors, he captured and slaughtered them, and the following morning—at play's opening—having recovered his reason, he is bowed down with shame at what he has done. He asks to see his young son Eurysaces, bids him farewell as though he is intent on suicide: "Nobly to live, or else nobly to die befits proud birth." Tecmessa, his loving concubine-wife, and the chorus of his warrior followers are in painful uncertainty, and dread his apparent decision to kill himself, until he emerges once more to reassure them.

But his speech of reassurance is riddled with ambiguity and double-meaning. His new calm, and the pity he feels for Tecmessa and their son, which presumably persuaded him to reconsider, he speaks of as "womanish." He will go to the sea's edge "to cleanse my stains [By prayer or suicide?]." He'll hide his sword "out of sight" [In the earth or in himself?]. He must give way to heaven and his army rulers "as dread strengths give way... in deference" [To their will? What is it? His death?]. He's learned to study friend as possible foe and foe as possible friend, but knowing that "most men have found friendship a treacherous harbor." He begs his wife to pray for the gods to fulfill "his soul's desire." He is going "where my way must go." And last, his friends may learn that he, though wretched now, may at the end "find safety." The wild determination of the previous episode has simply become his calm determination now.

Sophoclean irony clearly says one thing and darkly means another. The double intent of the speech: to calm his followers on the one hand; on the other, to hold to the integrity of his decision, and, as he sees it, to hold to the ultimate dignity of his being. Irony asks for immense subtlety of understanding and delivery: Ajax is persuading others of his comforting intent; and with the same words, he is confirming its comforting opposite for himself.

(Enter Ajax from the tent with a sword in his hand.)

AJAX
Strangely the long and countless drift of time
Brings all things forth from darkness into light,
Then covers them once more. Nothing so marvelous
That man can say it surely will not be—
Strong oath and iron intent come crashing down.
My mood, which just before was strong and rigid,
No dipped sword more so, now has lost its edge—
My speech is womanish for this woman's sake;
And pity touches me for wife and child,
Widowed and lost among my enemies.
But now I'm going to the bathing place
And meadows by the sea, to cleanse my stains,
In hope the goddess' wrath may pass from me.
And when I've found a place that's quite deserted,
I'll dig in the ground, and hide this sword of mine,
Hatefulest of weapons, out of sight. May Darkness
And Hades, God of Death, hold it in their safe keeping.
For never, since I took it as a gift
Which Hector, my great enemy, gave to me,
Have I known any kindness from the Greeks.

I think the ancient proverb speaks the truth:
An enemy's gift is ruinous and no gift.
Well, then,
From now on this will be my rule: Give way
To Heaven, and bow before the sons of Atreus.
They are our rulers, they must be obeyed.
I must give way, as all dread strengths give way,
In turn and deference. Winter's hard-packed snow
Cedes to the fruitful summer; stubborn night
At last removes, for day's white steeds to shine.
The dread blast of the gale slackens and gives
Peace to the sounding sea; and Sleep, strong jailer,
In time yields up his captive. Shall not I
Learn place and wisdom? Have I not learned this,
Only so much to hate my enemy
As though he might again become my friend,
And so much good to wish to do my friend,
As knowing he may yet become my foe?
Most men have found friendship a treacherous harbor.

Enough: this will be well. You, my wife, go in
And fervently and continually pray the gods
To grant fulfillment of my soul's desire.
And you, my friends, heed my instructions too,
And when he comes, deliver this to Teucer:
Let him take care for me and thought for you.
Now I am going where my way must go;
Do as I bid you, and you yet may hear
That I, though wretched now, have found my safety.

Hector, my great enemy…: after their duel on the battlefield, the Trojan, Hector, in acknowledgement of Ajax's prowess, made him a gift of his sword; it is with this sword that Ajax takes his life **sons of Atreus**: Agamemnon and Meneaus, leaders of the Greek army against Troy **Teucer**: Ajax's half-brother, who later pleads for his care and proper funeral after his death

6

AJAX BIDS FAREWELL TO THE GODS AND ATHENS, AND FALLS ON HIS SWORD

(450-440 BC) SOPHOCLES, Ajax, *tr. J. Moore*

Having reassured his followers that he was not going to his suicide [see II, #5], Ajax then goes to his suicide. The arc of his action during this scene at the sea's edge recapitulates the arc of the tragedy's action as a whole: the stages of his elevation from a contemptible lunatic to an icon of almost more than human value. In both instances, he quite literally "enlarges" beyond the prescriptive limits of a physical self. Note how at the beginning of this scene he is jabbing the sword into the ground, tamping the ground to fix the sword's position, testing the blade, figuring his angle of drop. To say the least, "object"(including himself)-oriented. Then, a loftier level of preparation: care for the dignity of his body after death—prayer for quick discovery (before birds and dogs come by), gentle removal of the sword from his body, a death in one swift motion (not bungled and mangled, but a clean death). Then, larger: revenge by the surrogate action of the Furies against the leaders of the army, and even the army itself, who brought him to his ruin (note the equivalence of the value the Furies are to place on his life and being, and that of the whole Grecian army). Then, enlargement of the theatre, or landscape, of his death by way of the spreading of the news. Finally, the propriety of his bidding farewell not only to his hearth and home, but to the Sun, to Athens, to all the "nurturers" of his life including, remarkably, the very nurturing waters of the plains of Troy, to whom he offers his final gratitude. The rest, he says, echoing a similar egoist, is silence.

*(Enter Ajax. Carefully fixes the sword in place, tamps
down the ground, and feels the edge of the blade)*

AJAX

He's firm in the ground, my Slayer. And his cut
(If I have time even for this reflection)
Should now be deadliest. For, first, the sword
Was Hector's gift, a token of guest-friendship,
And he of all guest-friends my bitterest foe;
Here, too, it stands, lodged in this hostile ground
Of Troy, its edge made new with iron-devouring stone.
And, last, I've propped it, so, with careful handling,
To help me soon and kindly to my death.
This preparation I have made. And now,
Making my invocation, as is right,
I call first, Zeus, on you. Grant me a little thing:
Rouse up some messenger for me, to bear
The news of my disaster first to Teucer,
So that he first may gently lift me up
When I have fallen on this reeking sword.
I would not have some enemy spy me out
And cast me forth, a prize for birds and dogs.
Grant me, O Zeus, this one thing. And do you,
Hermes, Conductor to the Nether World,
Waft me with one swift unconvulsive leap
Upon this piercing blade. And you, Dread Furies—
You who are ever maidens and do watch
Above all fates and sufferings of men—

Come with long strides, my helpers; mark my end,
How Atreus' sons have brought me to my ruin,
And sweep upon them for their ruin too.
They see me falling now by my own hand;
So too by loved and kindred hand may they!
Go, swift—and punishing Erinyes,
Taste the whole army's blood, and spare form nothing.
And you that drive your chariot up the steep

Of Heaven, Lord Helios—when you next shall see
My own dear country, check your golden reins,
And bring the tale of my distressful death
To my old father and to her that nursed me.
Poor mother! When she hears this wretched word,
How her grief's note will quaver through the town!
But I must leave this idle vein of weeping
And set about my business with some speed.
Strong God of Death, attend me now and come.
And yet I shall converse with you hereafter
And know you in the world below. But you,
Sweet gleam of daylight now before my eyes,
And Sun-God, splendid charioteer, I greet you
For this last time and never any more.
O radiance, O my home and hallowed ground
Of Salamis, and my fathers hearth, farewell!
And glorious Athens, and my peers and kin
Nurtured with me, and here all springs and streams,
My nurses, you that wet the plains of Troy,
Farewell! This last word Ajax gives to you;
The rest he keeps, to speak among the dead.

(Befalls on the sword and collapses behind the bushes.)

Hector's gift; **Teucer**; **Atreus' sons**; see II, #5 **Salamis**: an island in the Saronic Gulf

7

CREON ARGUES THE CASE TO HIS SON AGAINST DISLOYALTY AND ANARCHY
(441 BC) SOPHOCLES, Antigone, *tr. Nicholas Rudall*

After the long siege and final battle between the two sons of Oedipus for the rule of Thebes [see monologue 11, Volume I], both are dead, and Creon takes authority as the new king. He buries Eteocles, the defender of the city, with honors, but the "traitor" Polyneices is forbidden burial by anyone on pain of death. Antigone, Oedipus' daughter and Polyneice's sister, refuses to obey Creon's injunction, performs the burial rite, is arrested and brought before Creon. In perhaps the most famous confrontation in Greek tragedy, she poses her allegiance to the unwritten sacred laws against Creon's commitment to the supremacy of the laws of the state. Even though Antigone is engaged to his son Haemon, Creon condemns her to death.

Haemon confronts his father. At first, he offers him undivided loyalty. No marriage, he assures Creon, is more to him than his father's good counsel. On this cue, Creon responding, as he supposes, to assured accord, has little reason to withhold his real beliefs, and so treats his son to an unvarnished recital of his credo. But to Haemon's ears it turns out to be self-condemning. And not to his alone [see II, #8].

Creon's fixed principles are these: (1) first and foremost, there must be absolute obedience to the father's will—for offspring, "the heart's fixed law." (2) A man must never let a woman's (Antigone's) enticements subvert his reason—the enticements of the bed do not last, and once the man is so subverted, the woman is in fact the fixed enemy of his good. (3) As with the father of the household, so the ruler of the state—whoever rules, right or wrong, is owed implicit obedience. (4) The good ruler who knows to command obedience, and knows to submit to it as well, is therefore equally as good a subject and as loyal and trustworthy a companion on the battlefield. (5) Obedience is the guarantee of the safe, good life; chaos and anarchy alone derive from disobedience. Finally, (6) a woman must never best the man, for she will subvert order; her victory over the man *is* the subversion of order.

The most famous understanding of the confrontation between Creon and Antigone—and for decades the most influential—was the philosopher Hegel's, who understood the "principle" defended by Creon and that defended by Antigone to be on a par. Both absolutes, both equal in their moral force, their opposition subject to ultimate reconciliation only at the cost of the human agents'—Creon's and Antigone's—demise. The sacrifice of heroes to, and by, ultimate principle.

But in this expansive, not to say unguarded, speech of Creon's, it's clear that there's more than principle operating in him. Looked at closely, it's rarely the case in Greek tragedy that characters are walking precepts, and certainly not in Sophocles. There's an animus alive in Creon that transcends, or possibly undercuts, the "principle of the law of the state," which, one might notice, is not really what Creon is touting, but the authority of the man—that is, the male, and himself. It's clear that the power of opposition in both Creon and Antigone comes from a power of *person* that in their rhetoric is translated into, and borne by, statements of "principle."

It's the character, not the dicta, of Creon that lives comfortably inside his narrowness of soul, and makes possible the emanations of his dicta, and the tragedy of his acts.

CREON

My son, you have heard my judgment, my last word.

A father prays that he will breed sons who live with him in duty and obedience, hating his enemies and honoring his friends.

But when a son proves good for nothing, what has a man bred but trouble for himself and laughter for his enemies?

My son, do not let desire for a woman rule your mind.

This thing in your arms would soon grow cold when you knew you had a wicked woman for a wife.

A wicked lover in your bed—what knife could cut as deep?

No. Spit her out, devil that she is—let her be a bride in Hell!

She was the only one of all the city to disobey me.

She was caught in the act. She must die.

She can sing a prayer to Zeus, the god of kinship.

If I allowed disobedience in my own family, I would have to allow it everywhere.

If a man is honest and fair in the home, he will gain the public's confidence. I would trust such a man to rule his people well, even to *be* ruled well. In the thick of battle, when the hail of spears fall, he will be there, by your side. But if a man crosses the law, uses force, makes plans to subvert the power of the state, you will never find I have a word of praise for him!

Whoever the state has put in power must be obeyed—in all things, important and unimportant, just and unjust.

Anarchy! There is nothing worse.

Anarchy destroys great cities and hurls great families to the dust. Anarchy breaks the battle lines of great armies.

If men live decent lives it is because *rule of law* is their protector.
We must protect those who live within the law.

I will not be beaten by a woman. If we must lose, let it be to a man.

Is a woman to be seen as stronger than we are?

8

TIRESIAS VIOLENTLY CONDEMNS CREON'S STUBBORNNESS AND FOLLY

(441 BC) SOPHOCLES, Antigone, *tr. Nicholas Rudall*

As the result of the meeting between Creon and his son, Haemon—in rage against his father's inflexibility—determines to die with Antigone [see II, #7]. In the face of his son's rebellion, Creon reinforces his decree against Antigone, and orders her entombed alive.

The blind prophet Tiresias comes to him. He's compassionate toward Creon, who in the past has reverenced his priestly position and his counsel. And compassionately, sorrowfully, he recounts for Creon the results of his sacrificial ministrations: no flames emanate from the carrion that fed on the unburied body of Polyneices, no sacrificial offerings are being accepted by the gods. He begs Creon to reconsider: "Allow the claim of the dead." Tiresias assumes what the source of Creon's decree was—not in law, but in self-will and stubbornness, which add up to folly.

Tiresias' intent is to win Creon's concurrence by gentle persuasion. His speech, in its outcome, will have the opposite effect. Characteristic of these exchanges in Greek tragedy, persuasion comes up against the rock of a fixed intent and/or a level of intensity of intent that makes the persuasive speech seem either irrelevant, crudely calculating, or simply immoral. The rock is the rock of fixity of self-image; each character knows himself as right and reasonable, so much so that he will stand by that reasonableness to the point of madness. The stronger the personal conviction of reason, the more complete the isolation from communally held reasonableness. The consequence in this scene, for example, is that Creon will accuse Tiresias of greed—a priest's lust for money. Given the conviction of Creon's decree, no other explanation seems possible.

(Enter Tiresias led by a boy.)

TIRESIAS

Men of Thebes, we two have come here together, two with the eyes of one.
For this is how blind men walk.

(Creon enters.)

I will speak, but you must trust a prophet's words.
You walk upon a razor's edge.
You will understand when you have heard the meaning of my art.
I sat as of old in the secret haven where I listen to the sacred screams
of birds.
I heard bird cries I have never known.
They screeched mad and inarticulate.
I could hear the murderous tearing of their talons, heard the dying of
their wings.
I was afraid. I lit a fire of sacrifice upon the altar.
The flames refused the flesh and a slimy ooze dripped from the thighs,
sputtered, smoked, and died.
Gall spurted from the bladder and became vapor in the air.
The fat dripped, dripped. But did not burn.

The meaning of my art is clear. The ritual failed.
This boy was my eyes. As I am yours.
The city is diseased because of your decision. Every altar in the town is
glutted with the spewed-out flesh of Polyneices, regurgitated by dogs
and birds...the son of Oedipus.
The gods will accept no sacrifice from us, not prayer nor flesh nor flame.
The birds cry in the air, but I do not understand their cries.
For they are gorged with the oozing blood of the dead.
Think about these things, my son. All men make mistakes.
But a wise and determined man will change his course when he knows
that he is wrong.
He will cure the sickness.
Pride breeds disaster. Yield to the dead.

Why kill the dead a second time?
Listen to me. I speak only for your good.
To learn from such a man as me who knows what is right is not a
painful thing, especially if what he says will do you good.

I sat... birds: according to legend, Tiresias had an "observatory" in Thebes, a place
for watching for omens from birds

9

THE MESSENGER RECOUNTS THE DEATH OF
HAEMON TO HIS MOTHER

(441 BC) SOPHOCLES, Antigone, *tr. P. Arnott*

As in Sophocles' *Oedipus the King,* so in *Antigone* the Prophet
Tiresias becomes so enraged by the counter-accusations of his
king to whom he's offered timely warnings, that he blurts out the
whole of his terrible knowledge of what is to come [see II, #7, 8].
Oedipus ignores it, though it worries him. In this instance, Creon,
learning from the prophet's lips that his son will be dead as a result of
his stiff-necked inflexibility, rushes out in alarm to forestall what is by
now preordained.

This Messenger does not profess, as do other Messengers [see I, #3,
6, 10] significant personal attachment to the figures in his narrative or
to his interlocutor, but he does profess commitment to the most
essential of his obligations: to tell the exact truth, no matter how gruesome or painful. The recognition that he cannot afford to give false
comfort is in itself confession that he bears a painful burden, and that
there is little comfort in what he has to tell. For the actor, there is then
the underlying knowledge that he is delivering serious pain, and the
conflicting urgency for the sake of truth to tell it like it is. The obsta-

cle is his general human compassion; the forward momentum to overcome it is the need to tell the whole truth. But as in other Messenger
speeches, the intensity of the realization of the event itself—both
emotional and factual—and the mesmeric effect of realizing the past
as present, is the overriding intent—and power—of the Messenger's
speech.

MESSENGER
Dear lady, I shall tell you what I saw
Omitting nothing, exactly as it happened.
Why should I give false comfort? You would soon
Know I was lying. Truth is always best.
I attended on your husband to direct his way
Across the plain, where Polyneices' corpse,
Mangled by dogs, still lay unburied.
We prayed the goddess of the roads, and Pluto,
To have mercy on us and restrain their wrath,
Performed the ritual washing of the corpse,
Cut branches and cremated what was left of him
And raised a hillock of his native soil
Above him; then made for the cavern, where the girl
Waited for Death to share her rocky bed.
Far off, one of us heard a piercing cry
Coming from that unholy bridal chamber
And carne to report it to our master Creon.
As he approached, a cry of anguish came
To greet him, half-heard words; he groaned aloud
And in his grief said "Creon, you are doomed;
Can my fear be true? Is the path I tread today
To be the bitterest path I ever trod?
The voice that greets me is my son's; men, run ahead,
Make for the tomb; there is an opening
Where someone has wrenched the stones away. Squeeze inside
To the cell-mouth, see if it is Haemon's voice
I hear, or if the gods are mocking me."

And so, at our despairing master's bidding,
We made the search, and in the farthest corner
Of the tomb we saw her, hanged by the neck
In a noose of twisted linen, soft as silk,
While Haemon stood with his arms clasped round her waist
Weeping for his bride now with the dead,
For his father's actions and his foredoomed marriage.
When he saw him his father gave a fearful cry
And went to him and called to him through his tears,
"Oh Haemon, what is this that you have done?
What has possessed you? Have you gone insane?
Come out, my son, I beg you, I implore you."
But the boy glared back at him wild-eyed,
Spat in his face, and without a word of answer
Drew his cross-hilted sword and thrust at him
But missed, as he jumped aside. Then in wild remorse
The poor wretch threw his weight upon the point
And drove it half into his side. As long as sense
Was left him, he clasped the girl in a limp embrace
And as his breath came hard, a jet of blood
Spurted from his lips, and ran down her pallid cheek.
The bodies lie in each other arms. He has
Claimed his bride—in the next world, not in this.

10

THE CHORUS HYMNS THE WONDERS AND LIMITS OF MAN

(441 BC) SOPHOCLES, Antigone, *tr. Elizabeth Wycoff*

Together with Hamlet's "What a piece of work is man!" this chorus of Sophocles' stands as Western literature's most famous and most encouraging testimonial to human "wonder," with the qualification that Sophocles, unlike Shakespeare, adds a codicil to his eulogy: we're subject finally to death and, if we choose it, to evil.

But this chorus has a different intent from others that are distinctly relevant to the context of the ongoing action. This one is not so fitted, except in the most general way. In general reference, it is truly a hymn, a paean of praise, like the hymnal choruses in praise of random gods. More specifically, its warning at the end may possibly be taken to have relevance to Creon's and Antigone's divided commitments: "When he honors the laws of the land, *and* [that is, *both*] that justice" belonging to the gods, then his city will stand "proudly." But the *aim* of this choral song, its addressee, so to speak, is in fact—as it is in all such eulogies—its own subject; in this case, humanity.

> **CHORUS**
> Many the wonders but nothing walks stranger than man.
> This thing crosses the sea in the winter's storm,
> making his path through the roaring waves.
> And she, the greatest of gods, the earth—
> ageless she is, and unwearied—he wears her away
> as the ploughs go up and down from year to year
> and his mules turn up the soil.

Gay nations of birds he snares and leads,
wild beast tribes and the salty brood of the sea,
with the twisted mesh of his nets, this clever man.
He controls with craft the beasts of the open air,
walkers on hills. The horse with his shaggy mane
he holds and harnesses, yoked about the neck,
and the strong bull of the mountain.
Language, and thought like the wind
and the feelings that make the town,
he has taught himself, and shelter against the cold,
refuge from rain. He can always help himself.
He faces no future helpless. There's only death
that he cannot find an escape from. He has contrived
refuge from illnesses once beyond all cure.
Clever beyond all dreams
the inventive craft that he has
which may drive him one time or another to well or ill.
When he honors the laws of the land and the gods' sworn right
high indeed is his city; but stateless the man
who dares to dwell with dishonor. Not by my fire,
never to share my thoughts, who does these things.

11

TIRESIAS, PROVOKED BY OEDIPUS, REVEALS ALMOST THE WHOLE OF THE ORACLE'S PRONOUNCEMENT

(430-425 BC) SOPHOCLES, Oedipus the King, *tr. W.B. Yeats*

King Laius and Queen Jocasta of Thebes were warned by oracle that their offspring would kill his father and wed his mother. To forestall this eventuality, the son was given to a shepherd to be killed. Sparing the child instead, the shepherd gave him to a shepherd of

Corinth, and the child was raised by the Corinthian King and Queen. When Oedipus reached manhood, the Delphic oracle informed him of his destiny. To escape this fate, he fled Corinth, but in the course of a quarrel on the road with another chariot-rider, Oedipus killed him—his father Laius. At Thebes, the Sphinx was holding the city hostage by means of its riddle; failure to answer it meant death. Oedipus, quickly solving it, was hailed as the city's savior, and so won the hand of the recently-widowed Queen Jocasta—his mother. Celebrated for his wisdom, he reigned for many years, siring four children—Antigone, Ismene, Eteocles and Polyneices. Suddenly a plague struck Thebes, and Oedipus, responding to his people's pleas, sent Creon and the blind prophet Tiresias to consult the Delphic oracle as to its cause. Learning from Creon the cause—the still-unpunished murderer of Laius—Oedipus vowed to find him and punish him.

When confronting Tiresias, Oedipus is certain that the prophet knows the culprit's identity, and is angered by his refusal to divulge it. His humiliating taunting of the prophet finally causes Tiresias furiously to blurt out the truth: "You are yourself the murderer you seek." His intent? No longer compassionate, as his preliminary hesitation had been, longing to spare Oedipus the suffering of knowing. Now humiliated and enraged, he not only bares his horrible tidings, but bares them vindictively. His intent is plainly to cause Oedipus the deepest possible suffering, and the vindictiveness of that intent grows throughout his speech. But, as is so characteristic of Greek tragedy confrontation, self-image can be impervious to assault, though in this instance, a doubt is planted to which Oedipus later partially succumbs [see II, #12].

TIRESIAS

Rage if you have a mind to; bring out all the fierceness that is in your heart. I charge you to obey the decree that you yourself have made, and from this day out, to speak neither to these nor to me. You are the defiler of this land. You are yourself the murderer that you seek. I say that you are living with your next of kin in unimagined shame. And you are but a poor wretch flinging taunts that in a little while everyone will fling at you. You are your own enemy.

King though you are, the right to answer when attacked belongs to both alike. I am not subject to you, but to Apollo. And I tell you, since you have taunted me with blindness, that though you have your sight, you cannot see in what misery you stand, nor where you are living, nor with whom, unknowing what you do for you do not know the stock you come of—you have been your own kin's enemy be they living or be they dead. And one day a mother's curse and father's curse alike shall drive you from this land in dreadful haste with darkness upon those eyes. Therefore heap your scorn on my message if you have a mind to; for no one of living men shall be crushed as you shall be crushed.

This day shall you know your birth, and it will ruin you. I will go: boy, lead me out of this. But first I will do my errand. For frown though you may you cannot destroy me. The man for whom you look, the man you have been threatening in all the proclamations about the death of Laius, that man is here. He seems, so far as looks go, an alien; yet he shall be found a native Theban and shall nowise be glad of that fortune. A blind man, though now he has his sight; a beggar, though now he is most rich; he shall go forth feeling the ground before him with his stick; so you go in and think on that, and if you find I am in fault say that I have no skill in prophecy.

12

OEDIPUS CONFESSES HIS HAUNTING DOUBTS TO JOCASTA

(430-425 BC) SOPHOCLES, Oedipus the King, *tr. W. B. Yeats*

Oedipus confides in his wife Jocasta a horrible doubt, a terror overtaking him: that he is the guilty man he seeks [see II, #11]. His intent? Not simply to confess his doubt, but to win collaboration in removing his doubt, which, if it became certainty, would be beyond bearing. The arc of the speech is therefore this: by telling the facts, by reciting all the factors that weigh on his doubt, to make it *increasingly difficult* for Jocasta to offer comfort sufficient to remove the doubt. With increasing intensity and emotional/rhetorical investment in a gathering certainty, with an ever-growing barrage of damning facts and a solid case inescapably confirming his guilt, the burden of proof of his innocence is entirely given over to his confidante. Only if she succeeds in overriding this massive accumulation of damning facts and logic can he be free of this terror. Save me from my certainty! That is his yearning.

OEDIPUS
It shall not be kept from you now that my fear has grown so heavy. Nobody is more to me than you, nobody has the same right to learn my good or evil luck. My father was Polybus of Corinth, my mother the Dorian Merope, and I was held the foremost man in all that town until a thing happened—a thing to startle a man, though not to make him angry as it made me. We were sitting at the table, and a man who had drunk too much cried out that I was not my father's son—and I, though angry, restrained my anger for that day; but the next day went to my father and my mother and questioned them. They were indignant at the taunt and that comforted me—and yet the man's words

rankled, for they had spread a rumor through the town. Without consulting my father or my mother I went to Delphi, but Phoebus told me nothing of the thing for which I came, but much of other things—things of sorrow and of terror: that I should live in incest with my mother, and beget a brood that men would shudder to look upon; that I should be my father's murderer. Hearing those words I fled out of Corinth, and from that day have but known where it lies when I have found its direction by the stars. I sought where I might escape those infamous things—the doom that was laid upon me. I came in my flight to that very spot where you tell me this king perished. Now, lady, I will tell you the truth. When I had come close up to those three roads, I came upon a herald, and a man like him you have described seated in a carriage. The man who held the reins and the old man himself would not give me room, but thought to force me from the path, and I struck the driver in my anger. The old man, seeing what I had done, waited till I was passing him and then struck me upon the head. I paid him back in full, for I knocked him out of the carriage with a blow of my stick. He rolled on his back, and after that I killed them all. If this stranger were indeed Laius, is there a more miserable man in the world than the man before you? Is there a man more hated of Heaven? No stranger, no citizen, may receive him into his house, not a soul may speak to him, and no mouth but my own mouth has laid this curse upon me. Am I not wretched? May I be swept from this world before I have endured this doom!

13

OEDIPUS BIDS FAREWELL TO HIS DAUGHTERS

(430-425 BC) SOPHOCLES, Oedipus the King, *tr. P. Arnott*

It's more than likely that the greatest, most affecting reversal in dramatic literature is that of Oedipus' discovery of his human anomaly, as one critic put it, the journey—at a single word—*You*—from being One, unique, to being Zero, nothing.

Oedipus' doubt has been confirmed: he is in fact the one guilty of patricide and incest on whom the city's fate had hung. At their discovery, as reported by the Messenger [see I, #3], Jocasta fled into the palace and hung herself, and Oedipus, at the sight of her body, blinded himself with her brooch. He emerges, stumbling and blind, laments his misery, cries aloud his self-hatred [see II, #14] then begs Creon to bring his daughters to him: "Suffer me to touch them with my hands." He addresses his farewell to them, but also to Creon.

His intention is not only to sorrow with them, but to make clear to them their limits of life fulfillment, given, as will be known now, their heritage of shame. And so, no companionship, no marriages, no children. In consequence, he turns to Creon and visits on him the responsibility for preserving his daughters from utter misery and want. Winning Creon's assent—"Touch my hand and say yes"—he has, subsequently, only one more request: to be banished from his city.

It is, in other words, not merely a scene of tears. Still sensitive to more than his own grief, Oedipus makes his final, and practical, dispositions—reduced to negative injunctions though they may be.

> **OEDIPUS**
> Bless you for your trouble. May you find
> A kinder fate than what has come to me.
> Where are you now, my children? Over here:

Come to these hands of mine, your brother's hands,
Whose offices have made your father's eyes
That were once so bright, to see as they see now.
For the truth is out; your father, stupid, blind,
Begot you in the womb where he was born.
Sight have I none, but tears I have for you
When I think of how you will be forced to live
At men's hands in the bitter days to come.
What gathering of the folk will you attend,
What festival that will not send you home
In tears, instead of making holiday?
And when the time has come for you to marry,
Show me the man, my children, bold enough
To take upon his own head such disgrace,
The stain that you and your brothers will inherit.
What sorrow is not ours? Your father killed
His father, sowed his seed in her
Where he was sown as seed, and did beget you
In the selfsame place where he was once begotten.
That is how men will talk. Then who will marry you?
No-one, my children. Marriage is not for you.
You must be barren till your lives are done.
Son of Menoeceus, you are the only father
These girls have left, for we, their parents,
Are both of us gone. So do not let them wander
Beggared and husbandless. They are your kin.
And do not level them with my misfortunes
But pity them. You see how young they are.
You are the only friend they have in the world.
Touch me, kind heart, in token of your promise.
Children, if you were old enough to understand,
There is much I could say to help you. As it is,
Pray after me—to live with moderation
And better fortune than your father did.

Son of Menoeceus: Creon, the brother of Jocasta

14

OEDIPUS CONDEMNS HIMSELF TO EXILE AND DEATH

(430-425 BC) SOPHOCLES, Oedipus the King, *tr. D. Grene*

After his self-blinding [see II, #13], Oedipus stumbles out of the palace, and in a long wail of lamentation and knifing of his soul with words, makes words approximate in so far as they can the ultimate punishment of sin as great as his—the greatest, he conceives, of which a human soul is capable. But again, as in *Ajax* [see II, #5], it is not random howling—there is an arc to the utterance that mirrors its emotional logic. And again as in *Ajax,* the arc begins with the immediate, the physical—("This fog, this horrible darkness all around me!")—and step by step enlarges its emotional orbit with increasingly harrowing articulations of moral pain—("Men know nothing more abominable... hide me in some wilderness, or strike me dead, or throw me in the sea.")

> **OEDIPUS**
> O, O,
> where am I going? Where is my voice
> borne on the wind?
>
> Darkness!
> Horror of darkness enfolding, resistless, unspeakable visitant sped by
> an ill wind in haste!
> madness and stabbing pain and memory
> of evil deeds I have done!
>
> It was Apollo, friends, Apollo,
> that brought this bitter bitterness, my sorrows to completion.
> But the hand that struck me
> was none but my own.

Why should I see
whose vision showed me nothing sweet to see?
What can I see to love?
What greeting can touch my ears with joy?
Take me away, to a place out of the way!
Take me away
the most accursed, whom God hates
above all men on earth!
Curse on the man who took
the cruel bonds from off my legs, as I lay in the field.
He stole me from death and saved me.

Now I am godless and child of impurity,
begetter of the same seed that created my wretched self.
If there is any ill worse than ill,
that is the lot of Oedipus.
What I have done here was best done.
Do not give me further counsel.

Would the sight
of children, bred as mine are, gladden me?
No, not these eyes, never. And my city,
its towers and sacred places to the Gods,
of these I robbed my miserable self
when I commanded all to drive him out,
the criminal since proved by God impure.
To this guilt I bore witness against myself—
with what eyes shall I look upon my people?
No. If there were a means to choke the fountain
of hearing I would not have stayed my hand
from locking up my miserable carcass,
seeing and hearing nothing; it is sweet
to keep our thoughts out of the range of hurt.

O Polybus and Corinth and the house,
the old house that I used to call my father's—
what fairness you were nurse to, and what foulness
festered beneath! Now I am found to be

a sinner and a son of sinners. Crossroads,
the narrow way
at the crossroads, that drank my father's blood
offered you by my hands, do you remember
still what I did as you looked on, and what
I did when I came here? O marriage, marriage!
you bred me and again when you had bred
bred children of your child and showed to men
brides, wives and mothers and the foulest deeds
that can be in this world of ours.

Come—it's unfit to say what is unfit
to do.—I beg of you in God's name hide me
somewhere outside your country, or kill me,
or throw me into the sea, to be forever
out of your sight. Approach and deign to touch me
for all my wretchedness, and do not fear.
No man but I can bear my evil doom.

15

THESEUS CASTIGATES HIS SON HIPPOLYTUS FOR ADULTERY

(428 BC) EURIPIDES, Hippolytus, *tr. D. Grene*

Theseus' confrontation with his son [see I, #4, 5] following the suicide of his wife Phaedra and the note she left accusing Hippolytus of defiling her, focuses more on the outrage of the father than of the husband. What exacerbates his rage is what he takes to be the simple, ineffective play-acting of Hippolytus, pretending to know nothing of the reason for Phaedra's death, and to have no inkling of what his father means by his odd references to teaching fools the way to sense, and finding ways to test the truth of friends. But it's Hyppolytus' innocence of the charge that makes his performance seem so remarkably brazen to his father. And so Theseus storms first at the villainy of each generation outdoing the previous one, and wondering if the planet will be large enough to hold the coming race of villains.

This outburst is followed, though, by the characteristic Euripidean formal structuring of a speech's logic. From point to point: (1) The thesis to be substantiated: Hippolytus is vile and false, as proved by Phaedra's suicide note. (2) First argument: the evidence of his very person—a mocking, satiric characterization of what he supposes is his son's pretense of purity; so chaste he walks with the gods; so pure he's a committed vegetarian and worships art and music (Apollo); so studious he reads himself foolish in philosophy [Note the targets of distrust by the culturally crude old warrior]. (3) Second and clinching argument: But I've found out the villainous son behind that cover of purity; *from the evidence of Phaedra's note,* he's confirmed guilty. (4) Answer to the defense's first counter-argument, as Theseus anticipates it (that she hated Hippolytus as the bastard son of a former lover): if so, she chose a somewhat expensive way of destroying him, at the cost of her own life. (5) Answer to defense's second counter-argument, as anticipated (that kind of thing is inborn in women, it's their nature): young men disturbed by love are moved to become at least as untrustworthy, as false, as woman's nature. (6) Thesis proved: final verdict—exile.

So much for the logical intent of Theseus' speech; its emotional intent is to wither his son with a sarcasm that brooks no answer, its demeaning sneer implying so high a moral outrage that his attack must result in—at the very least—Hippolytus' confession of guilt. It does not [see I, #5].

THESEUS

The mind of man,—how far will it advance?
Where will its daring impudence find limits?
If human villainy and human life
shall wax in due proportion, if the son
shall always grow in wickedness past his father
the gods must add another world to this
that all the sinners may have space enough.
Look at this man! He was my son and he
dishonors my wife's bed! By the dead's
testimony he's clearly proved the vilest, falsest wretch.
Come,—you could stain your conscience with the impurity,—
show me your face; show it to me, your father.
You are the veritable holy man!
You walked with gods in chastity immaculate!
I'll not believe your boasts of gods' companionship:
the gods are not so simple nor so ignorant.
Go, boast that you eat no meat, that you have Orpheus
for your king. Read until you are demented
your great thick books whose substance is as smoke.
For I have found you out. I tell you all,
avoid such men as he. They hunt their prey
with holy-seeming words, but their designs
are black and ugly. 'She is dead' you thought,
'and that will save me.' Fool, it is chiefly that
which proves your guilt. What oath that you can swear,
what speech that you can make for your acquittal
outweighs this letter of hers? You'll say, to be sure,
she was your enemy and that the bastard son
is always hateful to the legitimate line.
Your words would argue her a foolish merchant
whose stock of merchandise was her own life
if she should throw away what she held dearest
to gratify her enmity for you.
Or you will tell me that this frantic folly
is inborn in a woman's nature; man
is different: but I know that young men

are no more to be trusted than a woman
when love disturbs the youthful blood in them.
The very male in them will make them false.
But why should I debate against you in words?
Here is the dead, surest of witnesses.
Get from this land with all the speed you can
to exile,—may you rot there! Never again
come to our city, god-built Athens, nor
to countries over which my spear is king.

16

PELEUS REVILES MENELAUS AND HIS WIFE HELEN

(417-415 BC) EURIPIDES, Andromache, *tr. M. Hadas and J. H. McLean*

Andromache is a domestic melodrama—particularly in the role of Andromache. It is some years after the fall of Troy. Neoptolemus, the son of the Greek hero Achilles, won the Trojan princess Andromache for his concubine and has since fathered a son by her, Molossus. But he has also married Hermione, the daughter of Menelaus and Helen (because of whose absconding to Troy the Trojan War was fought). Hermione's intense jealousy of Andromache moves her and her father to plan for the death of both the concubine and her son. The ruler of Thessaly is the dead Achilles' father Peleus, an old but still vigorous man of astonishing personal force.

Menelaus has now come from Sparta to help his daughter in carrying out the murder while, conveniently for them, Neoptolemus is away. Villainously, Menelaus offers spurious justifications for his authority—even in a foreign land—to execute his daughter's rival. With his soldiers, he's succeeded in tying up Andromache hand and foot, as her son clings to her. While Andromache is helpless and crying bitterly, on the verge of execution, old King Peleus arrives just in the nick of time. (Melodramatist Euripides had no shame.)

Not only does Peleus, in the face of Menelaus' troops, demand they instantly unbind Andromache, but in the same breath attacks Menelaus—a king in his native Sparta, but in Peleus' kingdom, a villain beneath contempt. Doing two things at once—supervising the unshackling of the maiden and tongue-lashing the foreign king— Peleus lays out a catalogue of incriminating indecencies of past conduct—of Menelaus, of his wife Helen's and Spartan girls' shamelessness, and of Sparta as such—that is intended to humiliate Menelaus into blushing shame. Of course, it doesn't; Menelaus replies subsequently at equal length and with equal vigor, but, as is Euripides' particular skill, abases his own argument even in its making.

Peleus is then provoked even further, and [in II, #17] raises both the decibel count of his wrath and the scope of his denunciatory argument against Menelaus. It is army generals like Menelaus who are given credit for the work of the footsoldiers braver and wiser than their stupid generals can ever be. As for foes, I will not only boot you out of Thessaly now, he yells, but have my son boot out his barren wife, your daughter, and we here in Thessaly will be more than happy to settle for the offspring of the concubine. Turning his back on the Spartans, with a single final insult tossed at them over his shoulder, he helps Andromache out of her bindings with compassion and care, ready to take her off.

For Peleus, the underlying focus of all this is his strong intent to guarantee total reassurance to Andromache and her son that they are as safe as though the Spartans were not even there. His roar of authority—he is accompanied by only one attendant—effectively outweighs the collective show of strength of Menelaus and his clutch of soldiers.

PELEUS

It's you I am asking—you who are supervising this slaughter—what
are you up to? What is the meaning of it? Whose word started this
rebellion? What do you mean by taking the law into your own hands?
What right had they to bind your arms with ropes and hale you off,
you and your child? Loose her, I command you. Untie the ropes that
bind her hands together.

Will you come here and meddle in my affairs? Isn't it enough for you
to lord it over the Spartans? Do you even count as a man, a coward
like your fathers before you? Where is your place in the catalogue of
men? Weren't you robbed of your wife by a mere Phrygian? You left
the rooms of your house without bolts or duennas, as if that wife you
had, the wickedest of her sex, were a chaste woman!

Spartan girls could not be chaste even if they wanted to. They leave
home, and with naked thighs and their dresses loosened, they share
the running tracks and gymnasiums with the young men. I call it
intolerable. And then are we to be surprised that the women you
bring up are not chaste? Helen might well have asked that question
when she left your palace and your sanctified love and went gallivanti-
ng off to another country with her young man. And what followed?
For her sake you assembled all that throng of Greeks and led them to
Ilium. When you discovered her wickedness, you ought to have reject-
ed her with loathing, instead of starting a war for her. Yes, you should
have let her stay where she was and even paid money not to take her
back home. But your mind took a different tack; you sacrificed many
good lives, you made old women look in vain for their children's
return, you robbed old fathers of their noble sons. I myself, alas! am
one of these. In my eyes you are the devil that murdered Achilles. You
alone came back from Troy without even a sword-scratch. Your untar-
nished armor in its fair coverings returned with you as good as it went.

I warned Neoptolemus, before the marriage, not to form any connec-
tion with you or take into his home the foal of an unchaste woman.
But there's more. The hideous wrong you did your brother, when you

stupidly demanded the sacrifice of his daughter. You were so afraid you would lose your worthless wife. And when you had taken Troy, you did not slay the woman when you had her at your mercy. No! as soon as you saw her breasts, you threw away your sword and took a kiss, fawning on the treacherous bitch, quite unable to resist her charms, you spineless creature! And after all that, you come to my grandson's house, in his absence, and pillage it. An unfortunate woman you put to a shameful death, and her son too.

Take your daughter back home with you. Men had better choose their friends and relations from the humble and honest than from the wealthy and wicked. But you are nothing at all.

Phrygian: Paris **foal**: a colt; here, a child, pejorative

17

PELEUS, OUTRAGED AT HIS ARMY'S TREATMENT OF ANDROMACHE, HELPS HER TO SAFETY
(417-415 BC) EURIPIDES, Andromache, *tr. M. Hadas and J.H. McLean*

[see II, #16]

PELEUS

How stupid is our Greek custom! When armies raise trophies over an enemy, we do not regard the victory as the work of the privates; it is the general who carries off the laurels. Yet he is only one man, wielding his lance with ten thousand others and doing no more than any one of them, but getting more credit than all of them. Seated solemnly in office, wherever they go, they think they are better than the common people; but they are themselves nobodies. The ordinary man is a thousand times cleverer than they; he only lacks their effrontery and ambition. So you and your brother sit back swollen with pride because of Troy and the service you saw there, but your glory rests on the labors and sacrifices of others. I shall teach you never to think Trojan Paris a more dangerous enemy than Peleus, if you don't get the devil out of this house as fast as you can, and your barren daughter with you. My grandson will drag her by the hair from room to room. A barren cow herself, with no children of her own, she cannot stand others having any. If she has the bad luck to be barren, is that a reason why we should be deprived of descendants? Take your cursed hands off her, you slaves. Let me see if anybody will stop me from untying this woman's hands.

(to Andromache) Lift yourself up. Trembling though I am, I shall loosen the twisted, knotted thongs. Oh look! you scoundrel, how you have disfigured her hands! Did you think you were roping a steer or a lion? Or were you afraid that she might seize a sword and drive you off? Come here, my child, come under my arms. Help me to untie your mother's bonds. I shall yet raise you up in Phthia to be an enemy to these Spartans. Lead on, my child. Stand here under my arms, and you too, poor woman. You ran into a fierce storm, but you have reached a sheltered anchorage. Go. Who will touch you? Whoever does will be sorry. By the favor of heaven I have hosts of horsemen and many foot-soldiers at my command in Phthia. I am not yet bowed down by age. A man like that I shall face alone and triumph over him. Even an old man, if his heart is in the right place, is a better man than many a youngster. What's the use of a young physique to a coward?

you and your brother: the two Greek generals Menelaus and Agamemnon
Phthia: a city in Thessaly (northern Greece), birthplace of Achilles, still ruled by his father Peleus

18

HERACLES, DYING IN AGONY, CURSES THE WIFE WHO SENT HIM THE POISONED SHIRT
(413 BC) SOPHOCLES, The Women of Trachis, *tr. M. Jameson*

Heracles is borne in on a litter by his son Hyllus and attendants; he is just waking, brought back to consciousness by the incredible pain he is suffering. Wrapped in a cloak, or shirt, glued to his body, the poison in it eats away at his flesh. It is the end of the saga of one of the most powerful and legendary of the heroes of Greek myth.

His agony is intermittent: excruciating jabs of pain, moments of remission. His cries and lamentations pursue three themes; first and foremost is his response to the agony of his pain and his pitiful anxiety at exhibiting the horrible condition of his body. Then, he appeals to his son to bring his wife Deianeira to him to destroy her, she who, he supposes, knowingly and treacherously inflicted the poisoned coat on him. Then, the recollection of who he was, and comparison of the exploits he accomplished and victories he won and pain he suffered "always without a groan," with the torment he is now undergoing and the "womanishness" of the wails with which he is responding to it. It is not just his pain, then, but the reduction of himself to a helpless sniveler that horrifies and disgusts him.

But Heracles is ignorant of the actual treachery that led to this suffering. After his rescue of Deianeira from the river-god Achelous and their marriage, in their flight they came to the river over which the centaur Nessus ferried travelers. During the crossing, Nessus' attempt to violate Deianeira caused Heracles, in a rage, to shoot him with a poisoned arrow. But as Nessus was dying, he urged Deianeira to take some of the blood from his wound and use it as a charm to win back Heracles should he ever prove unfaithful to her. It is the poisoned blood smeared on the Nessus shirt that Deianeira unwittingly sent to Heracles for his voyage home, following her fears of his unfaithfulness, that accomplishes Nessus' revenge.

In his agony now, Heracles remembers his heroic exploits—some of the labors imposed on him by Eurystheus (the famous Twelve Labors of Hercules):

1) "the lion that prowled the land of Nemea:" the rampaging lion Heracles killed, and then flayed, and then always afterward wore its pelt;

2) "the serpent of Lerna:" the Lernaen Hydra, who possessed a dog-like body and a multitude of heads, its venom so deadly that its breath or smell alone could kill. After defeating the Hydra, Heracles dipped his arrows in its gall, which rendered them forever poisonous.

3) "the double-bodied, hostile beasts:" the Centaurs, with human upper body and body of horse below, who assailed Heracles and his centaur host Pholis, tossing rocks, trees, firebrands and axes at them. In a raging battle, some were killed by Heracles, the rest fled;

4) "the boar of Erymanthus:" an enormous beast whom Heracles was to take alive, a task he accomplished by immobilizing it in a snow-drift, leaping on its back and so enchaining it.

5) "the hellhound with three heads:" Cerberus, the guardian dog of Tartarus, the world below. In Heracles' twelfth and most difficult labor, he was to capture the dog and bring him back to earth above. Under Hades' injunction to use no weapons, Heracles throttled the three heads with his bare hands, won the dog's surrender, and brought him forth.

6) "[the dragon] guarding the golden apples:" the dragon Ladon coiled around the golden apple tree, was set there by Hera to prevent the daughters of Atlas, the Hesperides, from stealing the apples. Heracles' task was to bring away some of the apples. He does, by killing the dragon, and tricking Atlas into surrendering the apples *he* had stolen.

But all Heracles' agonies and yearnings finally focus on one objective: to persuade his son Hyllus to bring his mother forward, so that Heracles—"even if I am nothing that can even crawl"—can revenge himself on her supposed treachery.

HERACLES
Many are the toils for these hands, this back,
that I have had, hot and painful even to tell of.
But neither the wife of Zeus nor hateful Eurystheus
has ever condemned me to such agony as this
that the false-faced daughter of Oeneus has fastened
upon my shoulders, a woven, encircling net
of the Furies, by which I am utterly destroyed.
It clings to my sides, it has eaten away
my inmost flesh; it lives with me and empties the channels
of my lungs, and already it has drunk up
my fresh blood, and my whole body is
completely killed, conquered by these unspeakable fetters.
Neither the spear of battle, nor the army of
the earth-born Giants, nor the violence of beasts,
nor Greece, nor any place of barbarous tongue, not all
the lands I came to purify could ever do this.
A woman, a female, in no way like a man,
she alone without even a sword has brought me down.

O my son, now truly be my true-born son
and do not pay more respect to the name of mother.
Bring her from the house with your own hands and put
her in my hands, that woman who bore you, that I may know
clearly whether it pains you more to see *my* body
mutilated or *hers* when it is justly tortured.
Come, my child, dare to do this. Pity me,
for I seem pitiful to many others, crying
and sobbing like a girl, and no one could ever say
that he had seen this man act like that before.
Always without a groan I followed my painful course.

Now in my misery I am discovered a woman.

Come close to me now, stand by your father and
look well at my misfortune, see what I suffer.
I shall take off the coverings and show you. Look,
all of you, do you behold this poor body?
Can you see how miserable, how pitiful I am?

Oh, oh, the pain!
That malignant tearing scorches me again,
it shoots through my sides, it will have me struggle,
it will not let me be—miserable, devouring sickness.
O King Hades, receive me!
O flash of Zeus, strike!
Drive against me, O King, hurl down the bolt
of lightning, Father. Now it feeds on me again,
it has sprung out, it blooms. O my hands, my hands,
O my back, my chest, O my poor arms, see
what has become of you from what you once were.
The lion that prowled the land of Nemea, that scourge of herdsmen,
that unapproachable, intractable creature,
with your strength once you overpowered it,
and the serpent of Lerna and that galloping army
of double-bodied, hostile beasts, violent, lawless,
supremely strong, and the boar of Erymanthus,
and under the earth the hell hound with three heads,
irresistible monster, the awful Echidna's whelp,
and guarding the golden apples the dragon at the end of the earth—
and I have had my taste of ten thousand other toils,
but these hands let no one set his trophies over me.
Now look at me, torn to shreds, my limbs unhinged,
a miserable ruin sacked by invisible disaster, I
who am called the son of the most noble mother,
I who claim to be begotten of Zeus in the heavens.
But I tell you this, even if I am nothing,
nothing that can even crawl, even so—

only let her come who has done this to me—
these hands will teach her, and she can tell the world: alive
I punished the evil, and I punish them in death.

> The **wife of Zeus**: Hera, Heracles' bitter enemy **Eurystheus**: a king of Argos and
> Mycenae, grandson of Pelops; by a decree of Zeus granted authority over
> Heracles, whom he forced to undertake the Twelve Labors **daughter of Oeneus**:
> Heracles' wife, Deianeira **earth-born Giants** (Titans): the first rulers of the uni-
> verse **"son of the most noble mother... begotten by Zeus**:" Alcmene,
> impregnated by Zeus, gave birth to Heracles

19

OEDIPUS, UNWILLING TO LEAVE THEBES, BEMOANS HIS DESTINY
(409 BC) EURIPIDES, The Phoenician Women, *tr. L. Katz*

Euripides' *The Phoenician Women* is a vastly different retelling of the Oedipus story from Sophocles' versions (which, from the one to the other—*Oedipus the King* to *Oedipus at Colonus*—also become substantially different.) The freedom with which the Greek tragedians could select and suppress and totally reinvent received versions of their myths makes absurd the notion that Greek audiences could comfortably anticipate the events and outcomes of their tragedies. Euripides was particularly sportive in this respect. This version sandwiches together, and radically changes, the numbers of events in the Oedipus story that follow the discovery of his double guilt.

The tragedy takes place on the day Polyneices, the banished brother, attacks the city of Thebes. In this version, Jocasta did not hang herself nor did Oedipus go into exile after the fateful discovery; both are still alive, Oedipus now old and self-blinded, confined to the palace and hidden from the world by his sons in the hope that his deeds will be forgotten. Bitter, almost mad with rage at his imprisonment, he hurls curses at his sons and prays that they will confront one another in a mutually fatal battle.

But to forestall the bloody battle between her sons, Jocasta arranges a truce for them to meet; the attempted reconciliation fails, and in the ensuing battle, both brothers die. At the grief of seeing her two sons dead, Jocasta kills herself. Antigone, the daughter of Jocasta and Oedipus, now enters followed by attendants bearing the bodies of Jocasta and her two slain brothers. Bewailing her triple loss and the ruin of the house of Oedipus, she cries out for Oedipus to appear and "disclose the misery of thy life" after so long imprisonment. When he does, groping his way out of the palace, Creon, now the ruler of Thebes, decrees his banishment to forestall further misfortunes to the city should the curse of Oedipus' presence still hang over it. Oedipus' response acknowledges the foreordained chain of miseries his life has been since birth; recognizes that they will now, in his helpless state when banished from his city, become altogether impossible to endure. And all this lamentation might, one would guess, be preamble to his pleading with Creon to spare him this final misery. "Why...slay me utterly," he cries to him. But precisely the function of this catalogue of woes is to underscore, in Oedipus' actual decision (*not* to "twine my arms about [Creon's] knees" in supplication), the scale of his heroic being, the measure of his implicit greatness. "I will not demean myself," he cries, "no matter what my evil state."

There's a remarkable resemblance between the last moments of Shakespearean and other Jacobean tragic heroes, and Euripides' Oedipus in his last moment: both *name* themselves. "Nothing before or after. I am myself alone," claims Flamineo in *The White Devil* as he is dying; "I am the Duchess of Malfi still," cries the Duchess as she goes to her death; "Aye, every inch a king," cries Lear, in his last miserable moments before expiring. They, like Oedipus, rise to the height of what they still remain internally, and name that as themselves, in willful contradiction of their outward, debased, bodily fact.

OEDIPUS
Daughter Antigone, why are you dragging me into the light?
I come, with blind footsteps, from my bed
Where I lay groaning like the ghost of a man,
Like a shadowless dead thing, a forgotten dream.
I have no place here in the waking world.
O my fate, from my beginning
Before I was born,
Before I was out of my mother's womb,
You marked me for suffering
Beyond all men's enduring.
Apollo spoke my end at my beginning,
Foretold how I would kill my father,
And he, my father, knowing I would
Be his murderer, tore me from my mother's breast,
And threw me to the beasts on Mount Cithaeron,
A meal for beasts off Mount Cithaeron…
But I, oh miserable destiny, was saved.
Oh, that place of desolation!
Why was it not sunk into the depths of Tartarus
For not destroying me? It rescued me,
It let me go. And I became a son again
In the house of Polybus. And then, O, Oedipus,
The slave of fate, fulfilled his destiny,
And killed his father, and wedded with his mother,
And got her sons who were his brothers,
Whom now, today, I've seen destroyed,
Passing to them the curse that Laius passed to me.
Was I mindless? Willess? Bereft of understanding
Of the holy ways of men? That I,
Out of myself, against my soul,

Against my sons, devised such horrors
Without the will, without contrivance, of the god?
It's done. It's past. What's left to do?
Who will tend the blind man, who will guide his step?
She, the wife and mother, who is dead?
Were she alive, ah well, were she alive.
My sons? Dead. Gone. And I?
Still young enough to make my way, to earn my bread?
You cast me out now, Creon. Why?
If you do, you slay me utterly.
But no, I will not twine my arms about your knees,
And show myself a beggar. I may be wronged,
But I will not demean my self,
No matter what my case,
No matter what my evil state

20

TIRESIAS HEATEDLY DEFENDS THE GOD DIONYSUS AGAINST PENTHEUS' CONDEMNATION

(c408 BC) EURIPIDES, The Bacchae, *tr. M. Hadas and J. H. McLean*

Pentheus, ruler of Thebes, is outraged at what has happened to the wives and mothers of his city: they're all outside the city on Mount Cithaeron in ecstasy celebrating the worship of a newly-arrived, indecent interloper claiming to be the god Dionysus. And, he understands, the women are gorging themselves on wine, and stealing off, one after the other, to "where love lies waiting." A God, this Lydian charmer? Hardly. Only a cunning fraud with "tossing curls" who spends his nights dangling a jar of wine in front of the lips of women. Having already arrested all the indecently celebrating women he could get his hands on, now Pentheus will go after the main criminal, the fake himself, and put an end to him.

In Euripides' prologue, Dionysus has already told us what *he* plans to do in Thebes. Though born out of a Theban woman Semele and the god Zeus himself, never have the Thebans acknowledged or worshipped him. Already long celebrated in the East as a "manifest god," now he's come to Greece—to Thebes first—to establish his worship there. To *inflict* it, if his godhead remains, as it has been until now, mocked and unacknowledged.

Two Thebans are taking no chances: Cadmus, the old king who turned over the kingship to his grandson Pentheus, and the blind prophet Tiresias. Wearing the ivy wand and the fawn-skin that marks them as worshippers of the Dionysian cult, they start to dance, ancient as they are, planning to join the worshippers on the mountain. But Pentheus, arriving, confronts them with what he supposes to be their criminal folly.

Tiresias, in this speech, responds. His argument point by point counters Pentheus', as follows:

1) There are "two chief blessings" in the world: food from the earth and wine from the grape, the latter great blessing given by this god.

2) The story of his being sewn up in the thigh of Zeus, out of which he had his second "birth," can be accounted for rationally, without destroying his claim to godhead (this, from a priest, persuading a "rationalist" in his own skeptical terms).

3) He has prophetic powers, and uses trance-states for humans to share them.

4) He is the god of madness (panic), with which he can destroy armies.

5) His victory over Greece is inevitable; don't imagine your power or wisdom can oppose him.

6) Those not corrupted in their nature will not be corruptible (refuting Pentheus' argument about corrupting women).

7) Your logic, your rationality, is madness.

This final point bears the intent of the whole argument: like Creon in *Antigone* [see II, #7], Pentheus is ready to hold to his fixed self-image of reasonableness to the point of madness, and like Tiresias in *Antigone,* the priest is warning the potential madman—but with the same tragic consequence for the mad "man of reason" as in *Antigone.*

TIRESIAS

Give a clever man a good theme to talk on, and it is easy enough to speak well. Your tongue, indeed, runs smoothly, as if you had wit, but there is no wit in what you say. The man whose strength is his impudence, whose ability is all in his tongue, makes a bad citizen—and a stupid one.

This new divinity whom you ridicule, words cannot describe how great will be his power throughout Hellas. Mankind, young man, has two chief blessings: goddess Demeter—the earth, that is; call her whichever name you will—who sustains men with solid food, and this son of Semele, who came later and matched her gift. He invented the liquid draught of the grape and introduced it to mortals. It stops the griefs of suffering humanity, when they get their fill of the flowing grape. It gives them sleep and forgetfulness of daily sorrows. There is no other medicine for trouble. The libations we pour—it is the god himself making our peace with the gods, so that through him mankind may obtain blessings.

You sneer at the story that he was stitched inside the thigh of Zeus. I will teach you the true interpretation of that. When Zeus snatched him from the thunderbolt's flame and brought the infant god to Olympus, Hera wanted to cast him out of heaven. But Zeus contrived a counter device, as a god might. He broke off a piece of the earth-enveloping sky and gave to jealous Hera an *incorporeal* Dionysus. But in time mortals got the word changed and said the child had been incorporated in Zeus. So they made up the story that he had been stitched inside the thigh of the god.

He is a prophetic god. Those whom his spirit fills, like people possessed, have no small prophetic power. Whenever the god enters the body in full strength, he takes possession of men, and makes them tell the future. He also has taken over a part of Ares' functions. A host under arms, ay already drawn up in line, is often scattered in panic before raising a spear. This also is a sort of madness sent by Dionysus.

A time will come when you will see him even on Delphi's rock, bounding over the double peak of Parnassus with his pine-torches, brandishing and tossing his bacchic wand. He shall be great throughout Hellas. Listen to me, Pentheus. Do not presume that mere power has influence with men. Do not be wise in your own diseased imagination. Welcome the god to the land, pour libations, wreathe your head, revel.

Not even Dionysus can compel women to be chaste. For that you must look to the women's own nature (for a chastity proof against all shocks). Even in bacchic revels the good woman, at least, will not be corrupted.

You see, *you* take pleasure when a multitude stands at your gates and the city magnifies the name of Pentheus. He, too, I judge, takes delight in being honored. I then, and Cadmus, whom you laugh at, shall crown ourselves with ivy and dance. A hoary old pair, but dance we must. I shall not be persuaded by your logic to combat gods. You are mad, most distressingly mad. No spells can cure a disease which is itself a spell.

Semele: mother by Zeus of Dionysus **made up the story**: after Zeus' lover Semele demanded to see him in his real form and was consumed by thunder and lightning, Hermes saved her six-months old son Dionysus and sewed him up inside Zeus' thigh for three more months, thus rendering Dionysus "double-born"
Delphi's rock: Apollo's temple where the oracle lived (see Pytho in Glossary)
Parnassus: a mountain in Phocis sacred to Apollo and the Muses; at its foot was Delphi **...pour libations, wreathe your head, revel**: manifestations of Dionysus worship

21

THE HERDSMAN REPORTS TO PENTHEUS THE MAGICAL FEATS OF THE BACCHANTS ON THEIR AWAKENING

(c408 BC) EURIPIDES, The Bacchae, *tr. M. Hadas and J. H. McLean*

The power of the god Dionysus has been already confirmed for Pentheus when, imprisoning him, the "Lydian Stranger" burst the walls of his prison and left [see II, #20]. But while Pentheus is refusing still to countenance his divinity, a Herdsman arrives from the mountain, breathless with astonishing news.

The Herdsman is of two minds: on the one hand, frightened of Pentheus' wrath should he confirm irrational wonders in his report, and ready to say nothing if his king signifies his unwillingness to hear; on the other hand, bursting to recapitulate the wonder of what he's witnessed, to relive the awesome thing. But what he is describing, though he gets the picture right, quite possibly exceeds his own comprehension. Two separate phases, and therefore two separate conditions of the god's power, are being described. The first, the sanctified condition of the women's absolute at-one-ness with the god himself, the condition in which the human completely shares his magic and his power—becoming, in effect, the god's surrogate. This is the condition of the women on their first awakening on the mountain top. But when jarred by intrusion or threat, disturbed in that condition and brought down a single notch from its height of pure ecstasy and benignity, their implicit and equal-to-divine power, so completely benign at first, becomes—with equal force—the absolute savagery of power, being still equal to divinity's.

The threat that Pentheus should heed in this narrative is that of the god's potential savagery, given the occasion—as Pentheus has given it to him twice over—of threat to or intrusion on his godly equanimity. The burden of the Herdsman's address is, at its conclusion, totally geared to persuading his king to surrender all his opposition. The powerful evocation of the magical, the supermundane, has brought the herdsman's narrative from its initial hesitancy to open, unabashed glorification.

HERDSMAN
Pentheus, ruler of the Theban land, I come from Cithaeron, where I have seen the raving bacchants, who rushed barefooted from their homes in frenzy. I am here all eager to tell you and the city, king, the fearsome things they do, things surpassing wonder.

Our herds of pasturing kine had just begun to ascend the steep to the ridge when I saw three bands of women dancers; Autonoe was leader of the first choir, your mother Agave of the second, and Ino of the third. They all lay in the sleep of exhaustion. Some were reclining with their backs against branches of fir, others had flung themselves at random on the ground on leaves of oak.

Then your mother rose up in the midst of the bacchants and called upon them to bestir their limbs from sleep when she heard the lowing of the horned kine. The women then cast their sleep from their eyes and sprang upright, a sight of wondrous comeliness.

First they let their hair fly loose about their shoulders and tucked up their fawnskins, those whose fastenings had become unloosed, and girt the speckled skins about them with serpents that licked their cheek. One took her thyrsus and struck it against a rock, and there sprung from it a dewy stream of water. Another struck her fennel wand upon the ground, and the god sent up a fountain of wine for her. Those who had a desire for the white drink scraped the earth with the tips of their fingers, and had rich store of milk. From the wands of ivy there dripped sweet streams of honey. If you had been there to see, you would have approached with prayers the god whom you now revile.

We cowherds and shepherds came together to argue and debate on the fearful and wonderful things they did. One fellow spoke out: "Do you vote that we chase Pentheus' mother, Agave, from her bacchic revels and do our king a kindness?" And so we set an ambush amidst the leafy thickets and hid ourselves.

Agave happened to come racing by me and I jumped out and made to seize her, evacuating the ambush where I was hiding. But she raised a cry: "Ah, my fleet hounds, we are being hunted by these men! But follow me, follow with your wands in your hands for weapons."

We fled and escaped a rending at the bacchants' hands. But the women attacked the heifers, that were grazing on the grass, with naked, unarmed, hands. You could see one holding wide the legs of a well-fed calf which bellowed and bellowed. Others rent heifers apart. You could see ribs or cloven hooves tossed here and there, and pieces smeared with gore hanging from the firs, dripping blood. The wanton bulls were tripped and dragged to the ground by the hands of countless young women. Quicker were their coverings of flesh torn asunder than you could close the lids of your royal eyes. Like birds they soared off the ground in their flight as they scoured the spreading plains by the streams of Asopus.

Like an invading army they everywhere wrought confusion and havoc. They pillaged homes at random. Their loot they put upon their shoulders, and though it was not tied on, it held fast; nothing fell to the dark earth, neither brass nor iron. They carried fire in their curls and it did not burn them. Some of us, angered by the depredations of the bacchants, resorted to arms. And *there* was a terrible sight to see, O king. Their pointed spears drew no blood, whereas the women flung wands from their hands and wounded their assailants till they turned tail and ran.

There was a god with them. Then they went back whence they had started, to the fountains which the god had shot up for them. They washed off the blood, while the serpents licked clean the clots from their cheeks.

This deity then, whoever he is, O king, receive into the city. In many things he is powerful. This also they say of him, that he gave mortals the wine which ends sorrow. If *he* exists not, then neither does Cypris, nor any other joy for men at all. I am fearful of speaking out freely to one who is my master, but I shall have my say: there is no god greater than Dionysus.

kine: cows, cattle **Autonoe, Agave, Ino**: local princesses and leaders of the Bacchants; Agave is the mother of Pentheus **fawnskins**: the skins of young deer worn by the followers of Dionysus **thyrsus**: the Bacchants' staff tipped with a pine cone and sometimes twined with ivy and vine branches **fennel wand**: the Bacchic staff trimmed with yellow flowers and aromatic fruits **heifers**: calves **Asopus**: the river running through the valley at the north front of Mt. Cithaeron **gave mortals the wine**: Dionysus originated the wine cult which spread from India to Britannia

22

OEDIPUS DENOUNCES HIS SON POLYNEICES AND PROPHESIES HIS DOOM
(406 BC) SOPHOCLES, Oedipus at Colonus, *tr. R. Fitzgerald*

In Oedipus' reply to Polyneices' plea [see I, #11] for blessing on his coming battle with his brother, Oedipus reaches the height of his heretofore frustrated rage against this son as well as the other. It is also the

height of denunciatory rhetoric in extant Greek tragedy. Its intent is quite literally to condemn his sons to the ultimate punishments of death and the underworld, and more immediately, for his sons "to divide the honors" of his curse on their battle: double doom. It is the rhetoric of pure rage, unmitigated judgment, pure hate. And it gathers momentum in emotion, *and* in decibel count.

OEDIPUS

You scoundrel! When it was you who held
Throne and authority—as your brother now
Holds them in Thebes—you drove me into exile:
Me, your own father: made me a homeless man
Insuring me these rags you blubber over
When you behold them now—now that you, too
Have fallen on evil days and are in exile.

Weeping is no good now. However long
My life may last, I have to see it through;
But I regard you as a murderer!
For you reduced me to this misery,
You made me an alien. Because of you
I have begged my daily bread from other men.
If I had not these children to sustain me,
I might have lived or died for all your interest.
But they have saved me, they are my support,
And are not girls, but men, in faithfulness.
As for you two, you are no sons of mine!

And so it is that there are eyes that watch you
Even now; though not as they shall watch
If those troops are in fact marching to Thebes.
You cannot take that city. You'll go down
All bloody, and your brother, too.

For I have placed that curse upon you before this,
And now I invoke that curse to fight for me,
That you may see a reason to respect
Your parents, though your birth was as it was;
And though I am blind, not to dishonor me.
These girls did not.

And so your supplication and your throne
Are overmastered surely,—if accepted
Justice still has place in the laws of God.

Now go! For I abominate and disown you!
You utter scoundrel! Go with the malediction
I here pronounce for you: that you shall never
Master your native land by force of arms,
Nor ever see your home again in Argos,
The land below the hills; but you shall die
By your own brother's hand, and you shall kill
The brother who banished you. For this I pray.
And I cry out to the hated underworld
That it may take you home; cry out to those
Powers indwelling here; and to that Power
Of furious War that filled your hearts with hate!

Now you have heard me. Go: tell it to Thebes,
Tell all the Thebans; tell your faithful fighting
Friends what sort of honors
Oedipus has divided among his sons!

these children: Oedipus' daughters Antigone and Ismene

23

OEDIPUS GIVES HIS BLESSING TO ATHENS AND GOES TO HIS DEATH
(406 BC) SOPHOCLES, Oedipus at Colonus, *tr. R. Fitzgerald*

After Oedipus' denunciation of his son Polyneices [see II, #22], bolts of lightning and peals of thunder signal from the gods that his "destined end" has come, and he calls anxiously for his daughters to summon Theseus. At his arrival, Oedipus fulfills his promise to his protector with prophecy and instruction for the future blessing of Colonus.

It is a speech that should not be summarized or characterized too particularly, since it opens onto mysteries that neither Sophocles nor Oedipus divulges. The destiny of Oedipus, and the very action he is engaged in during this last episode of the tragedy, are given a scale of meaning and grandeur of implication that depend entirely on dark intimation rather than enlightenment. The blessings and the prognosis he offers to Colonus and Theseus, his blind eyes that suddenly see more clearly than those with sight, and his clarity as he approaches his resting place, of how and where his passing from life is to be accomplished, signify a figure as transcendent over the ordinary conditions of human experience as those that attended the ends of Moses and Christ. Oedipus is, so to speak, gathered to the gods; and remarkably, his last words are an echo in anticipation: "When this you see, remember me."

For the actor, nothing is so effective and so believable in moments such as this as uncluttered simplicity.

> **OEDIPUS**
> My lord, I longed for you to come! This is
> God's work, your lucky coming.
> My life sinks in the scale: I would not die
> Without fulfilling what I promised Athens.
>
> I shall disclose to you, O son of Aegeus,
> What is appointed for you and for your city:
> A thing that age will never wear away.
> Presently now, without a soul to guide me,
> I'll lead you to the place where I must die;
> But you must never tell it to any man,
> Not even the neighborhood in which it lies.
> If you obey, this will count more for you
> Than many shields and many neighbors' spears.
> These things are mysteries, not to be explained;

But you will understand when you come here
Alone. Alone, because I cannot disclose it
To any of your men or to my children,
Much as I love and cherish them. But you
Keep it secret always, and when you come
To the end of life, then you must hand it on
To your most cherished son, and he in turn
Must teach it to his heir, and so forever.
That way you shall forever hold this city
Safe from the men of Thebes, the dragon's sons.

For every nation that lives peaceably,
There will be many others to grow hard
And push their arrogance to extremes: the gods
Attend to these things slowly. But they attend
To those who put off God and turn to madness!
You have no mind to that, child of Aegeus,
Indeed, you know already all that I teach.

Let us proceed then to that place
And hesitate no longer; I am driven
By an insistent voice that comes from God.
Children, follow me this way: see, now,
I have become your guide, as you were mine!
Come: do not touch me: let me alone discover
The holy and funeral ground where I
Must take this fated earth to be my shroud.

This way, O come! The angel of the dead,
Hermes, and veiled Persephone lead me on!

                    (He leads them, firmly and slowly.)
O sunlight of no light! Once you were mine!
This is the last my flesh will feel of you;
For now I go to shade my ending day
In the dark underworld. Most cherished friend!
I pray that you and this your land and all

Your people may be blessed: remember me,
Be mindful of my death, and be
Fortunate in all the time to come!

son of Aegeus: Theseus **men of Thebes, the dragon's sons**: by oracle's command, Cadmus, after slaying a dragon and sewing its teeth in the soil, saw
warriors grow at once out of the teeth, and fight one another. With the five sur-
viving warriors, Cadmus founded the city of Thebes.

24

OEDIPUS DEFENDS HIMSELF AGAINST THE CHARGE OF INCEST AND PATRICIDE

(c50-65 AD) SENECA, Oedipus, *tr. E. I. Harris, ad. L. Katz, Act 3, Sc. 1*

As in Sophocles' play, Oedipus is here confronted by Creon and
Tiresias, who report the oracle's accusation of Oedipus' patricide
and incest as the cause of the city's plague [see II, #11]. And as in
Sophocles, Oedipus, unable to square the facts of the accusation with
what he supposes are the known facts of his parentage and past life,
finds no alternative but to accuse Creon and Tiresias of private
motives for so accusing him.

But there the resemblance ends. From the beginning, Seneca's
Oedipus is a haunted man. At play's opening, he considers that,
although he has avoided the oracle's prediction by fleeing from his
supposed parents, "yet even now, the dreadful fear remains." It is a
feeling of implicit guilt, unshakeable and terrifying, so that unlike
Sophocles' Oedipus, whose certainty of his innocence justifies his
counter-accusation against Creon and Tiresias, when Seneca's
Oedipus is so accused, his instant response is, "A chilling tremor penetrates my bones. The very thing that I have feared to do, they say that
I have done it."

It's the Roman, not the Greek Oedipus, that is closest to Freud's understanding of the Oedipal dilemma: that in daylight's reason, the consciousness of innocence of the deed has little bearing on the abiding, guilty suspicion of having in fact done it. And so carefully, this Oedipus uses the fulcrum of reason—the facts—to pry himself free from his haunting suspicion, and carefully arraying the facts one after the other, with effort, with the hope of relief, succeeds in turning the tables on his accuser. The vigor of his condemnation of Creon at the end of his speech is itself the measure of its uncertainty—and the punishment he visits on Creon—to bury him "deep in some rocky dungeon"—is itself the measure of its necessity.

OEDIPUS
A chilling tremor penetrates my bones.
The very thing that I have feared to do,
They say that I have done it.
But Merope my mother wed my father.
The crime's disproved of marriage with my mother.
And Polybus my father, still unharmed, absolves me
Of the crime of patricide.
Father and mother living and sound: how have I
Sinned in murder and adultery?
What thought was there of murder? Against Laius?
Thebes mourned for Laius' death long, long before
My journey found the road to Laius' kingdom.
Is he, blind seer, priest Tiresias,
Mocked by his blindness and his old man's folly?
Or is the God Apollo faithless to his priests?
Ah yes! I see! I see these shrewd accomplices,
I see their guile! The priest invents the lie,
Uses the God Apollo for a cloak,
And promises my scepter to his ally.

(To Creon)
You! Creon! You have counseled me
To lay aside the scepter of the King.

To rest, give up my rule, give up
The heavy burden of my crown.
The smoothest way to power, is it not?
Counseling the King to moderation,
To temper fortune, seek his ease, his sleep?
The restless often urge such counterfeits.
But is my fate so fully known to you?
Or does Tiresias see beyond my innocence?
Yet I seem guilty. Why? Because your words,
Your terrible words have beckoned to me,
And, terrified, I blindly followed them.
Men fear these unknown, dark uncertainties
No less than all their known and certain crimes.
Since he who once has sinned, when he is pardoned
Comes back again to be one's enemy,
Let doubt, let all my doubts, be put away.
For he who trembles at his enemy's hate
Has never learned to rule. Fear, only fear,
Will permeate his realm.

(To his followers)

Arrest this man!
Shut up this criminal.
Bury him
Deep in some rocky dungeon,
And guard him well.
I, I will examine once again
The safety of my palace walls.

25

OEDIPUS, BLINDED AND SELF-EXILED, FEELS RELIEVED BY HIS FATE

(c50-65 AD) SENECA, Oedipus, *tr. E. I. Harris, ad. L. Katz, Act 5, Sc. 2 and 3*

Seneca's Stoicism emerges fully in this last gesture of Oedipus, in which the tragic king matches the calm of mind and sense of well-being that Seneca himself must have felt—in accordance with his philosophy—at the moment of his own suicide enjoined by the Emperor Nero. Extraordinarily, Oedipus anticipates the Christian sense of the efficacy of punishment and the propriety of fate itself— "I've paid the debt I owed—my crime's forgiven."

The squaring of crime with punishment—"Now all is well and finished"—introduces a different sense of human value from that evidenced in Sophocles' tragedy: the value of human suffering *not* as in the Greek tragedians, for the wisdom of learning the limited measure of the self, but instead for its possible gift to community. Oedipus offers his guilt and its punishment, willingly taking on the role of pariah, outcast, as a cleansing of the community. His final function he recognizes as the *enwrapping* about himself of all the pestilences, the "blasting Fates," the "mad despairs" of the city—and by his wearing them so, in his exodus, the city is cleansed and made whole.

The notion is repeated in Sartre's *The Flies,* in which Orestes assumes the same purgative role, leaving the city enwrapped in and taking with him "the Flies," the paralyzing mythic oppressions under which the populace is intellectually and morally enslaved. The "healing pariah" becomes one of the profound themes of Western literature.

OEDIPUS

Now all is well and finished. I have paid in full
The debt I owed—my crime's forgiven. Welcome, blessed night!
What friendly god has spattered on my head
Black darkness? What kindly god forgave the criminal?
I have escaped the Sun's all-seeing eye.
I, murderer of my father, know no more its light
It's fled; and such a blinded face
Is meet for Oedipus.

Phoebus Apollo, foreteller of the truth
And god of truth, I make my prayer to you:
Only a father's murder was foretold,
But I am twice a parricide, guilty
Beyond my greatest fear.
I've slain my mother; she lies dead
Through this my guilt. O Phoebus, truthful, lying god,
I have exceeded all the ills foretold.
Now, with faltering steps, I'll walk my gloomy way
Through obscure nights, with apprehensive feet
Advance, and with a shuddering hand feel out
A pathway; and stumble on with trembling steps.
Now, fly from here!—But slowly, carefully, lest you stumble
Over your mother's corpse.
Suffering ones, infected with the plague's disease,
I go. Draw breath again,
Lift up your heads. A milder sky will shine
When I am gone. Whoever still retains
His life, though weak and prostrate, still shall draw
The breath of life. God Apollo, leave our city! End your work in
    Thebes!
The earth's death-dealing poison I will take with me.
The blasting fates, the mad despairs, the chill
Of dreadful sickness, and wild grief will leave
With me—with me!
These are meet for my companionship.

corse: corpse

26

ATREUS PLANS HIS GRUESOME REVENGE ON HIS BROTHER THYESTES

(c50-65 AD) SENECA, Thyestes, *tr. E. I. Harris, ad. L. Katz, Act 2, Sc. 1*

Thyestes, the brother of Atreus, King of Mycenae, seduces Atreus' wife and is driven from the city. But subsequently Atreus, pretending to be reconciled to his brother, recalls Thyestes and his sons to Mycenae with the lure of a promise to share the throne, and executes his barbaric revenge: he kills Thyestes' sons, and serves them to his brother at a banquet. It is the psychology of such blatant savagery that Seneca studies in Atreus.

At the furthest remove from rational self-control—which was the ideal of the Stoics and of Seneca—is *ira,* wrath. It is ungoverned, boundless beyond reason, the state that is most fundamentally evil. It *is* evil, the thing itself, outside of harmony with God, outside the cosmically inclusive mind of God within which the two ideals of human conduct reside: inner tranquility and social duty.

Atreus is the very presentiment of *ira.* Study his speech closely, and recognizably his logic is not the logic of reason but the logic of psychological aberration. It is a deliberate structuring of the path of *ira* working independently of human will, of human autonomy. A rage, Atreus recognizes, is rising out of "the lowest depths" within him, hurrying "I know not whither." It is accompanied not by his words or his thought but by moanings and crashings, frightening the very gods of the hearth, themselves afraid to look or think on these thunderous rumblings. And out of these chaotic blasts in the dark recesses of his soul there rises, without his will or understanding, a "monstrous deed," one which gradually clarifies itself, becomes recognizable to Atreus as so unspeakable—"the perfect image of the slaughter"—as to be worthy of his revenge against Thyestes. As it formulates of its own volition, Atreus, its observer rather than its instigator, sees it particularizing, gaining a hideous reality before his eyes, so hideous that the conscious, reasoning side of Atreus draws back, frightened.

Only then does the "consciously reasoning" Atreus come into play, and only then when the volition of *ira* has constructed its own perfect model does Atreus begin to calculate how to realize it. And cunningly, he intuits the one motive in his brother Thyestes that could possibly bring him into the orbit of *ira's* revenge: his ambition for the throne.

What is notable is Seneca's separation of the emotional frenzy lying *within* "character," and the inadequate, helpless, "rational," onlooking self that is, even to the self, one's ostensible "character." It's small wonder that the Elizabethan and Jacobean playwrights, studying the same psychological terrain, found inspiration in Seneca's tragedies—and *not* for his ghosts and mayhem alone. The multi-layering of character in the classical tradition of tragedy became distinct from the single-layered, single-trait characterization almost universal—though not entirely so—in the classical tradition of comedy. And it is this multi-layering that causes characters in tragedy to speak of their own inwardly governing impulses rhetorically, objectively, as though they are their mere observers—sometimes with amusement (Iago, Flamineo), sometimes with horror (Macbeth).

> **ATREUS**
> There is no deed, even beyond the bounds
> Of evil, that I will not do against this brother,
> This Thyestes. I will leave no crime untried,
> Because none is great enough for him. The sword?
> Too poor. Fire? Fire's not enough.
> What weapon shall arm such hate as mine?
> Thyestes' self, his very self.

This crime I long to do is worse than hate.
I own it. In my breast a tumult reigns;
It rages deep within, and I am urged
I know not whither, yet it urges me.
Earth from its lowest depths sends forth a groan,
It thunders, though the daylight is serene,
The whole house shakes as though the house were rent,
The trembling Lares turn away their face.
This shall be done, this evil shall be done,
What evil? I know not yet.
There is a passion in my heart,
Wilder than I have ever known, beyond the bounds
Of human nature. It rises, and urges on
My sluggish hands. I know not what it is,
But it is something great. Be it what it will,
Be quick, my soul! This crime must be
Fit for Thyestes' fate, and worthy of me, of Atreus.
Both shall serve together, brother joined with brother.
A feast, a hideous feast, once seen
In Tereus' house. I know, the crime is great,
And yet it has been done. May grief invent
Some greater crime. Inspire my soul,
O Daulian Procne; you were siblings too.
Our cause is so alike. Assist me, move my hand.
Together, we will bring about this monstrous deed.
The father, hungrily, will tear with joy
His children's limbs, and eat their very flesh
It is well; it is enough. This punishment
Is so far pleasing. Quick! Where can he be?
My brother is too long innocent of the deed.
I see all the sacrifice already,
The perfect image of the slaughter.
I see the morsels placed
Within the father's mouth. Now why, my soul,
Are you afraid? Why fail before the deed?
Forward! It must be done. He himself shall

Perpetrate the greater crime. And will,
He will, for reason.
He hopes with all his soul to gain my kingdom;
And for this hope,
He would not hesitate to face
The threatening thunderbolts of Jove himself.
For this hope; he would endure
The very whirlpool's threats, and dare to sail
Even within the fatal shoals of Lybia.
And to confront his brother, whom he thinks
The last and worst of evil obstacles. — Yes,
Hope, malicious hope, will lead him on.

Lares, Roman: household gods **Daulian Procne**: Princess Procne of Daulis killed her
son and fed him to her husband Tereus in revenge for his cutting her tongue out
and locking her up with the slaves in order to marry her sister **shoals**: sandbanks

27

ATREUS, GLOATING, OBSERVES THYESTES
WAKING AFTER FEASTING ON HIS SONS
(c50-65 AD) SENECA, Thyestes, *tr. E. I. Harris, ad. L. Katz, Act 5, Sc. 1 and 3*

"There renounce the gods, for I have gained the height of my desire,"
exults Atreus. [See II, #26 for brief summary of the Thyestes-Atreus
myth.] It is a declaration of freedom from the ultimate of moral
restraint, and the cue for exercising the pleasures of ultimate moral
release. His only anxiety is to realize the end of possibility, to get to
the verge. And the structure of the speech is based on a breathless urge
to overcome each pleasure already won, to exceed the last, always,
once again. Atreus, happy, revels in his increasingly successful ingenu-
ities. Handing Thyestes the cup containing the blood of his sons, his

own cup is full. It is the same intent as the Marquis de Sade's, in pursuit of the same end, the final possibility of unhampered inventive ingenuity, the savor of terminal success, termination of desire, always eluded by the Marquis—but Atreus, here, grasps it, as he hands the cup.

ATREUS
It is enough; I am replete; I'm satisfied.
I here renounce the gods, for I have gained
The height of my desire.
High above all, and equal to the stars,
My proud head brushes heaven itself
At last I hold the crown, at last I hold
My father's throne. At last. It is enough.
No shame restrains me; day has taken flight;
It's time to act now while the sky is dark.
Oh, if I could keep the gods from flight,
Or drag them back by force, that they might see
The feast of Atreus spelling out revenge!
Ah well, it is enough that he, Thyestes,
Will be witness to the best of this night's pleasures.
Daylight's unwilling, brother, to observe,
But I myself will rid us of the dark
That cloaks your misery. It will not, no.
It's far too long that you've been feasting merrily.
No more wine, Thyestes; no more meat.
You must not be too drunk with wine
To taste the best of this night's banquet.
There's need in this, your crowning moment,
To be awake.

Slaves, open wide the temple doors
And show the splendors of our house of feasting.
I long to see his pallor when he sees at first
His dead sons' heads, to hear his groans when he
First shocked, in horror, sits, dumbstruck and motionless.

This is the recompense for all my toil.
I want to see his wretchedness grow on him
From the first, first instant that he sees—and then
Note how, each moment, he plumbs his misery.
Now the great hall is bright with many torches,
And he—ah, beautiful! he lies supine
On gold and purple. His left hand holds his head
That is so heavy now with wine. He vomits, ah!
I am, this moment, the mightiest of the gods,
The king of kings. My wish has been outdone.
He's fall, but still he lifts the silver cup
To drink. Spare not the wine! There still remains in it
Some of the victims' blood; the old wine's red conceals it.
And with this cup, the feast will end.
His children's blood is mixed with wine he drinks.
Ah well, he would have drunken mine. And now he sings!
Sings festal songs! His mind is dimmed with wine.

Brother, let us together celebrate this festal day.
It is the day that makes my scepter firm,
The day that binds our deathless pact.
Believe me, brother, that your sons
Are close in your embrace. They are here, with you,
And shall be. No single part of your loved. ones
Is lost to you. Ask, and whatever is your wish,
I'll give to you. I'll satisfy the father with his sons.
Fear not, you will be more than satisfied.
Now with my own, your sons will lengthen out
This joyous feast. Mine will be sent for. Drink
The wine. It is a precious heirloom of our house.

28

HERCULES, HAVING IN HIS MADNESS DESTROYED HIS WIFE AND SONS, NOW LONGS TO DESTROY HIMSELF

(c50-65 AD) SENECA, Mad Hercules, *tr. E. I. Harris, Act 5, Sc. 1*

The goddess Juno is enraged by the behavior of her libertine husband. Jupiter has enthroned in her place the mortal Alcmene with whom he fathered Hercules. Juno is also afraid that the mighty hero Hercules, when he's admitted to Heaven—as Jupiter intends—might well, following Jupiter's own example, dethrone his father and become Olympus' tyrant. Juno reasons that since no adversary on earth or heaven is likely to defeat Hercules, there's left only the alternative that he be compelled to destroy himself. In Seneca's version of the myth, the murderous politics of heaven remarkably resemble the politics of Seneca's, and his Emperor Nero's, Rome.

Hercules, after the last of his labors—his mission to the underworld [see II, #18]—returns with Theseus to his wife Megara, his sons, and the city of Thebes. When he learns that the usurper Lycus, after assassinating Megara's father and brothers, is now threatening Megara with death if she refuses marriage, he rushes at Lycus and kills him. Then Juno, observing, finds her moment. She causes Hercules to be overcome by madness, and supposing he is killing Lycus' children, kills his own children and his wife. He falls into deep sleep, and when he wakes, sees the slaughter around him and wonders: who was the author of this monstrous crime?

Seneca follows, and in some critics' estimation improves on, Euripides' Heracles. In this scene of Hercules' slowly dawning realization of his overwhelming guilt, Seneca duplicates the pattern of

Euripides' scene, and also the great scene of Agave's growing recognition of her slaughter of her son Pentheus in *The Bacchae*. There's left only one resolution for him: "the criminal must be by death made whole" by suffering return to the torment of the Underworld.

But following this scene of Hercules' agonizing guilt, Seneca, philosopher of Stoicism. elevates Hercules to Stoic endurance and resignation. Of all mythological figures, he was the paradigm of Stoicism's ideal: the ultimate conquest of the self.

HERCULES

(Awaking and looking around in wonder.)
What place is this? What realm?
What air is this I breathe? on what soil rest
My wearied limbs?
Why prostrate lie those bloody bodies there?
Has not my mind put by the shapes of hell?
Although returned does hell's sad throng still move
Before my eyes? It shames me to confess :—
I fear! I know not what my soul forebodes
Of heavy ill. My father, where art thou?
Where are my sons, my wife? Why is my side
Bare of the lion's spoil? Whither has fled
My lion's skin that served as cloak and couch?
Where are my bow and arrows? Who could take
My weapons from me and I still alive?
What is this?
My sons lie bathed in blood, my wife is dead!
Ye who besides Ismenus' waters dwell,
Show the author of these savage deeds.
But why do Theseus and my father shun
My glance? Why hide their faces? Stay your tears,
Speak, who has slain my all? What, father, dumb?
Yet speak thou, Theseus, Theseus, faithful friend.
Speak, who o'erthrew my house?
Whose prey am I?

Have pity, father; supplicating hands
I stretch. He turns away.
What shaft is that with children's murder wet?
Alas! My own, in Hydra's venom dipped!
I need not ask what hand could bend that bow,
Or draw the bowstring that reluctant yields
To me. My father, speak, is mine the crime?
He speaks not, it is mine.
Now send thy thunders from all parts of heaven,
O great progenitor; forgetting me,
Avenge thy grandsons, though with tardy hand.
The starry heavens roar, the sky shoots flame.
To Caspian cliffs bound fast, let eager birds
Upon my body feed.
Should not this blood-stained form be burned with fire?
Grim country of the Furies, prison house
Of hell,
If place of banishment
Lies hid beyond the shades of Erebus,
There hide me. I will lurk beyond the bounds
Of Tartarus. O heart, too fiercely tried!
Who worthily might mourn for you, my sons,
Scattered through all the house? My tearless eyes
Have not the power to weep these heavy ills.
Give back my bow, my arrows; give my club.
For thee, my sons, I break my shaft, for thee
Destroy my bow; this heavy club shall burn
An offering to thy shades; this quiver, full
Of Hydra-poisoned arrows, shall be laid
Upon thy funeral pile; the arms that slew
Shall pay the penalty.
Frenzy has not so quenched my sense of shame
That I can see all peoples flee my face.
My weapons, Theseus! Give me back, I pray,
In haste my stolen arms; if I am sane,
Give back my spear; if madness holds me yet,

Fly, father, for I take the road to death.
There is no healing for a soul defiled,
The criminal must be by death made whole.
The deed is mine.
Give back
My weapons, let my hand avenge my fate.
Lip, hand, begin
This heavy labor, greater than them all.
Unless my arms are given back to me,
The woods of Thracian Pindus I will fell,
Or all the Theban homes,
The citizens, the temples of the gods,
Above my body I will heap, will lie
Entombed beneath a city overthrown;
And if the ruined walls should prove too light
For my strong shoulders, and the seven gates
Too lightly rest, in the world's heart, I'll hide,
Pressed down beneath the burden of the earth.
Whither fly?
Where hide myself? In what land lie concealed?
What Nile can wash this right hand clean?
Murderer, whither flee?
There is no place of exile, earth rejects
And all the stars flee from me.
Theseus, faithful friend, seek out for me
Some secret, far-remote abiding place;
Since, looking on another's guilt, thou still
Canst love the guilty, show me now, I pray,
The gratitude thou owest: take me back
To hell's dark shades, endue me in thy chains,
That place will hide me.
That place alone.

Ismenus: river near Thebes sacred to Apollo; the river god Ismenus was killed by Hercules with a lyre **Hydra**: see monologue 147 **Erebus**: the threshhold to Hades

ELIZABETHAN/JACOBEAN

29

THE SPANISH GENERAL NARRATES A TALE OF BATTLE VICTORY

(c1587; 1602) THOMAS KYD, The Spanish Tragedy, *Act 1, Sc. 2*

At the play's opening, the war between Spain and Portugal has already concluded with Spanish victory. The Spanish King commands his returning General to "unfold in brief discourse... thy blissful victory." And so the General obliges by reciting, we would presume, the classical Messenger's speech. But with a major difference.

The speech in no way follows a path of personal feeling, but only of narrative continuity. It is a rhetorical exercise detachable from person or dramatic occasion. Messengers' reports in Greek tragedy [compare, for example, I, #3, 6, 7, 12; II, #9, 21] were deeply personal, deeply embedded in the emotional condition or dramatic intent of the speaker. Not so here. The speech is in the mode not of dramatic but of epic discourse—Virgil, Ariosto, Homer. Like similar narratives in epic poems, its intent is of course to bring to vivid life the event recounted, but also and most important to stupefy the reader's or auditor's senses with the sound and fury, the grandiloquence, of the rhetoric itself.

The speech returns us to the battlefield. As noted in Volume I [see I, #3], it is the verbal equivalent of the flashback in film, and we hear and "see" in its recitation the life, the noise, the bustle, the horror, the chivalry and the heroism of the bloody but exhilirating event. Like the event itself, the recitation rises to climax after climax in following the successive waves of the battle's violence, from the gathering of the forces to its triumphant conclusion—very much like the musical architecture it emulates—until the speech, at its end, resolves battle and rhetoric with a note of calm repose, of closure.

SPANISH GENERAL

Where Spain and Portingale do jointly knit
Their frontiers, leaning on each other's bound,
There met our armies in their proud array;
Both furnish'd well, both full of hope and fear,
Both menacing alike with daring shows,
Both vaunting sundry colours of device,
Both cheerily sounding trumpets, drums and fifes,
Both raising dreadful clamours to the sky,
That valleys, hills and rivers made rebound,
And heaven itself was frighted with the sound.
Our battles both were pitch'd in squadron form,
Each corner strongly fenc'd with wings of shot;
But 'ere we join'd and came to push of pike,
I brought a squadron of our readiest shot
From out our rearward to begin the fight.
They brought another wing t' encounter us.
Meanwhile, our ordnance play'd on either side,
And captains strove to have their valours tried.
Don Pedro, their chief horsemen's colonel,
Did with his cornet bravely make attempt
To break the order of our battle ranks.
But Don Rogero, worthy man of war,
March'd forth against him with our musketeers,
And stopp'd the malice of his fell approach.
While they maintain hot skirmish to and fro,
Both battles join, and fall to handy-blows,
Their violent shot resembling th' ocean's rage,
When, roaring loud, and with a swelling tide,
It beats upon the rampiers of huge rocks,
And gapes to swallow neighbour-bounding lands.
Now, while Bellona rageth here and there,
Thick storms of bullets ran like winter's hail,
And shiver'd lances dark'd the troubled air.
On every side drop captains to the ground,
And soldiers, some ill-maim'd, some slain outright:

Here falls a body sund'red from his head,
There legs and arms lie bleeding on the grass,
Mingled with weapons and unbowell'd steeds,
That scattering overspread the purple plain.
In all this turmoil, three long hours and more,
The victory to neither part inclin'd;
Till Don Andrea, with his brave lanciers,
In their main battle made so great a breach,
That, half dismay'd, the multitude retir'd.
But Balthazar, the Portingales' young prince,
Brought rescue, and encourag'd them to stay.
Here-hence the fight was eagerly renew'd,
And in that conflict was Andrea slain,
Brave man at arms, but weak at Balthazar.
Yet while the prince, insulting over him,
Breath'd out proud vaunts, sounding to our reproach,
Friendship and hardy valour join'd in one
Prick'd forth Horatio, our knight marshal's son,
To challenge forth this prince in single fight.
Not long between these twain the fight endur'd,
But straight the prince was beaten from his horse,
And forc'd to yield him prisoner to his foe.
When he was taken, all the rest they fled,
And our carbines pursu'd them to the death,
Till, Phoebus waving to the western deep,
Our trumpeters were charg'd to sound retreat.

Portingale: Portugal **colours of device**: insignia on standards **pitch'd**: drawn up
shot: musketeers **push of pike**: fighting at close range **ordnance**: artillery **cornet**: wing of an army **fell**: deadly **handy-blows**: hand-to-hand combat **battles**:
battle-lines **rampier**: rampart, fortifications **Bellona**: the Roman Goddess of War
vaunts: boasts **prick'd**: spurred

30

HIERONYMO DISCOVERS THE BODY OF HIS MURDERED SON

(c1587; 1602) THOMAS KYD, The Spanish Tragedy, *Act 2, Sc. 5*

Horatio, Hieronymo's son, returns from the Spanish-Portuguese war a hero, having fought honorably beside his Prince, Lorenzo, and having captured and brought home for ransom the Portuguese Prince, Balthazar. But the two Princes form an alliance against Horatio, who has won their enmity because of rivalry for the love of Bel-Imperia. Together, they plot his murder, and accomplish it by hanging him in Hieronymo's orchard. Hieronymo's recognizing his son hanging in his orchard occasions one of the most powerful scenes in Elizabethan drama.

But the scene is not by Kyd. Since *The Spanish Tragedy* was the most popular play in Elizabethan theatre, revived repeatedly over a period of 25 years, playwrights—among them Ben Jonson—were hired on several occasions to add interpolations to the text, updating its style and relieving it of its sometimes depressing early-Elizabethan-tragedy sophomorisms. The interpolations added on one occasion (either for the 1597 or 1602 revival) elevated the study of Hieronymo from the serviceable melodrama of the original to a profoundly tragic, profoundly alive character who anticipates some of the characteristics of Shakespeare's Hamlet and Lear.

Hieronymo runs mad. The sight of his murdered son overwhelms him with so sudden and so unbearable a shock that—in the interpolated text—he at first denies it. He then tests the possibility that his son is still alive; studies the body, the clothes, the arrangements his son made for the evening, as evidence of his still being alive. But gradually, the props of his delusion fall away, and he succumbs to the pain of the reality of his son's death, from which he does not recover for the rest of the play.

Hieronymo's monologues—made up as they are of updated text and bits of the original—offer the rare instance in Elizabethan drama of language that follows the flow and echoes the flexibility of the human mind in the very act of thinking-saying, in the moment of thought tumbling out of that very same moment's feeling, not pre-meditated, not formally structured. But most affecting of all, the true and full residue of that instant's emotion, overwhelming as it is, some-times fails to achieve its whole articulation, the failure itself constituting its eloquence. When the rush of feeling surfaces entirely, and language hurtles to the limit of its expressive possibility, emotion yells through the barrier of language sometimes monosyllabically: Lear's "Kill, kill, kill, kill, kill, kill;" Hieronymo's "Confusion, mis-chief, torment, death and hell."

HIERONYMO
Who calls Hieronymo? Speak, here I am.
I did not slumber; therefore `t was not a dream.
No, no, it was some woman cried for help,
And here within this garden did she cry,
And in this garden must I rescue her.—
But stay, what murd'rous spectacle is this?
A man hang'd up and all the murderers gone!
And in my bower, to lay the guilt on me!
This place was made for pleasure, not for death.

(He cuts him down.)
These garments that he wears I oft have seen—
Alas, it is Horatio, my sweet son!
O no, but he that wilom was my son!
O, was it thou that call'dst me from my bed?
O speak, if any spark of life remain:
I am thy father. Who hath slain my son?

What savage monster, not of human kind,
Hath here been glutted with thy harmless blood,
And left thy bloody corpse dishonoured here,
For me, amidst these dark and deathful shades,
To drown thee with an ocean of my tears?
He supp'd with us tonight, frolic and merry,
And said he'd go visit Balthazar
At the duke's palace: there the prince doth lodge.
He hath no custom to stay out so late:
He may be in his chamber; some go see.
Roderigo, ho!

True, all Spain takes note of it.
He is so generally belov'd;
His majesty the other day did grace him
With waiting on his cup: these be favours,
Which do assure me he cannot be short-liv'd.

I wonder how this fellow got his clothes!—
Sirrah, sirrah, I know the truth of all.
Jaques, run to the Duke of Castille's presently,
And bid my son Horatio to come home:
I and his mother have had strange dreams to-night.
Do ye hear me, sir?

Well, sir, he gone.
Pedro, come hither; know'st thou who this is?
Who, who is it? Peace, Isabella!
Nay, blush not, man.

My lord Horatio?
Ha, ha, St. James! but this doth make me laugh,
That there are more deluded than myself.
I would have sworn myself, within this hour,
That this had been my son Horatio:
His garments are so like.
Ha! are they not great persuasions?

Isabella, dost thou dream?
Can thy soft bosom entertain a thought
That such a black deed of mischief should be done
On one so pure and spotless as our son?
Away, I am ashamed.

It was a man, sure, that was hang'd up here;
A youth as I remember: I cut him down.
If it should prove my son now after all—
Say you? say you?—Light! lend me a taper;
Let me look again.—O God!
Confusion, mischief, torment, death and hell,
Drop all your slings now in my cold bosom,
That now is stiff with horror: kill me quickly!
Be gracious with me thou infective night,
And drop this deed of murder down on me;
Gird in my waste of grief with thy large darkness,
And let me not survive to see the light
May put me in the mind I had a son.

whilom: formerly

31

MAD HIERONYMO CONSIDERS:
'WHAT IS A SON?'

(c1587; 1602) THOMAS KYD, The Spanish Tragedy, *Act 3, Sc. 11*

"Think not too precisely on the event" runs one example of reasonable advice, "That way madness lies." But the genius of Hieronymo's madness lies precisely in his denial of that common sense. Obsession opens his curiosity to detailed, unrelenting, unstoppable questioning. He goes back to the roots of the assumed—questioning the obvious, the never-before examined. Why?

Elizabethan and Jacobean tragic heroes, with the loss of faith in any one absolute, one stable certainty—honor, justice, love, virtue, hierarchy, idealized person—almost immediately loses his moorings altogether, doubts, despairs, and so to speak, "runs mad." Having suddenly and overwhelmingly recognized the fragility of the structures in which he had believed, he becomes altogether disoriented from the familiar community of common beliefs. And he obsessively tests, questions, searches through the norms he had formerly assumed. That is his "madness," his craving to reconstitute stability out of his intellectual derangement.

Hieronymo interrogates the concept: *Sons.* Defines it, exemplifies it, rejects it. And what is left for him after his purgation of the word is a single glimmer still remaining within it of pure gold: the name, Horatio. That that newly-defined, newly-tested gold is lost to him reawakens his frenzy. But frenzy for what? For justice. Frenziedly, he imagines and invokes total annhilating retribution.

> **HIERONYMO**
> 'T is neither as you think, nor as you think,
> Nor as you think; you're wide all.
> These slippers are not mine, they were my son Horatio's.
> My son? and what's a son? A thing begot
> Within a pair of minutes—thereabout;
> A lump bred up in darkness, and doth serve
> To ballace these light creatures we call women;
> And, at nine months' end, creeps forth to light.
> What is there yet in a son,
> To make a father dote, rave, or run mad?
> Being born, it pouts, cries, arid breeds teeth.
> What is there yet in a son? He must be fed,
> Be taught to go, and speak. Ay, or yet
> Why might not a man love a calf as well?
> Or melt in passion o'er a frisking kid,
> As for a son? Methinks, a young bacon,

Or a fine little smooth horse-colt,
Should move a man as much as doth a son:
For one of these, in very little time,
Will grow to some good use; whereas a son,
The more he grows in stature and in years,
The more unsquar'd, unbevell'd, he appears,
Reckons his parents among the rank of fools,
Strikes care upon their heads with his mad riots,
Makes them look old before they meet with age.

This is a son!—And what a loss were this,
Consider'd truly? O, but my Horatio
Grew out of reach of these insatiate humours:
He lov'd his loving parents;
He was my comfort, and his mother's joy,
The very arm that did hold up our house:
Our hopes were stored up in him,
None but a damned murderer could hate him.
He had not seen the back of nineteen year,
When his strong arm unhors'd
The proud Prince Balthazar, and his great mind,
Too full of honour, took him us to mercy,
That valiant, but ignoble Portingale!
Well, heaven is heaven still!
And there is Nemesis, and Furies,
And things call'd whips,
And they sometimes do meet with murderers:
They do not always scape, that's some comfort.
Ay, ay, ay; and then time steals on,
And steals, and steals, till violence leaps forth
Like thunder wrapp'd in a ball of fire,
And so doth bring confusion to them all.

wide of the mark: far from the truth **ballace**: ballast **frisking**: frolicsome, playful
bacon: swine **unsquar'd, unbevell'd**: unreadied, immature **insatiate**: insatiable

32

MAD HIERONYMO DIRECTS A PAINTER TO PAINT A MURDER

(c1587; 1602) THOMAS KYD, The Spanish Tragedy, *Act 3, Sc. 12a*

The ultimate irony of Hieronymo's plight is that he, the Marshall—that is, the Chief Justice—of Spain, has no recourse to Justice. It's in the power of the King's son Lorenzo, the murderer himself, to contravene it. And he does. Hieronymo's uncontrollable rage for justice, with which he concluded his previous monologue [see II, #31] is the measure of the intensity of this frustration.

How does he deal with this double torment, the murder of his son and the impossibility of winning justice? By play-acting, or mad-acting, or (questionably) by madness itself. In other words, by distancing the tormenting reality, dealing with it by translating it into metaphor (a painting, a mere hypothesis, a figment of the imagination). Meeting the Painter who comes to ask for justice for the murder of his own son, Hieronymo engages him at once in play-acting: let us paint a picture (know the murder, know our loss and frustration in the guise of a painting.) But in the very process of stipulating the painting's necessary details, leaning heavily as it does on invasively precise memory, dwelling so on the event enlarges it into nightmare, and then the fabric of the pretense is breached, then destroyed, and the initial horror of the reality reemerges for him with redoubled fury.

> **HIERONYMO**
> What woudst thou have, good fellow?
> Justice? O ambitious beggar!
> Wouldst thou have that that lives not in the world?
> Why, all the undelved mines cannot buy
> An ounce of justice!

'Tis a jewel so inestimable. I tell thee
God hath engross'd all justice in his hands,
And there is none but what comes from him.
Thy son murder'd? I had a son
Whose least unvalued hair did weigh
A thousand of thy sons: and he was murdered.
But all is one.
Pedro, Jaques, go in a-doors; Isabella, go,
And this good fellow here and I
Will range this hideous orchard up and down,
Like to two lions reaved of their young.
Go in a-doors, I say.

(Exeunt.)

Come, let's talk wisely now.
Was thy son murder'd? So was mine.
How dost take it? Art thou not sometimes mad?
Is there no tricks that comes before thine eyes?
Art a painter? Canst paint me a tear,
or a wound, a groan, or a sigh? Canst paint
me such a tree as this? Look you, sir, do you see?
I'd have you paint me for my gallery, in your oil-colors
matted, and draw me five years younger than I am—
do ye see, sir, let five years go; let them go
like the marshal of Spain—my wife Isabella
standing by me, with a speaking look
to my son Horatio, which should entend to this
or some such-like purpose: "God bless thee, my
sweet sort," and my hand leaning upon his head,
thus, sir; do you see? may it be done?
Nay, I pray, mark me, sir. Then, sir,
would I have you paint me this tree,
this very tree. Canst paint me a doleful cry?
Seemingly? Nay, it should cry; but all is one.
Well, sir, paint me a youth run through and through
with villains' swords, hanging upon this tree.
Canst thou draw a murderer? I have the pattern

of the most notorious villains in Spain,
but let them be worse, worse: stretch thine art,
and let their beards be of Judas his own color;
and let their eyebrows jutty over: in any case,
observe that. Then, sirrah, after some violent
noise, bring me forth in my shirt, and my gown
under mine arm, with my torch in my hand,
and my sword reared up, thus:—and with these words:
"What noise is this? Who calls Hieronymo?"
May it be done?

Well, sir; than bring me forth, bring me through alley and alley, still
with a distracted countenance going along, and let my hair heave up
my night-cap. Let the clouds scowl, make the moon dark, the stars
extinct, the winds blowing, the bells tolling, the owl shrieking, the
toads croaking, the minutes jarring, and the clock striking twelve. And
then at last, sir, starting, behold a man hanging, and tottering and tottering, as you know the wind will wave a man, and I with a trice to
cut him down. And looking upon him by the advantage of my torch,
find it to be my son Horatio. There you may show a passion, there
you may show a passion! Draw me like old Priam of Troy, crying,
"The house is a-fire, the house is a-fire, as the torch over my head!"
Make me curse, make me rave, make me cry, make me mad, make me
well again, make me curse hell, invocate heaven, and in the end leave
me in a trance—and so forth.

There is no end; the end is death and madness! As I am never better
than when I am mad; then methinks I am a brave fellow, then I do
wonders; but reason abuseth me, and there's the torment, there's the
hell. At the last, sir, bring me to one of the murderers; were he as
strong as Hector, thus would I tear and drag him up and down.

(He beats the painter in.)

reave: forcibly deprived **matted**: dulled **entend**: to tend **jutty over**: to project
alley: garden-walk **involate**: to invoke

33

MAD HIERONYMO MISTAKES A SUPPLIANT FOR HIS DEAD SON

(c1587; 1602) THOMAS KYD, The Spanish Tragedy, *Act 3, Sc. 13*

Madness is reckoned in Elizabethan and Jacobean drama not so much as the derangement of a mind into verbal incoherence (as was was the practice in Italian *commedia dell'arte),* but rather as the madman imagining he is undergoing sudden and successive shifts of scene and circumstance, each experienced with absolute clarity, almost with the swiftness of thought (as in the rapid shifts of subjective time and place in Ophelia's and Lear's scenes of "madness"). In this monologue, Hieronymo undergoes four such transitions.

Petitioners come to Marshal of Spain Hieronymo, each begging him to plead his case before the King. One of them stands apart, an old grieving man who brings a "humble supplication" for his murdered son. Hieronymo (like Hamlet overcome by the acted grief of the Player) is shamed by the old man's example into confronting his own guilt for "neglect[ing] the sweet revenge of [my] Horatio."

As with Hamlet, Hieronymo's longing for revenge is accompanied by the guilt of having not yet accomplished it. But unlike Hamlet, Hieronymo moves to immediate remedy: the old man will lead him into Hell where, like Orpheus, he will plead his cause and win from Hell's monarch the right to "rent and tear [the murderers]... shivering their limbs in pieces with [his] teeth."

Running off stage, he returns to find his son—in the body of the Old Man—risen from Hell, wanting revenge. The son's image is soon displaced, and becomes a Fury from Hell arresting him for so long "seeking not vengeance." But at a cue from the Old Man, he recognizes him once again as the bereaved father of another murdered son.

The monomania of Hieronymo is now fixed on his longing for justice, his guilt at not achieving it, and simultaneously on the impossibility of his ever reaching it.

HIERONYMO

See, see, O see thy shame, Hieronymo
See here a loving father to his son!
Behold the sorrows and the sad laments,
That he delivereth for his son's decease!
If love's effects so strives in lesser things,
If love enforce such moods in meaner wits,
If love express such power in poor estates,
Hieronymo, when as a raging sea,
Toss'd with the wind and tide, o'erturneth then
The upper billows, course of waves to keep,
Whilst lesser waters labour in the deep,
Then sham'st thou not, Hieronymo, to neglect
The sweet revenge of thy Horatio?
Though on this earth justice will not be found,
I'll down to hell, and in this passion
Knock at the dismal gates of Pluto's court,
Getting by force, as once Alcides did,
A troop of Furies and tormenting hags
To torture Don Lorenzo and the rest.
Yet lest the triple-headed porter should
Deny my passage to the slimy strand,
The Thracian poet thou shalt counterfeit.
Come on, old father, be my Orpheus,
And if thou canst no notes upon the harp,
Then sound the burden of thy sore heart's grief,
Till we do gain that Proserpine may grant
Revenge on them that murdered my son.
Then will I rent and tear them, thus and thus,
Shivering their limbs in pieces with my teeth.
Tush, no; run after, catch me if you can.

*(Exeunt all but the Old Man. Bazulto remains till
Hieronymo enters again, who, staring him in the face,
speaks.)*

And art thou come, Horatio, from the depth
To ask for justice in this upper earth,
To tell thy father thou art unreveng'd,
To wring more tears from Isabella's eyes,
Whose lights are dimm'd with over-long laments?
Go back, my son, complain to Aeacus,
For here's no justice; gentle boy, begone,
For justice is exiled from the earth:
Hieronymo will bear thee company.
Thy mother cries on righteous Rhadamanth
For just revenge against the murderers.
But let me look on my Horatio.
Sweet boy, how art thou chang'd in death's black shade!
Had Proserpine no pity on thy youth,
But suffer'd thy fair crimson-colour'd spring
With wither'd winter to be blasted thus?
Horatio, thou art older than thy father.
Ah, ruthless fate, that favour thus transforms!

What, not my son? Thou then a Fury art,
Sent from the empty kingdom of black night
To summon me to make appearance
Before grim Minos and just Rhadamanth,
To plague Hieronymo that is remiss,
And seeks not vengeance for Horatio's death.

Ay, now I know thee, now thou nam'st thy son.
Thou art the lively image of my grief;
Within thy face my sorrows I may see.
Thy eyes are gumm'd with tears, thy cheeks are wan,
Thy forehead troubled, and thy mutt'ring lips
Murmur sad words abruptly broken off
By force of windy sighs thy spirit breathes;

And all this sorrow riseth for thy son:
And selfsame sorrow feel I for my son.
Come in, old man, thou shalt to Isabel.
Lean on my arm: I thee, thou me, shalt stay,
And thou, and I, and she will sing a song,
Three parts in one, but all of discords fram'd.
Talk not of chords, but let us now be gone
For with a cord Horatio was slain.

(Exeunt.)

Alcides: a surname of Heracles, who for his twelfth labor descended into Hades **triple-headed porter** (Cerberus): the dog-guard of Hades **Thracian poet**: Orpheus, who gained entry into Hades by subduing Cerberus with his lute and song **canst**: knowest **Proserpine**: Persephone, identified with spring during her six months a year on earth joins "the winter" of Hades for the rest of the year **Aeacus**: one of the three judges who stand at the gates of Hades and direct the souls inside according to their virtuous or sinful life **Rhadamanth**: another one of the judges; the third one is **Minos**

34

HIERONYMO BRINGS THE PLAY-WITHIN-THE-PLAY TO ITS GRUESOME END

(c1587; 1602) THOMAS KYD, *The Spanish Tragedy, Act 4, Sc. 4*

Hieronymo at last plots with the Princess Bel-Imperia to effect their revenge against the Princes Lorenzo and Balthazar, the murderers of Horatio, Hieronymo's son and Bel-Imperia's lover. At the ceremonies dedicated to reconciling the Kings of Portugal and Spain after their bloody war, Hieronymo wins permission to entertain the monarchs with a play of his own devising. In the course of the action, played in a scramble of languages, both Hieronymo and Bel-Imperia have occasion to stab to death the criminal Princes, and Bel-Imperia, having suffered the loss of her lover Horatio, devises her own death.

Standing over the strewn corpses—not an unusual arrangement at the conclusion of an Elizabethan tragedy—Hieronymo recites his bitter, vengeful epilogue, explaining to the assembled Kings that these deaths are not play-acting but real, and recounting for the Kings the tale that led to this horrible conclusion. His final words, "Urge no more words: I have no more to say," are indeed final. When, after this account to the Kings, they demand his justification for his action, Hieronymo, in a sort of terminal gesture of incapacity *even to begin* to express his whole feeling, bites out his tongue.

HIERONYMO
Here break we off our sundry languages,
And thus conclude I in our vulgar tongue.
Haply you think—but bootless are your thoughts—
That this is fabulously counterfeit,
And that we do as all tragedians do,—
To die to-day, for fashioning our scene,
The death of Ajax or some Roman peer,
And in a minute starting up again,
Revive to please tomorrow's audience.
No, princes; know I am Hieronymo,
The hopeless father of a hapless son,
Whose tongue is tun'd to tell his latest tale,
Not to excuse gross errors in the play.
I see, your looks urge instance of these words;
Behold the reason urging me to this!

(Shows his dead son.)
See here my show, look on this spectacle!
Here lay my hope, and here my hope hath end;
Here lay my heart, and here my heart was slain;
Here lay my treasure, here my treasure lost;
Here lay my bliss, and here my bliss bereft:
But hope, heart, treasure, joy, and bliss,

All fled, fail'd, died, yea, all decay'd with this.
From forth these wounds came breath that gave me life;
They murd'red me that made these fatal marks.

The cause was love, whence grew this mortal hate;
The hate, Lorenzo and young Balthazar;
The love, my son to Bel-imperla.
But night, the coverer of accursed crimes,
With pitchy silence hush'd these traitors' harms,
And lent them leave, for they had sorted leisure
To take advantage in my garden-plot
Upon my son, my dear Horatio.
There merciless they butcher'd up my boy,
In black, dark night, to pale, dim, cruel death.
He shrieks: I heard—and yet, methinks, I hear—
His dismal outcry echo in the air.
With soonest speed I hasted to the noise,
Where hanging on a tree I found my son,
Through-girt with wounds, and slaught'red as you see.
And griev'd I, think you, at this spectacle?
Speak, Portuguese, whose loss resembles mine:
If thou canst weep upon thy Balthazar,
'T is like I wail'd for my Horatio.
And you, my lord, whose reconciled son
March'd in a net, and thought himself unseen,
And rated me for brainsick lunacy,
With "God amend that mad Hieronimo!"—
How can you brook our play's catastrophe?
And here behold this bloody handkercher,
Which at Horatio's death I weeping dipp'd
Within the river of his bleeding wounds:
It as propitious, see, I have reserv'd,
And never hath it left my bloody heart,
Soliciting remembrance of my vow
With these, O, these accursed murderers:
Which now perform'd, my heart is satisfied.
And to this end the bashaw I became

That might revenge me on Lorenzo's life,
Who therefore was appointed to the part,
And was to represent the knight of Rhodes
That I might kill him more conveniently.
So, Viceroy, was this Balthazar, thy son,
That Soliman which Bel-imperia,
In person of Perseda, murdered;
Solely appointed to that tragic part
That she might slay him that offended her.
Poor Bel-imperia miss'd her part in this:
For though the story saith she should have died,
Yet I of kindness, and of care to her,
Did otherwise determine of her end;
But love of him whom they did hate too much
Did urge her resolution to be such.
And, princes, now behold Hieronymo,
Author and actor in this tragedy,
Bearing his latest fortune in his fist;
And will as resolute conclude his part,
As any of the actors gone before.
And, gentles, thus I end my play;
Urge no more words: I have no more to say.

sundry languages: the parts spoken in the play-within-the-play, which Hieronymo here interrupts **sorted**: chosen **through-girt**: pierced through **net**: transparent disguise **bashaw**: pasha, an Arabic or Turkish nobleman **knight of Rhodes**: the isle of Rhodes controlled by the Christian order was the farthest Christian outpost, closest to the Muslim world **Soliman** (Suleiman) **and Perseda**: an anonymous tragedy sometimes attributed to Kyd tells the tragic tale of the Turkish sultan Suleiman II and Perseda

35

SEJANUS COMMITS HIMSELF TO A SANGUINE AND LIMITLESS REVENGE

(1603) BEN JONSON, Sejanus, *Act 2, Sc. 2*

The most formal, the most classically rhetorical, the least Shakespeare-like metaphor-mongering tragic verse in popular Elizabethan/Jacobean tragedy is Ben Jonson's. Its ideal? A noble but uncluttered simplicity of utterance, one that is precise, clear, and hard-edged. Shakespeare nodding sometimes settles for verse this untangled; Jonson, never nodding, stays that way.

It's a mistake, though, to see Jonson's tragic characters as stoic bores; they can be, and are, as mad, sinister and impassioned as the most decadent of Elizabethan tragedy's devils. Take Sejanus. Proud, ambitious, corrupt of soul, he has insinuated his way into the graces of Tiberius, the degenerate Emperor who became the ultimate symbol of Rome's moral decline. So successful was Sejanus in his conquest that, as Jonson puts it in his prefatory "Argument" to the play, "there wanted nothing but the name to make him a co-partner of the empire." But Drusus, the Emperor's son, "after many smothered dislikes" of the interloper, one day in quarrel with Sejanus, is moved to anger and temerity violent enough to slap Sejanus in the face.

For Sejanus, the insult is galvanizing, but at the moment of the blow, he makes no move, says nothing, but waits, in silence. Slowly, over days, he gathers together the pieces of his revenge, one that will not only satisfy his vengeance, but will also be delectable to his intellect, and satisfy further his ultimate purpose: power over the Emperor and the Empire. Part of his vengeance is already in place: he's already seduced Drusus' wife Lydia, and persuaded her that the death of her husband will elevate her, together with Sejanus, to power, and Lydia has already readied the poisoned draught for her husband. But before continuing to build his increasingly wide-ranging and incredibly complex plot, Sejanus stops for a moment to imagine its final happy consequence.

SEJANUS
If this be not revenge, when I have done
And made it perfect, let Egyptian slaves,
Parthians, and barefoot Hebrews brand my face,
And print my body full of injuries.
Thou lost thyself, childe Drusus, when thou thought'st
Thou couldst outskip my vengeance, or outstand
The power I had to crush thee into air.
Thy follies now shall taste what kind of man
They have provoked, and this thy father's house
Crack in the flame of my incensed rage,
Whose fury shall admit no shame or mean.
Adultery? It is the lightest ill
I will commit. A race of wicked acts
Shall flow out of my anger, and o'erspread
The world's wide face, which no posterity
Shall e'er approve, nor yet keep silent—things
That, for their cunning, close, and cruel mark,
Thy father would wish his, and shall, perhaps,
Carry the empty name, but we the prize.
On, then, my soul, and start not in thy course;
Though heav'n drop sulphur, and hell belch out fire,
Laugh at the idle terrors. Tell proud Jove,
Between his power and thine there is no odds.
'Twas only fear first in the world made gods.

Egyptians, Parthians (West Asians), **Hebrews**: all subjects of Rome; Sejanus means, "may I suffer punishment from the lowest of Roman slaves" **childe**: used contemptuously **outstand**: withstand

36

SEJANUS PLANS THE SECRET ASSUMPTION OF CAESAR'S AUTHORITY

(1603) BEN JONSON, Sejanus, *Act 3, Sc. 2*

Sejanus' plotting [see II, #35] has reached a comfortable stage of success. He has already made the Emperor Tiberius suspicious of his own wife and two sons, and Sejanus is preparing for their removal from his path to power. He's ready for his next important step: gaining Tiberius' consent to his marriage with Lydia, the widow of Tiberius' son Drusus, whose undetected murder he and Lydia have already accomplished. But Sejanus, nothing if not attuned to subtleties of discourse, hears a subtle note of warning in Tiberius' carefully worded refusal to allow the match. The Emperor cites as his reasons Sejanus' lack of noble station, and more to the point, the people's growing disaffection toward him as possibly reflecting on Tiberius' devotion to him. And he recognizes—possibly before Tiberius himself does—the sinister implication of this: that in the future Tiberias might well use this excuse to win back popular favor "by forfeiture of" Sejanus—in other words, by throwing him to the wolves. Catching that note, Sejanus at once, "with winged haste," prepares to checkmate the Emperor's anticipated move. He has already laid the groundwork for getting Tiberius out of Rome altogether, and into retirement in the country—a delicious possibility for Tiberius, since he could indulge his "proneness to lust," and indulge in those "unnatural pleasures which he could not so publicly practice" in Rome. (The Emperor, both in the play and historically, was deeply devoted to male sex in its most creative mutations.) And turning possible threat to happy advantage, Sejanus, acting for the absent Emperor, could then "remove him both from thought/ And knowledge" of the Empire's affairs, and become himself the chief and commanding power in Rome.

In the consequence, his calculation is brilliantly successful up to a point. But as Sejanus anticipated, the Emperor does in the end "forfeit" Sejanus, whose horrible fate is to be literally—as Jonson notes in his "Argument"—"torn in pieces by the rage of the people." But before that grisly conclusion, Sejanus, in the silent mental maneuvers of this monologue, plays masterly chess opposite one he conceives of as a contemptibly dull and stupid opponent.

> **SEJANUS**
> Dull, heavy Caesar!
> Wouldst thou tell me thy favors were made crimes,
> And that my fortunes were esteemed thy faults,
> That thou for me wert hated, and not think
> I would with winged haste prevent that change,
> When thou might'st win all to thyself again
> By forfeiture of me? Did those fond words
> Fly swifter from thy lips than this my brain,
> This sparkling forge, created me an armor
> T' encounter chance and thee? Well, read my charms,
> And may they lay that hold upon thy senses,
> As thou hadst snuffed up hemlock, or ta'en down
> The juice of poppy and of mandrakes. Sleep,
> Voluptuous Caesar, and security
> Seize on thy stupid powers, and leave them dead
> To public cares; awake but to thy lusts,
> The strength of which makes thy libidinous soul
> Itch to leave Rome—and I have thrust it on,
> With blaming of the city business,
> The multitude of suits, the confluence
> Of suitors, then their importunacies,
> The manifold distractions he must suffer,
> Besides ill-rumors, envies, and reproaches,
> All which a quiet and retired life,

Larded with ease and pleasure, did avoid,
And yet for any weighty and great affair,
The fittest place to give the soundest counsels.
By this shall I remove him both from thought
And knowledge of his own most dear affairs;
Draw all despatches through my private hands;
Know his designments, and pursue mine own;
Make mine own strengths by giving suits and places,
Conferring dignities and offices;
And these that hate me now, wanting access
To him, will make their envy none, or less;
For, when they see me arbiter of all,
They must observe, or else with Caesar fall.

(Exit.)

hemlock... poppy... mandrake: potions inducing sleep or death **libidinous**:
lustful, lewd **designments**: intentions

37

DE FLORES, SUFFERING THE CONTEMPT OF HIS BELOVED BEATRICE, BIDES HIS TIME
(1622) THOMAS MIDDLETON AND WILLIAM ROWLEY, The Changeling, *Act 2, Sc. 1*

De Flores, a retainer in the household of the Governor Vermandero, is obsessed by his sexual attraction for the Governor's daughter Beatrice. However, she detests the very being of this ugly, unappealing servant, and is incensed by his determination to keep her always in his sight.

As many readers have noted, there is more than one "changeling" in this tragedy other than Beatrice in the main plot and the sane-mad-sane Antonio in the subplot. De Flores is a candidate for "changeling" as well. He begins as a man obsessed, full of self-contempt and hopeless longing, fixed on an object of distant worship who loathes the sight of him, and ends as the sexual tyrant and corrupting scourge over this same woman. The astonishing shifts in sexual negotiation in this play seem more at home in Strindberg than in the more "fixed character" scenarios of the 17th century. Middleton and Rowley graph the steps from stage to stage of a psychology that accomplishes total character reversal.

Here is stage one for De Flores: a man in "servitude" but who "tumbled into the world a gentleman," his contempt for his own helpless condition of sick longing for this woman is countered by his equally sick pleasure in being in her presence, even when—possibly particularly when—her vilification of him is at its most abusive. He shares with other Elizabethan/Jacobean soliloquizers the peculiar strategy of their self-examination: at once both crying out their helplessness, and at the same time, from a perspective of sobriety and rationality, mourning and even loathing it. A sick self and a rational self, side by side. But for De Flores, it is the sick self that dreams of a magical eventuality that easily brushes aside reason: that even one such as he can follow in the footsteps of even more loathed men who have found their way at last, and by invitation, into women's beds.

DE FLORES
(aside) Yonder's she;
Whatever ails me, now a-late especially,
I can as well be hanged as refrain seeing her;
Some twenty times a-day, nay, not so little,
Do I force errands, frame ways and excuses,
To come into her sight; and I've small reason for't,
And less encouragement, for she baits me still
Every time worse than other; does profess herself
The cruellest enemy to my face in town;
At no hand can abide the sight of me,

As if danger or ill luck hung in my looks.
I must confess my face is bad enough,
But I know far worse has better fortune,
And not endur'd alone, but doted on;
And yet such pick-hair'd faces, chins like witches',
Here and there five hairs whispering in a corner,
As if they grew in fear one of another,
Wrinkles like troughs, where swine-deformity swills
The tears of perjury, that lie there like wash
Fallen from the slimy and dishonest eye;
Yet such a one pluck'd sweets without restraint,
And has the grace of beauty to his sweet.
Though my hard fate has thrust me out to servitude,
I tumbled into th' world a gentleman.
She turns her blessed eye upon me now,
And I'll endure all storms before I part with't.
Now't begins again;
I'll stand this storm of hail, though the stones pelt me.
Soft and fair!
The shower falls amain now.
(Aloud.) My lord, your father, charg'd me to deliver
A message to you.
Signor Alonzo de Piracquo, lady,
Sole brother to Tomazo de Piracquo—
The said Alonzo,
With the foresaid Tomazo—
Is new alighted.
My lord, your father,
Charg'd me to seek you out.
So;
(Aside.) Why, am not I an ass to devise ways
Thus to be rail'd at? I must see her still!
I shall have a mad qualm within this hour again,
I know't; and, like a common Garden-bull,
I do but take breath to tie lugg'd again.
What this may bode I know not; I'll despair the less,
Because there's daily precedents of bad faces

Belov'd beyond all reason; these foul chops
May come into favour one day 'mongst his fellows
Wrangling has prov'd the mistress of good pastime;
As children, cry themselves asleep, I ha' seen
Women have chid themselves abed to men.

(Exit.)

baits: harasses **pick-hair'd**: thin-bearded **swine-deformity**: swine pox, which causes pustules in the swine's skin **swills the tears of perjury**: i.e. washes the "tears of perjury" through the faces' wrinkles (which are "like troughs") **to his sweet**: for his mistress **alighted**: arrived **Garden-bull**: Paris Garden, on the Bankside, where bulls were baited **lugg'd**: dragged by the ear **chop**: jaw **chid**: scolded, faulted

38

DE FLORES WINS HIS WHOLE RECOMPENSE FROM BEATRICE
(1622) THOMAS MIDDLETON AND WILLIAM ROWLEY, The Changeling, *Act 3, Sc. 4*

As in Strindberg, it is the weapons available at the moment that rule in sexual politics and transform the contenders. Circumstance, along with his "contender" Beatrice herself, drop new weapons into the hands of De Flores, and he is transformed [see II, #37].

Beatrice became engaged to Alonzo, a noble lord, before she had the good fortune to meet and love Alsemero, and she is determined to correct Fortune's error. Refusing to allow Alsemero to challenge her fiancé to a duel, and so risk his own life or the threat of banishment, she stumbles on another plan. If the loathsome De Flores could be persuaded to murder Alonzo, she will be rid of two inconveniences at once, one by assassination, the other by necessary flight. De Flores takes up the task eagerly, more than eagerly, but he calculates the outcome differently: once the deed is done, he and his beloved at once become confederates, and his hold over her will bring him to his bliss.

He is transformed. At the very interview between them, as she is slowly disclosing her plan, he is on his knees begging the favor of its execution, while also experiencing the heretofore unknown joy of hearing kind words from her and reveling in the unimagined ecstasy of feeling the touch of her hand. He is also calculating his new advantage. She promises him money for his flight that he might "live bravely in another country." He, on the other hand, "feel[s] her in [his] arms already;/ Her wanton fingers combing out this beard,/ And, being pleased, praising this bad face."

When the deed is done, they meet; she offers him thanks, reward, and safe passage. He refuses gold of any value, to her bewilderment, and gradually makes known to her what his reward must be. And in the course of his explanation, the haughty Beatrice is gradually reduced to the condition of a silenced, frightened bedmate, and the cringing De Flores to a commanding, adroit wooer, much like the murderer Richard III in his wooing of Lady Anne over the coffin of her dead husband in Shakespeare's play. At scene's end, De Flores bears the lady off, with reassuring lover's words, to bed.

> **DE FLORES**
> Do you place me in the rank of verminous fellows,
> To destroy things for wages? Offer gold?
> The life-blood 'of man? Is anything
> Valued too precious for my recompense?
>
> I could ha' hired
> A journeyman in murder at this rate,
> And mine own conscience might have slept,
> And have had the work brought home.
> Double the sum?
> You take a course
> To double my vexation, that's the good you do.

You must fly too,
I'll not stir a foot else.
Why, are not you as guilty, in (I'm sure)
As deep as I. And we should stick together:
Come, your fears counsel you but ill; my absence
Would draw suspect upon you instantly,
There were no rescue for you.
Nor is it fit we two, engaged so jointly,
Should part and live asunder.
What makes your lip so strange?
This must not be betwixt us.
Come, kiss me with a zeal now.
I will not stand so long to beg 'em shortly.
Faith, you're grown much forgetful. You are to blame in't.
I have eased you
Of your trouble, think on it; I am in pain,
And must be eased of you; 'tis a charity,
Justice invites your blood to understand me.
Quickly!
Soft, lady, soft!
The last is not yet paid for! Oh, this act
Has put me into spirit; I was as greedy on't
As the parched earth of moisture, when the clouds weep.
Did you not mark, I wrought myself into't,
Nay, sued and kneeled for't? why was all that pains took?
You see I've thrown contempt upon your gold;
Not that I want it not, for I do piteously,
In order I'll come unto't, and make use on't,
But 'twas not held so precious to begin with,
For I place wealth after the heels of pleasure,
And were not I resolved in my belief
That thy virginity were perfect in thee,
I should but take my recompense with grudging,
As if I had but half my hopes I agreed for.

Look but into your conscience, read me there;
'Tis a true book, you'll find me there your equal:
Pish! Fly not to your birth, but settle you

In what the act has made you, you are no more now.
You must forget your parentage to me;
You are the deed's creature; by that name
You lost your first condition, and I challenge you,
As peace and innocency has turned you out,
And made you one with me.

Yes, my fair murderess; do you urge me?
Though thou writ'st maid, thou whore in thy affection!
'Twas changed from thy first love, and that's a kind
Of whoredom in thy heart; and he's changed now
To bring thy second on, thy Alsemero,
Whom (by all sweets that ever darkness tasted)
If I enjoy thee not, thou ne'er enjoyest!
I'll blast the hopes and joys of marriage,
I'll confess all; my life I rate at nothing.

I shall rest from all lover's plagues then;
I live in pain now; that shooting eye
Will burn my heart to cinders.
She that in life and love refuses me,
In death and shame my partner she shall be.
The wealth of all Valencia shall not buy
My pleasure from me;
Can you weep Fate from its determined purpose?
So soon may you weep me.

(raising her)
Come, rise and shroud your blushes in my bosom;
Silence is one of pleasure's best receipts:
Thy peace is wrought for ever in this yielding.
'Las! how the turtle pants! thou'lt love anon
What thou so fear'st and faint'st to venture on.

(Exeunt.)

brought home: done by an agent as "home employment," i.e., in his own place
and time **suspect**: suspicion **parentage**: birth, position **receipts**: recipes **turtle**:
turtle dove

39

FRIAR BONAVENTURA CONDEMNS GIOVANNI AND URGES PENITENCE FOR HIS THOUGHT OF INCEST

(1629-33) JOHN FORD, 'Tis a Pity She's a Whore, *Act 1, Sc. 1*

Friar Bonaventura is responding with dismay to the youth Giovanni's justification of his incestuous desire for his sister Annabella [see I, #45]. The Friar's response is not so much an argument as a prohibition against argument, since to his mind, the sin lies in venturing on argument at all. But his attempt to forestall Giovanni's pleas altogether ("No more! I may not hear it!") is argument by diversion, for to his mind he is confronting neither reason nor unreason, but disease, "the leprosy of lust that rots the soul." And since the source of aberration is lodged in the soul rather than the mind, remedy, rather than morality's counter-justification, lies in prescriptive treatment (varied over time: analysis, group therapy, lobotomy, flagellant prayer; in this instance, the last). Friar Bonaventura's prescription is specific: self-mortifying prayer six times a day for seven mortifying days.

Giovanni's argument and Bonaventura's prescriptive cure are not joined—they are, in fact, not even talking to one another—in itself a symptomatic condition of moral orthodoxy engaging the unorthodox. But while the Friar's blandishments subsequently become increasingly irrelevant to Giovanni, he achieves deadly relevance for Annabella, who, succumbing to his exhortations, abandons her incestuous love. This initiates her lover's determination to keep their love "unsullied," which he does at the cost of both their lives.

FRIAR

Dispute no more in this; for know, young man,
These are no school-points; nice philosophy
May tolerate unlikely arguments,
But Heaven admits no jest: wits that presumed
On wit too much, by striving how to prove
There was no God with foolish grounds of art,
Discovered first the nearest way to hell,
And filled the world with devilish atheism.
Such questions, youth, are fond: far better 'tis
To bless the sun than reason why it shines;
Yet He thou talk'st of is above the sun.
No more! I may not hear it.

Hie to thy father's house; there lock thee fast
Alone within thy chamber; then fall down
On both thy knees, and grovel on the ground;
Cry to thy heart; wash every word thou utter'st
In tears—and if't be possible—of blood:
Beg Heaven to cleanse the leprosy of lust
That rots thy soul; acknowledge what thou art,
A wretch, a worm, a nothing; weep, sigh, pray
Three times a-day and three times every night:
For seven days' space do this; then, if thou find'st
No change in thy desires, return to me:
I'll think on remedy. Pray for thyself
At home, whilst I pray for thee here.—Away!
My blessing with thee! we have need to pray.

XVII CENTURY FRENCH

40

THE FATHER OF RODRIGUE DETERMINES TO BE REVENGED

(1638) PIERRE CORNEILLE, Le Cid, *tr. Paul Landis, Act 1, Sc. 4*

Don Diegue, now old, has won the most highly prized of offices: the King has given him the post of tutor to his son, the young Prince [see I, #48]. Oddly enough, it is the cap of a courtier's ambition to win this office; it signifies not only the King's trust in his knowledge, wisdom, manners, and attainments, but recognition of his valor on the battlefield. It's the reward of an unblemished reputation after a lifetime of courtier's and warrior's service to the Crown.

The Count, Don Gormez, enraged that the office did not fall to him, taunts Don Diegue: his age, he sneers, has incapacitated him, and he offers a poor example for the young Prince of a warrior's prowess. It should have been a younger man, Don Gormez himself, who was given the honor. Words lead to insult, insult to a blow. Don Diegue is struck, and in his attempt to defend his honor, suffers the humiliation of being easily disarmed by the younger man.

Revenge is in order: whatever his rage at the insult, the code of honor demands it. His son Rodrigue must take his sword, "useless ornament of feeble age," and effect his revenge. His hatred of his own helplessness is joined with his fierce determination to redeem the "honor" of his sword.

> **DON DIEGUE**
> Rage and despair! O villainous old age!
> Have I lived so long to suffer this disgrace?
> Shall laurels gained with slowly whitening locks
> In years of warlike toils fade in a day?

And does the arm all Spain has wondered at,
Whose might has often saved the king his throne,
And kept the rod of empire in his grasp,
Betray me now and leave me unavenged?
O sad remembrance of my vanished glory!
O years of life, undone in one short hour!
New honor, fatal to my happiness!
New eminence, from which my honor falls!
Must the Count's triumph add the final pang,
To die without revenge, or live in shame?
The office, Count, is yours, yours the high place
Of tutor to my prince, that dignity
Demands a man of honor and your hand,
In spite of the king has rendered me unworthy.
And you, brave instrument of my exploits,
But useless ornament of feeble age,
Sword, once so feared, which now in this affront
Served only to parade my impotence.
Go, quit henceforth the least of mortal men,
Pass to avenge me into worthier hands.

41

THE EMPEROR AUGUSTUS RUMINATES ON
THE FUTILITY OF POWER
(1640) PIERRE CORNEILLE, Cinna, *tr. Paul Landis, Act 2, Sc.1*

In France and England in the late 17th and 18th centuries, the Roman Emperor Augustus was revered, and Augustan Rome emulated. The first years of the Roman Empire under Augustus were taken to be its greatest moment, and Augustus himself its model governor. Corneille in *Cinna* pays tribute to this devotion in one of his greatest, if not his greatest, character: the Augustus who withstands sedition, relying on the tempered wisdom of the Stoic, deeply committed to Reason, profoundly alert to the dangers of Passion, superbly endowed with the Will to withstand the one and live by the other. Reason, Passion, Will, the triad within which Corneille's characters find their moral center.

In a deeply ruminative vein, he asks his two trusted counselors to hear him as he debates with himself on the wisdom of keeping or surrendering his office altogether. His speech is a kind of summary of the vanity of human wishes in which he counters the examples of "barbarous" Sulla, who, during the days of the Republic, retired from public office and died beloved, and Augustus' father, "gentle" Julius Caesar, who continued to enjoy office and was assassinated. Of these examples, he concludes, "One beckons me to follow, one breeds fear." But examples themselves, he argues, can be deceptive, since "What destroys one man preserves another." And so, he concludes, the decision of whether to remain as King or resign and leave Rome a republic will wait on the advice of these trusted advisers, whom he admonishes to speak, as he has done, with candor "as to a friend."

A classic speech of justification, the most distinctive rhetorical device of French Classical tragedy, is one in which the protagonist weighs at length and with great specificity the pros and cons of his last or his next move. Since in these speeches it isn't practical but ethical determinants that weigh most powerfully, they characteristically reveal the moral measure of the man. And as characters tortuously reason their way to a decision, weighing the impulses of passion against codified injunctions, they provide the essential drama of French Classical tragedy. The issue is not so much the tragedy's outcome as the tangle of justifications that bring about that outcome, and the sometimes ironic, sometimes symmetrical relation between morally-engendered causes and their consequences.

Augustus' speech, then, like all speeches of justification, is an arduous reaching-toward, a troubled journey through pros and cons, toward resolution. His intention is fixed—to arrive at that resolution—but the manner, the sagacity, the reasonableness with which he arrives at what is in itself a tempered, exemplary decision (to take into account the advice of trusted counselors) gives us our first insight into the moral stature of Augustus.

Ironically, these counselors, Cinna and Maximus, will advise in bad faith; they are the two leaders of the conspiracy making plans to assassinate Augustus.

> **AUGUSTUS**
> Let all retire and no one enter here.
> You, Cinna, stay and, Maximus, you too.
>
> *(Exit Courtiers)*
> This absolute power over land and sea,
> This sovereign sway I hold o'er all the world,
> This grandeur without limit, this high rank,
> Which has already cost such suffering;—
> Yes, all which in my noble eminence
> Calls admiration from a flattering court,
> Is but a shining bauble, dazzling first,
> But losing all attraction once enjoyed.
> Ambition palls when once it is accomplished;
> And an opposing passion takes its place.
> So now our spirit, having striven ever
> To the last breath to gain some certain end,
> Turns on itself, with nothing more to conquer,
> And having reached the peak would fain descend.
> I longed for empire, and I won to it,
> But while I longed for it, I knew it not:
> Possessing it, I found that all its charms
> Turned into heavy cares and constant fears.

A thousand secret foes deserving death,
No pleasure without trouble, no repose.
Sulla before me held this power supreme:
Great Julius, my father, too, enjoyed it.
But with what different eyes they looked upon it.
One gave it up, the other would have held it.
One, cruel and barbarous, died well beloved,
Like any worthy citizen, at home;
The other, ever gentle, met his end
In the senate house by an assassin's hand.
These fresh examples ought to serve to teach me;
If solely by example one may learn.
One beckons me to follow, one brings fear;
Yet an example often proves to be
A mirror of deception, and the plan
Of destiny which so disturbs our thoughts
Not always written in the chosen steps.
Now one is broken and another saved,
And what destroys one man preserves another.
There, my good friends; you see what troubles me.
Think not at all of this great state of mine,
Hateful to Romans, wearying to myself;
Deal with me as a friend, not as a sovereign:
Augustus, Rome, the empire, rest on you:
You shall decide if Europe, Asia,
Or Africa be governed by a king
Or a republic. Yours to say if I
Be emperor or simple citizen.

Lucius Cornelius **Sulla** (138-78 BC): Roman general and dictator **met his end...
hand**: Julius Caesar was murdered by conspirators in the senate

42

THE EMPEROR AUGUSTUS UNDERGOES HIS DARK NIGHT OF THE SOUL

(1640) PIERRE CORNEILLE, Cinna, *tr. Paul Landis, Act 4, Sc. 2*

The favor of Augustus toward his two most trusted subjects, Cinna and Maximus [see II, #41], is outweighed for them by the cruelties suffered during his bloody path to the throne and in his reign, which leaves "fields full of horrors, Rome piled high with dead." At first emulating the republican idealism of Brutus and Cassius in their assassination of Caesar, they organize a conspiracy. But Maximus, out of jealousy of Cinna, his rival in love, betrays the conspirators. Augustus, shocked by the betrayal of his two closest allies, nevertheless instinctively responds, "There is no crime against me that repentance/ Will not erase."

But this is followed by a remarkable episode in which Augustus, alone, undergoes his dark night of the soul. Self-accusing, castigating the crimes of his past, denigrating his "omnipotence," and judging his treasonous subjects just. Enraged against himself, he suffers ultimate self-betrayal by abandoning himself to "passion." "Ah, how my reason fails me in my need!" he cries, and it fails him utterly. His decision flails between murdering his betrayers and murdering himself; finding revenge by dying and so cheating his assassins of their revenge, and taking a tyrant's total revenge against the Rome that "hates us." Recovering, he looks back on his momentary derangement, and mourns his helplessless to overcome "the awful battle of a wavering heart." At the end, the battle remains unresolved: he prays for "some command," some counsel to tell him what to "follow, what avoid,/ And either let me die, or let me reign." He's undergone the torment of a man of conscience looking implacably into himself, but still ending with his total bafflement altogether unresolved.

AUGUSTUS

O Heaven, to whom is it your will that I
Entrust my life, the secrets of my soul?
Take back the power with which you have endowed me,
If it but steals my friends to give me subjects,
If regal splendors must be fated ever,
Even by the greatest favors they can grant,
To foster only hate, if your stern law
Condemns a king to cherish only those
Who burn to have his blood. Nothing is certain.
Omnipotence is bought with ceaseless fear.
Look in your heart, Octavius, and cease
Your lamentations. What! Would you be spared,
Who have spared none yourself? Think of the waves
Of blood in which your arms are bathed. How much
Reddened the fields of Macedonia;
How much was shed in Antony's defeat;
How much in Sextus' fall. Then look once more
Upon Perugia drowned in its own blood,
With all its citizens. Recall again,
After all this, your murderous proscriptions
In which you were yourself the butcherer;
Sink the knife in your own tutor's breast,
And dare to cry injustice against fate,
Seeing your subjects armed for your destruction,
Taught by your own example how to kill you,
Ignoring rights, which you did not respect!
Their treason is deserved, sanctioned by heaven:
Leave your throne as you acquired it;
Shed faithless blood for infidelity;
Suffer ingratitude for having showed it.
Ah, how my reason fails me in my need!
What madness, Cinna, that I should accuse
Myself and pardon you. You, whose deceit
Convinced me to retain the sovereignty,
For which you wish to punish me, who think
Me criminal, yet make my only crime;
You who sustain a throne usurped solely
To strike it down and cover your intention

With shameless zeal, and set yourself against
The welfare of the State to murder me?
Should I forget this and withhold my wrath?
Let you live safely who have threatened me?
No! No! The very thought is treasonable;
Who pardons freely, but invites attack;
Punish the assassins, and proscribe the plotters!
Ah! Always blood! Always punishment!
I weary of cruelty, yet cannot stop it.
I would be feared, and yet can only anger.
Rome is a hydra bent upon my ruin,
One head struck off a thousand take its place.
And blood shed by a thousand traitors renders
My life more cursed, yet no more assured.
Octavius, wait not for the stroke of some
New Brutus. Die, and rob him of his glory;
The attempt to live were cowardly and vain
When such a host of brave men vow your death;
If every noble youth of Rome is stirred,
Time after time, to plot against your life.
Die, since it is a sore you cannot heal.
Die, since you must lose everything or die.
Life is a little thing, and what small part
Of life remains for you is not worth buying
At such a grievous cost. Die, but at least
Go grandly off, put out your spirit's torch
In this mad ingrate's blood, and, dying, offer
This traitor to yourself in sacrifice;
Fulfill his wishes, punish him for murder;
Make your own death his torture in arranging
That he shall witness it, but not enjoy it.
But let us more enjoy his punishment,
And if Rome hates us, triumph o'er its hate.
O Romans! O revenge! O sovereign power!
O awful battle of a wavering heart,
Which shrinks at once from all that it decides!
Give some command to this unhappy prince,
What counsel he should follow, what avoid,
And either let me die or let me reign.

43

THE EMPEROR AUGUSTUS REASONS WITH HIS WOULD-BE ASSASSIN

(1640) PIERRE CORNEILLE, Cinna, *tr. Paul Landis, Act 5, Sc. 1*

The Augustus who emerges after his painful "battle of a wavering heart" [see II, #42] is renewed; his resolve, his reason, are fully restored, and he approaches Cinna, his would-be assassin, having accomplished in the interim what is literally the triumph of his will. The force of will guides Augustus through his meeting with Cinna to persuade rather than to avenge, and in the path of reason he takes— reciting with studied equanimity the favors he's heaped on Cinna, the mercy he's granted him in the past ("My only vengeance was to give you life"), the complete confidence he's placed in him subsequently— carries in its very tone as well as in its argument the magnanimity to which Augustus is aspiring.

So much for Part One of his brief, by which Cinna is meant to be persuaded toward gratitude. Part Two persuades towards shame, by underscoring—through the mere recitation of the details of the plot and the listing of its followers—the baseness of the enterprise. The tactic obviously succeeds: Cinna apparently responds with "confusion," his sense of dishonor awakened.

Part Three: persuasion toward recognition of the plot's pointlessness. "What was your plan, what did you mean to do?" asks Augustus, and spells out the inherent absurdity of conspirator Cinna's logic. If it was liberty—freedom from monarchy—the conspirators aimed at, murdering Augustus was hardly necessary: nothing was more to his taste than to be free of monarchy's burdens. "You might have had it without the trouble of assassination." If, on the other hand, it was Cinna's intention to become monarch in Augustus' place, he would need the homage, the "trembling," of Rome. That, Augustus lays down as gospel, was unlikely, since the homage paid to Cinna by the public was not to him but to the "star" to which Augustus raised him. "My favor makes your glory, out of that/ Your power grows," and abandoned by Augustus' sustaining hand ("There needs but the withdrawal of my hand"), he will be left with neither power nor authority nor "glory."

But the final argument is the most deadly: were he, who was "raised up" to his position by Augustus, to become monarch, the "old nobility," the conspirators who joined him, would not for long "sink their pride" to be ruled by such an upstart. And so, Augustus implies, the chain of conspiracy and assassination would simply be perpetuated.

In the end, it is not this speech alone which persuades Cinna and the other conspirators to submit loyally to Augustus' rule; in his reply, Cinna holds to his deepest grievances, and so, he warns, "Expect no cringing penitence from me." He knows what he has done, he says, and what Augustus must do. But it is Augustus' sagacity that, after several further trials, wins victory for himself, for Rome's political stability, for reason's rule.

> **AUGUSTUS**
> Be seated, Cinna, and on every point
> Follow the orders which I lay upon you;
> In silence lend your ear to what I say;
> Neither by word nor cry break in upon me;
> Hold your tongue captive, and if silence stir
> Some violence in your feelings, afterwards
> You shall be able to reply at leisure.
> Afterwards clear yourself, if possible.
> Meanwhile, give ear to me, and keep your word.
> You planned to kill me in the Capitol
> Tomorrow during the sacrifice, your hand
> From which I should have taken the incense

Was to have struck the fatal blow as signal;
Half of your people were to hold the door,
The other half to follow you and help.
Are these true words, or simply base suspicion?
Shall I recite for you the murderers' names?
Proculus, Glabrius, Virginius,
Rutilus, Plantus, Lenas, Pomponius,
Marcellus, Albinus, Icilius,
Maximus, whom next yourself I loved;
'Twere too much honor even to name the rest;
A mob of men sunk deep in debt and crime,
On whom my just decrees rest heavily,
And who, despairing of escape, knew well
They could not live if all were not o'erthrown.
You are silent now, and you preserve your silence
More from confusion than obedience.
What was your plan, what did you mean to do
When I lay in the temple at your feet?
To free your country from a monarch's sway?
If I interpreted your words aright,
Her future welfare hung upon a sovereign
Who, to preserve all, holds all as his own;
And if her liberty was your desire,
No force was needed to make me give it back.
In the name of all the State you might have had it
Without the trouble of assassination.
What was your plan? To reign here in my place?
It were a strangely evil destiny
If in your mounting to the royal throne
You found in Rome no obstacle but me.
If she be sunk to such a state that you
Are, after me, her greatest, that the weight
Of the Roman Empire, after I am dead,
Could fall into no better hands than yours.
Know yourself, Cinna, look into your heart:
They honor you in Rome. They court you, love you,
Tremble before you, offer you their homage;
Your star is high. What you would do, you can:

But none would be too mean to pity you
If I abandoned you to your deserts.

Deny it if you dare, tell me your worth,
Recount your virtues and your glorious deeds,
Those rare accomplishments with which you pleased me
And all that raised you up above the herd.
My favor makes your glory, out of that
Your power grows; that only raised you up,
And held you there, 'tis that the Romans honor,
Not yourself. You have no rank or power
Except I give it you, and for your fall
There needs but the withdrawal of my hand,
Which is your sole support. But I prefer
To yield to your desire. Reign, if you will,
Even if it cost my life. But dare you think
That Cassius, Servilius, Metellus,
Paulus and Fabius and all the rest
For whom the noble heroes of their blood
Are living images, will sink the pride
Of such an old nobility as theirs
Only that you may rule them in my stead?
Now speak, I give you leave.

44

THESEUS ACCUSES HIS SON OF ADULTERY
(1677) JEAN RACINE, Phaedra, *tr. R. Henderson, Act 4*

As in Euripides' *Hippolytus* [see II, #15], Theseus condemns his son
to exile and death because of his wife Phaedra's false charge that
he seduced her. But it is a different Theseus and a different Hippolytus
that confront one another in Racine. The father is not confronting a
son, as he does in Euripides, whose character and lifestyle he found
contemptibly unmanly, contemptibly unmartial, and with the sup-

posed discovery of his adultery, giving voice to his outrage along with his contempt. Racine's Theseus has held his son in the high esteem automatically granted by one man of honor to another. Both, he believed, were on a par in their honor and virtue. But just as no grey area exists for women in honor-code legalism between virgin and whore, so none exists between the man of perfect integrity and the man of none. It's Theseus' intent in the first part of his speech to, in effect, "rename" his son, to put him in another light, to supplant his former image.

There is no brief, as there is in Euripides, in which the father spells out the evidence of his son's betrayal: no need for it here. The whiff of scandal is enough; the report of Phaedra's nurse is enough; the conclusion is not in doubt. He addresses, then, this "traitor," this "creature," this "foul remnant." So converted in image, it's impossible for Theseus to comprehend how such an insolent thing could "dare to rear before me [his] hostile face," how he could not have already fled to "unheard-of lands" where Theseus' name is unknown.

Given so "abhorrent," so reduced a sight, Theseus' justice is fitting: the sea-god's wrath, promised by the god to Theseus for a single act of vengeance. He invokes it, and with a last, vestigial pang of conscience, "his vitals wrung" recalling how he had once loved his son, he sends him to his horrible doom.

> **THESEUS**
> Ah, there he is! Great gods! That noble manner
> Might well deceive an eye less fond than mine!
> Why should the sacred mark of virtue shine
> Bright on the forehead of an evil wretch?
> Why should the blackness of a traitor's heart
> Not show itself by sure and certain signs?
> Traitor, how dare you show yourself before me?
> Monster, whom Heaven's bolts have spared too long!

A last survivor of that robber hand
Whereof I cleansed the earth, your brutal lust
Scorned to respect even my marriage bed!
And now you dare—my hated foe—to come
Here to my presence, here where all things are filled
And foul with infamy, instead of seeking
Some unknown land, that never heard my name.
Fly, traitor, fly! Stay not to tempt my wrath!
I scarce restrain it. Do not brave my hatred.
I have been shamed forever; 'tis enough
To be the father of so vile a son,
Without your death, to stain indelibly
The splendid record of my noble deeds.
Fly! And unless you yearn for punishment
To make you yet another villain slain,
Take heed that this sun, shining on us now
Shall see your foot no more upon this soil.
I say it once again—fly!—and in haste!
Rid all my realms of your detested person.
On thee—on thee, great Neptune, do I call!
If once I cleared thy shores of murderers,
Remember, then, thy promise to reward me
For these good deeds, by granting my first prayer.
I was held long in close captivity.
I did not then demand thy mighty aid,
For I have saved so great a privilege
To use in greatest need. That time is come.
And now I ask—avenge a wretched father!
I leave this traitor subject to thy wrath.
I ask that thou shouldst quench his fires in blood,
And by thy fury, I will judge thy favor!

Were you beyond the Pillars of Alcides,
Your perjured presence still were far too near me!
Go seek for friends who praise adultery,
And look for those who clap their hands at incest!—

Low traitors, lawless,—steeped in infamy—
Fit comforters for such a one as you!
Go from my sight!—
This last time I will say it—traitor, go!
And do not wait until a father's anger
Drives you away in public execration!

(Exit Hippolytus. Theseus alone.)
Wretch! Thou must meet inevitable ruin!
Neptune has sworn by Styx—an oath most dreadful
Even to gods—and he will keep his promise.
Thou canst not ever flee from his revenge.
I loved thee, and in spite of this offense
My heart is moved by what I see for thee.
Nay, but thy doom is but too fully earned.
Had father ever better cause for rage?
O you just gods, who see my crushing grief,
Why was I cursed with such an evil son?

Pillar of Alcides: door-post erected in honor of Hercules at the entrance of hell
(Hades)

RESTORATION

45
SAMSON IN TORMENT YEARNS FOR HIS DEATH
(1668-70) JOHN MILTON, Samson Agonistes, *Lines 606-651*

Milton's verbal obfuscations are so obsessive, latinate, and over-riding to modern ears on first sounding that, for the casual ear, his language exhibits only its thick texture, but not its sense, and certainly not its emotional power. Let's parse it slowly, and get to what is for most of us below the surface—its clear sense and its overwhelming, brooding emotion.

Samson Agonistes is a rare example in English drama of the direct and faithful imitation of Greek tragedy, very close in form to Aeschylus: a series of stationary monologues or duologues separated by choral interludes. Like *Prometheus Bound,* it focuses on a single protagonist in fixed torment, and through the episodes charts the progress of his inward reasoning, its emotional course and its developing intent.

For Samson, that inner development leads to a paradoxically triumphant catastrophe: the destruction of the temple of the Philistines and of himself. "Disciplined in temperance," as one critic put it, he "grows perfect in strength."

In the first stage of that progress toward "temperance," he's remote from its discipline. Captured and blinded by the Philistines, bound in chains like Prometheus, and living through the physical torment of a captive's labors, he cries out, first, against his most painful suffering: his blindness. "O dark, dark, dark, amid the blaze of noon,/ Irrecoverably dark, total eclipse/ Without all hope of day." His father Manoah comes to comfort him, promising to petition the Philistines for his ransom, a proposal Samson rejects. Conquered though he is, the God of Abraham will yet "rise, and his great name assert," despite

Samson's own betrayal of Him—all fault, he insists, belonging to himself alone, and none to Fate or God. His faults of marriage to the Canaanite Delilah, of succumbing to laxity and sensuality, of whispering to her the secret of his strength, are sins of his own contriving.

With so much gained—his assumption of all fault as his own—he laments a deeper anguish than the physical ones of blindness and bodily harm: the torments of the mind. There, in the mind, is the greater anguish: pain like the pain of wounded "entrails, joints and limbs," only more intense.

Next sentence (Milton's sentences take on the burden of paragraphs, or, poetically, are the equivalent of stanzas, and are sometimes as long): the intensification of mental pain. It does not merely last, but rankles, "ferments," produces rage, reaches a level of "black mortification." And—next sentence—his thoughts (and here analogy to medicine takes over) are "armed with deadly stings." The "stings" Milton has in mind are the effects of poisonous salts in the stomach, which according to an early commentator on the tragedy, "stimulate, tear, inflame and exulcerate the tender fibres" in the stomach, a torment which hopefully ends in "death's benumbing opium." Since sleep provides no relief, nothing but the opium of death can relieve the mind's perpetually increasing pain. And since death's relief does not come, he reaches the climax, or nadir, of his intellectual torment: despair, and "the sense of Heaven's desertion."

There's the crux of this stage of Samson's "progress," his belief in God's desertion at the time of his most unendurable pain. But it is, paradoxically, the pain of his own guilt, and of his own betrayal of God. And this in turn leads—next three sentences—to his almost blissful recollection of when he was at one with God, when he was God's right arm—from birth elected; two later signs from Heaven; guided by God's hand toward "abstemiousness," toward a life without temptation; guided by God's hand to victories over their common enemies.

And now, by contrast—next two sentences—abandoned to the "cruelty and scorn" of the very enemies God caused him to provoke.

With what alternatives, Sampson argues, is he now left? "Remediless," he has only one remaining prayer: the balm of death.

From this descent into longing for death, each subsequent confrontation—contending with Delilah, with the giant Harapha, with the messenger from the Philistine ruler Dagon—brings Samson, stage by stage, once more to a sense of oneness with God. Samson leaving for the temple by Dagon's command, "with inward eyes illuminated," makes his final gesture, once again as God's arm.

> **SAMSON**
> Oh, that torment should not be confined
> To the body's wounds and sores,
> With maladies innumerable
> In heart, head, breast, and reins,
> But must secret passage find
> To th' inmost mind,
> There exercise all his fierce accidents,
> And on her purest spirits prey,
> As on entrails, joints, and limbs,
> With answerable pains, but more intense,
> Though void of corporal sense!
> My griefs not only pain me
> As a lingering disease,
> But, finding no redress, ferment and rage;
> Nor less than wounds immedicable.
> Rankle, and fester, and gangrene,
> To black mortification.
> Thoughts, my tormentors, armed with daily stings,
> Mangle my apprehensive tenderest parts,
> Exasperate, exulcerate, and raise
> Dire inflammation, which no cooling herb
> Or med'cinal liquor can assuage,

Nor breath of vernal air from snowy Alp.
Sleep hath forsook and given me o'er
To death's benumbing opium as my only cure;
Thence faintings, swoonings of despair,
And sense of Heaven's desertion.
I was his nursling once and choice delight,
His destined from the womb,
Promised by heavenly message 'twice descending.
Under his special eye
Abstemious I grew up and thrived amain,
He led me onto mightiest deeds,
Above the nerve of mortal arm,
Against the uncircumcised, our enemies:
But now hath cast me off as never known,
And to those cruel enemies,
Whom I by his appointment had provoked,
Left me, all helpless with th' irreparable loss
Of sight, reserved alive to be repeated
The subject of their cruelty or scorn.
Nor am I in the list of them that hope;
Hopeless are all my evils; all remediless.
'This one prayer yet remains, might I be heard,
No long petition—speedy death,
The close of all my miseries and the balm.

reins: kidneys **accidents**: chances occurences **answerable**: commensurate, proportional **void of corporal sense**: without bodily effect **immedicable**: incurable **apprehensive**: intellectual, mental **vernal**: spring-like **His destined** champion **amain**: exceedingly, greatly **nerve**: strength, vigor **reserved alive**: deliberately kept alive

46

MILTON'S TRAGIC CONCLUSION: 'CALM OF MIND, ALL PASSION SPENT'

(1668-70) JOHN MILTON, *Samson Agonistes*, *Lines 1708-1758*

It is Manoah, Samson's father, who delivers the eulogy over the tragedy's event. This is one of the great expressions in Western literature not only of purged feeling at tragedy's end, but of a remarkable and perfect equanimity of intellect and emotion in appraising, overcoming, and entering into accord, into voluntary oneness, with what is. The state of things, or, as Nietzsche's Zarathustra put it, uttering "The Great Yea-saying." "Nothing is here for tears, nothing to wail/ Or knock the breast," writes Milton. "His [God's} servants he with new acquist [acquisition]/ Of true experience from this real event,/ With peace, and consolation hath dismissed, / And calm of mind, all passion spent." Or, to put it grossly, after witnessing this tragedy, He, God, sends us home in this perfectly equilibrated, emptied/full condition.

What is left of tragic perception? Its overcoming. "Nothing but well and fair," asserts Manoah, "And what may quiet us in a death so noble." But as in *Oedipus at Colonus* [see II, #23], it is not merely the death so noble of the protagonist but the sensibility so noble of the poet that accomplishes this transcendent assent. "Now let the weeping cease," sings Sophocles' chorus at his play's end. "Let no one mourn again. These things are in the hands of God." These things are as they are. These things are so. Calibrating that exact middle register is the quietest and most spectacular of literary triumphs. I add one more, though it's probably impertinent to interject a writer whom I'm one of very few to consider to be one of the greatest writers of the 20th century. At the conclusion of Gertrude Stein's *Four Saints in Three Acts,* when the chorus of "Saints" have finished with the human experience—"Wed dead led said" is their chant as they approach their transcendent "place"—and after arranging themselves in the unanticipated fourth act of their "play," sitting in Heaven, calm, comfortable, "Last act," they sing. "Which is a fact."

MANOAH

Come, come; no time for lamentation now,
Nor much more cause. Samson hath quit himself
Like Samson, and heroicly hath finished
A life heroic, on his enemies
Fully revenged—hath left them years of mourning
And lamentation to the sons of Caphtor
Through all Philistian bounds; to Israel
Honor hath left and freedom; let but them
Find courage to lay hold on this occasion;
To himself and father's house eternal fame;
And, which is best and happiest yet, all this
With God not parted from him, as was feared,
But favoring and assisting to the end.
Nothing is here for tears, nothing to wail
Or knock the breast; no weakness; no contempt,
Dispraise, or blame; nothing but well and fair,
And what may quiet us in a death so noble.
Let us go find the body where it lies
Soaked in his enemies' blood, and from the stream
With lavers pure, and cleansing herbs, wash off
The clotted gore. I, with what speed the while
(Gaza is not in plight to say us nay),
Will send for all my kindred, all my friends,
To fetch him hence, and solemnly attend,
With silent obsequy and funeral train,
Home to his father's house. There will I build him
A monument, and plant it round with shade
Of laurel evergreen and branching palm,
With all his trophies hung, and acts enrolled
In copious legend, or sweet lyric song.

Thither shall all the valiant youth resort,
And from his memory inflame their breasts
To matchless valor and adventures high;
The virgins also shall, on feastful days,
Visit his tomb with flowers, only bewailing
His lot unfortunate in nuptial choice,
From whence captivity and loss of eyes.
All is best, though we oft doubt
What th' unsearchable dispose
Of Highest Wisdom brings about,
And ever best found in the close.
Oft he seems to hide his face,
But unexpectedly returns,
And to his faithful champion hath in place
Bore witness gloriously; whence Gaza mourns,
And all that band them to resist
His uncontrollable intent.
His servants he, with new acquist
Of true experience from this great event,
With peace and consolation hath dismissed,
And calm of mind, all passion spent.

quit: acquitted **Caphtor** and his sons are Philistines **lavers**: basins, vessels for washing **speed**: assistance, aid **will send... obsequy**: based on the Scriptures, Judges XVI.31, "Then his brethren, and all the house of his father, came down and took him, and brought him up, and buried him..."; the "silent obsequy" alludes to the Jewish funeral custom of the near relations of the deceased sitting down on the floor of the mourning house in silence **all his trophies hung**: Milton might be alluding to the custom of hanging the sword, helmet and ensignia over the tombs of eminent persons **unsearcheable dispose**: unknowable dispensation **band**: bind, coerce **acquist**: acquisition, gain

47

ANTONY MOURNS HIS FALLEN STATE
(1671) JOHN DRYDEN, *All for Love, Act 1, Sc. 1*

After his defeat at the battle of Actium, Antony was prostrate. Five years earlier, after his division of the Roman world with Octavius—the brother of his wife, Octavia—Antony became the ruler of the Eastern empire, and returned to Alexandria and the comforts of Cleopatra, Egypt's Queen. But because of the ease with which he disposed of kingdoms and provinces in her favor, and the dissipation of his life with her, he alienated his supporters, and the Roman senate declared war against Cleopatra and himself. After two years of military preparation, he was defeated at Actium, and ignominiously followed Cleopatra, who had escaped with 60 ships, from the scene of the sea battle.

Now he is not only in despair, but in delusion. His despair is expressed in his certainty that his ashes will soon be borne by his abandoned wife Octavia, and mourned *pro forma* and cynically by his rival Octavius. His delusion is self-willed: unable to bear the image he's conjured up of his death, he conjures up another image of himself alone and abandoned, a primitive shepherd lying in a bucolic setting along with his flocks, sighing, a captive of melancholy music.

Considerably distant though it is from Shakespeare's portrait of Antony in his despair, still in Dryden's newly explored vein of softened tragic heroics, there is a deep sensitivity in his portrayal of this self-condemned anti-hero longing for pastoral oblivion.

ANTONY

(Having thrown himself down)

Lie there, thou shadow of an emperor;
The place thou pressest on thy mother earth
Is all thy empire now; now it contains thee;
Some few days hence, and then 'twill be too large,
When thou'rt contracted in thy narrow urn,
Shrunk to a few cold ashes; then Octavia
(For Cleopatra will not live to see it),
Octavia then will have thee all her own,
And bear thee in her widowed hand to Caesar;
Caesar will weep, the crocodile will weep,
To see his rival of the universe
Lie still and peaceful there. I'll think no more on't.
Give me some music; look that it be sad.
I'll soothe my melancholy till I swell
And burst myself with sighing.

(Soft music)

'Tis somewhat to my humor. Stay, I fancy
I'm now turned wild, a commoner of nature;
Of all forsaken and forsaking all,
Live in a shady forest's sylvan scene,
Stretched at my length beneath some blasted oak,
I lean my head upon the mossy bark
And look just of a piece as I grew from it;
My uncombed locks, matted like mistletoe,
Hang o'er my hoary face; a murm'ring brook
Runs at my foot. The herd come jumping by me
And, fearless, quench their thirst while I look on,
And take me for their fellow-citizen.
More of this image, more; it lulls my thoughts.

48

ANTONY ACCUSES CLEOPATRA OF BEING THE INSTRUMENT OF HIS DOWNFALL

(1671) JOHN DRYDEN, *All for Love*, *Act 2, Sc. 1*

After Antony's bout with despair, Ventidius, Antony's still loyal lieutenant, succeeds in bringing him once again into war-like, soldier-like demeanor, and they are readying for battle against Octavius to reverse the outcome of Actium [see II, #47]. Cleopatra's eunuch, her wily champion Alexis, intercepts their departure, pleads Cleopatra's "millions of sighs and tears" of remorse for her catastrophic flight from battle, and expertly persuades Antony to face her once more before his military departure. To the despair of Ventidius, Antony, "bred," as he says, "to the rules of soft humanity," assents to the interview.

On meeting, Cleopatra quickly puts Antony on the defensive to justify his leaving her. He takes the occasion to justify himself fully, and to accuse her for her defection and treachery. He recounts, with sober reason—careful not to weaken the force of his argument with too much of a show of emotion—the history of their love from its beginning: her years of attachment to Caesar, when as a young officer Antony had already fallen in love with her, to her betrayal of their cause at Actium.

Carefully measured statement, the recitation of facts, the accurate recall of their history: an unanswerable case against further dalliance, or further trust in Cleopatra. And yet at once following this, Cleopatra's reply in her defense, once more, and entirely, seduces him.

ANTONY

We have loved each other
Into our mutual ruin.
If I mix a lie
With any truth, reproach me freely with it;
Else, favor me with silence.
That I derive my ruin
From you alone—
You promised me your silence,
And you break it
Ere I have scarce begun.
When I beheld you first, it was in Egypt.
Ere Caesar saw your eyes, you gave me love,
And were too young to know it; that I settled
Your father in his throne was for your sake;
I left the acknowledgment for time to ripen.
Caesar stepped in and with a greedy hand
Plucked the green fruit ere the first blush of red,
Yet cleaving to the bough. He was my lord,
And was, beside, too great for me to rival.
But I deserved you first, though he enjoyed you.
When, after, I beheld you in Cilicia,
An enemy to Rome, I pardoned you.
I loved you still and took your weak excuses,
Took you into my bosom, stained by Caesar,
And not half mine. I went to Egypt with you,
And hid me from the business of the world,
Shut out inquiring nations from my sight
To give whole years to you.

How I loved,
Witness, ye days and nights and all your hours
That danced away with down upon your feet,
As all your business were to count my passion!
One day passed by and nothing saw but love;
Another came and still 'twas only love.

The suns were wearied out with looking on,
And I untired with loving.
I saw you every day, and all the day;
And every day was still but as the first,
So eager was I still to see you more.
While within your arms I lay,
The world fell moldering from my hands each hour,
And left me scarce a grasp—I thank your love for't.

Fulvia died
(Pardon, you gods, with my unkindness died);
To set the world at peace I took Octavia,
This Caesar's sister; in her pride of youth
And flower of beauty did I wed that lady,
Whom, blushing, I must praise, because I left her.
You called; my love obeyed the fatal summons.
This raised the Roman arms; the cause was yours.
I would have fought by land where I was stronger;
You hindered it. Yet, when I fought at sea,
Forsook me fighting; and (O stain to honor!
O lasting shame!) I knew not that I fled,
But fled to follow you.
All this you caused.
And would you multiply more ruins on me?

Twelve legions I have left, my last recruits,
And you have watched the news, and bring your eyes
To seize them, too. If you have aught to answer,
Now speak, you have free leave.

Fulvia: Antony's first wife **this Caesar**: Augustus Caesar, Julius Caesar's adopted son

49

THE GREAT CONSTABLE EXPLAINS THE FOLLY OF VIRTUE TO HIS SON, HIS PRISONER

(1679) JOHN CROWNE, The Ambitious Statesman, *Act 5, Sc. 1*

The Great Constable is the great villain of *The Ambitious Statesman.* At the play's opening, he has been deposed from his high offices which had been, in his ambitious mind, a stepping-stone to rebellion against his King; with his son's alliance, he would take over the monarchy and its succession. In revenge for his disgrace, and with the intention of getting to his ultimate objective nevertheless, he resolves to implement his long-laid plans of rebellion at once. The complications of those plans, and the cunning with which they've been set, have one major loophole: the virtue of his son, the Duke of Vendosme; in the Constable's mind, a crippling defect. Loyalty to monarchy would balk at rebellion. His efforts to undermine it by the one avenue open to him—his son's anticipated and certain rage should he believe the defection of his fiancee in favor of the King's son— eventually fails; even in the face of personal rage against the throne's heir, Vendosme is proof against sedition. In the end, the Constable's plots fail so spectacularly that, in order to save himself, he is left in the gruesome position of himself having to be his son's executioner.

Even at this juncture, he makes one last attempt to overcome that stubborn virtue, and to enlist his son in a final attempt at rebellion. The attempt is made in the context of a last debate between them, a debate that threads through the play and serves as its fundamental thesis: though both are in melancholy agreement about the world's iniquities, their remedies are opposite. One wants to triumph over them by the example of inflexible moral conduct; the other wants to labor with craft using the world's ways to gain the only blessings they afford: power and position.

The Constable so far fails in persuading him that his son, out of his unblemished "reverence for Princes," for his King and even for the King's son who betrayed him, becomes, even at his death, the instrument of the Constable's undoing.

The Constable's intelligence, his cunning and his unscrupulousness echo Sejanus' in Ben Jonson's play [see II, #35, 36] Like Sejanus, he projects his plans deep into the future; they involve multiple steps, and therefore multiple safeguards along their projected way. It is the Constable's single-mindedness both in his plannings and in his beliefs that make possible his extraordinary interim successes; but, given the natural limits of his station with respect to both God and King, it is the overreaching of his ambition that inevitably defeats him. The play was clearly intended for and succeeds in being a powerful apologia for Royalist sentiment during the troubled latter days of Charles II's reign. The Great Constable is portrayed as the most hated of all villains: a conniving traitor to his King.

> **CONSTABLE**
> So, Sir, are you here ?
> Now you'll believe my principles are true.
> Who ever wou'd be vertuous, is a fool:
> For he endeavours to plant Vertue here
> In a damn'd world, where it no more will grow
> Than Oranges in Lapland. It is true,
> 'Twill peer sometimes a little above ground.
> But never but in dung of poverty;
> And then it smell's so ill, people of quality
> Ne're take it in their bosoms.
> Flay, the projecting fool that aims at Vertue,
> Is a ridiculous Chymist, that wou'd make
> A vertuous thing out of a man or woman,
> Who have not a grain of honesty about 'em;
> And they have some parts can never be made honest.
> Nay, there is no false fellow like your fool.

Who wou'd be virtuous ? for your steady villain
Who sticks at nothing, is most true to every thing;
But your lame fool who halt's 'tween Vice and Vertue.
Is false to both, and so is true to nothing,
And so has no friends in Heaven or Hell.
And that's the reason he never thrives.
Perhaps there never were such things as Vertues,
But only in men's fancies like the Phenix.
Or if they once have been, they'r now but names
Of natures lost, which came into the world,
But cou'd not live nor propagate their kind.
How shou'd they propagate? Your virtuous fellow
Is an Hermophradite, he has two sexes,
Virtue and Vice, and such a monster thou art:
To glory thou art a girl, but to woman
Thou art a vig'rous Man! Oh! thou poor sinner!
To scorn ambition, the sin of angels,
And stoop to be a goat.

Are you here?: addressing his son, in prison, awaiting execution **Lapland:** a
region in Scandinavia (mainly in Norway, in the frozen north) **chymist:** alchemist
Phenix: the Phoenix, consumed by fire, rose out of its ashes

50

ABOAN, OROONOKO'S LOYAL FOLLOWER, ROUSES HIM TO REBELLION AGAINST THE ENGLISH
(1695) THOMAS SOUTHERNE, Oroonoko, *Act 3, Sc. 2*

Aboan is Malcolm X to Oroonoko's Martin Luther King. Unlike
Oroonoko, but like all the other captives who arrived in Surinam
in chains, Aboan is suffering bitterly in enslavement, and expects
no—and suffers no—accomodation to the white plantation owners

[see I, #60]. Oroonoko himself has been side-blinded by the exceptional courtesies extended to him, a Prince in the eyes of his owners, though technically their slave. The courtesies: his own master, Blanford, dazzled by Oroonoko's princely bearing and civility, reverses their roles: "I'll wait on you," he promises, "attend, and serve you," and miraculously lives up to his promise. In a bit of a side skirmish, Oroonoko, leading the planters, beats back rebelling Indians, and as a result of the encounter, discovers his long-lost wife Imoinda, a captive slave like himself; they are at once given the privilege of their marital status, and remain blissfully together. Oroonoko does not see his slavery as brutal; given his circumstances, he regrets, but in a distant way, his loss of liberty. He also argues—as an African businessman who was once in the slave trade himself, and does not forget appropriate business ethics—that though they are slaves, "they did not make us Slaves; but bought us in an honest way of trade,/ As we have done before 'em, and never thought it wrong." But Aboan does, and reminds him of what slaves have always been subjected to by these planters, oppressions that Oroonoko has never known.

It is Aboan who reminds him too of the potential price of his own enslavement. Not only the loss of freedom in itself, but, for Oroonoko, the loss of his extraordinary but dubiously lasting privileges: the possible forced separation from Imoinda, and—the clincher—the certain fact that his unborn child will be born into slavery. "Shall the dear Babe, the eldest of my hopes,/ Whom I begot a Prince, be born a Slave?" This consideration alone counters Oroonoko's potential feelings of ingratitude, and his abhorrence of not only rebelling against but necessarily killing his erstwhile protectors.

Aboan persuades him and Oroonoko leads the rebellion. He is inevitably defeated, and dies, in a mutual pact with Imoinda, in high poetic fervor, praising liberty.

Southerne, like Aphra Behn's novel out of which he made his play, sits on the cusp concerning the question of slavery: African Princes win our admiration and profound sympathy with their pride in, and ideal of, liberty; but slavery in itself is legitimate business, wrong only when it violates decent business practice. The values of commerce and colonialism, in 1695, were practical and persuasive; the values of universal liberty and equality were young and still admirably abstract.

ABOAN
Sir, I must not blame you.
But as our fortune stands
A brave resentment inspired by you,
Might kindle and diffuse a generous rage
Among the slaves, to rouse and shake our chains,
And struggle to be free.
We have hands sufficient,
Double the number of our master's force,
Ready to be employed. What hinders us
To set 'em then at work? We want but you
To head our enterprise, and bid us strike .
Remember, sir,
You are a slave yourself, and to command,
Is now another's right.
Since the first moment they put on my chains,
I've thought of nothing but the weight of 'em,
And how to throw 'em off: can yours sit easy?
You do not know the heavy grievances,
The toils, the labours, weary drudgeries,
Which they impose; burdens, more fit for beasts,
For senseless beasts to bear than thinking men.
Then if you saw the bloody cruelties
They execute on every slight offence;
Nay, sometimes in their proud, insulting sport,
How worse than dogs they lash their fellow creatures,
Your heart would bleed for 'em. Oh, could you know

How many wretches lift their hands and eyes
To you, for their relief!
O royal sir, remember who you are,
A prince, born for the good of other men,
Whose god-like office is to draw the sword
Against oppression, and set free mankind
And this, I'm sure, you think oppression now.
What though you have not felt these miseries,
Never believe you are obliged to them:
They have their selfish reasons, may be, now,
For using of you well; but there will come
A time, when you must have your share of 'em.

Oh, my lord!
Rely on nothing that they say to you.
They speak you fair, I know, and bid you wait.
But think what 'tis to wait on promises,
And promises of men who know no tie
Upon their words, against their interest:
And where's their interest in freeing you ?

Nay, grant this man you think so much your friend
Be honest, and intends all that he says:
He is but one; and in a government
Where, he confesses, you have enemies
That watch your looks, what looks can you put on
To please these men who are before resolved
To read 'em their own way? Alas! my lord!
If they incline to think you dangerous,
They have their knavish arts to make you so.
And then who knows how far their cruelty
May carry their revenge?
I know you are persuaded to believe
The Governor's arrival will prevent
These mischiefs, and bestow your liberty:
But who is sure of that? I rather fear

More mischiefs from his coming: he is young,
Luxurious, passionate, and amorous.
Such a complexion, and made bold by power,
To countenance all he is prone to do,
Will know no bounds, no law against his lusts.
If, in a fit of his intemperance,
With a strong hand he should resolve to seize,
And force my royal mistress from your arms,
How can you help yourself?

I have mustered up
The choicest slaves, men who are sensible
Of their condition, and seem most resolved:
Summon 'em, assemble 'em: You command in all.
We shall expect you, sir.

XVIII CENTURY ENGLISH/GERMAN

51

CATO CONTEMPLATES THE ALLUREMENT OF IMMORTALITY

(1713) JOSEPH ADDISON, Cato, *Act 5, Sc. 1*

Cato is encamped in Utica with a small clutch of followers and a tiny army still loyal to his lost cause, awaiting the arrival of Caesar's victorious army and his own inevitable defeat. As the heroic embodiment of the Roman Republic's ideal of liberty, he is the last bulwark against the inevitable victory of the "tyrant" Caesar's conquest of the Roman provinces, and the inevitable submergence of the Republic and of Rome's liberty.

So much is Cato held in awe by his followers that neither defection nor sedition have any power to destroy his cause; he and they hold firm until the inevitable day comes when submission to Caesar's army is a certainty. It's then that Cato rises to his full stature: the great Stoic, unbending in his determination never to submit to the shackles of "tyranny," contemplates the alternative with perfect equanimity. And it's then, too, that the play rises to its highest level of moral and intellectual dignity, when Cato turns his deliberation from the ideal of earthly freedom from contingencies to the ultimate ideal: the soul's immortality. His deliberations spell out Stoicism's and the Stoic's argument for suicide.

That argument, somewhat knotted in his speech, unknots as follows: (1) The evidence that there is "a power above us:" Nature itself is its earthly exhibit and proof; (2) the evidence that that divine power "stirs within us:" our dread of falling back into "naught" after death, and our "pleasing hope" for its opposite, immortal existence, both can only be inspired [literally, inspirited into us] by that "divinity;" (3) and so, it's that "divinity" again that tells us inwardly, "intimates," that there's a hereafter, an eternity beyond death. But (4), the certainty that there is an eternity, does not tell us with equal certainty what its nature is. And the way to find out (5) is covered with "shadows, clouds and darkness." It may necessitate our passing through new bodily states, "new scenes and changes" [i.e., a process of metempsychosis] before we discover its nature. But (6) since that "power above" must of necessity "delight in virtue," it stands to reason that that eternity "which he delights in must be happy."

(7) There's another certainty: since the soul is eternal, "secured in her existence," it will survive in that eternal place of virtue and delight long after matter itself, the elements, worlds, the sun itself, will have vanished. Therefore (8), the choice of the sword for suicide and Plato's doctrine of immortality, is in fact one choice, death by the sword leading to eternal life.

Despite the fact that the argument is derived from Plato, plainly it has wide gaps; but it did yeoman work for the Stoics, though Hamlet, confronted by the same dilemma, remembered what Cato had no reason to remember: that that same "everlasting" had fixed his canon 'gainst self-slaughter. But Cato, having by this argument divested himself of the last allegiance to this world "made for Caesar," falls asleep in perfect tranquility, whether to sleep or die a matter of profound indifference to him.

> *(Cato solus, sitting in a thoughtful posture: in his hand
> Plato's book on the immortality of the soul. A drawn
> sword on the table by him.)*

CATO
It must be so—Plato, thou reason'st well!—
Else whence this pleasing hope, this fond desire,
This longing after immortality?
Or whence, this secret dread, and inward horror,
Of falling into nought? why shrinks the soul
Back on herself, and startles at destruction?

'Tis the divinity that stirs within us;
'Tis heav'n itself, that points out an hereafter,
And intimates eternity to man:
Eternity! thou pleasing, dreadful thought!
Through what variety of untried being,
Through what new scenes and changes must we pass!
The wide, th' unbounded, prospect, lies before me;
But shadows, clouds, and darkness, rest upon it.
Here will I hold. If there's a pow'r above us,
(And that there is all Nature cries aloud
Through all her works) he must delight in virtue:
And that which he delights in must be happy.
But when! or where!—This world was made for Caesar.
I'm weary of conjectures—this must end 'em.

(Laying his hand on his sword.)
Thus am I doubly armed: my death and life,
My bane and antidote, are both before me:
This in a moment brings me to an end;
But this informs me I shall never die,
The soul, secured in her existence, smiles
At the drawn dagger, and defies its point.
The stars shall fade away, the sun himself
Grow dim with age, and nature sink in years;
But thou shalt flourish in immortal youth,
Unhurt amidst the wars of elements,
The wrecks of matter, and the crush of worlds.
What means this heaviness that hangs upon me?
This lethargy that creeps through all my senses?
Nature, oppressed and harassed out with care,
Sinks down to rest. This once I'll favor her,
That my awakened soul may take her flight,
Renewed in all her strength, and fresh with life,
An off'ring fit for heav'n. Let guilt or fear
Disturb man's rest: Cato knows neither of 'em,
Indiff'rent in his choice to sleep or die.

bane: deadly poison

52

THOROWGOOD CATECHIZES
THE BLESSINGS OF COMMERCE
(1731) GEORGE LILLO, The London Merchant, *Act 3, Sc. 1*

The merchant Thorowgood forgives his apprentice Barnwell his first indiscretion—not returning for the night—and prevents his suffering the "torment" of confessing the cause, since Thorowgood is certain that it was harder for Barnwell to offend than for himself to pardon [see I, #61, 62]. Barnwell's "remorse makes [him] dearer to me than if he had never offended." In the same vein, Thorowgood offers his other apprentice, Trueman, the benefit of his credo: his profound belief in the moral efficacy of global trade.

Thorowgood, unlike many of the global free trade apologists who follow him, lives up to his name. He is without guile or greed, and believes in his heart in the convergence of commercial and Christian principles, "by mutual benefits diffusing mutual love from pole to pole." How they do it is classic 18th century economic "win-win" theory, to which Thorowgood wholeheartedly subscribes: advanced trading countries take from the primitive ones "with their own consent... their useless superfluities" of gems, spices, silver, gold, and so on, and give them in return the beliefs and the manufactured goods (the clothing, guns and bibles) "they stand in need of." And then, most tellingly, the industrious merchant, after collecting "the various blessings of each soil and climate" does not primarily enrich himself, but "his native country." The profits of this good-Samaritan exchange, though not altogether unselfish, in principle accrue to something higher than the self. Profit and patriotism, like commerce and christian virtue, merge. And in this benign exchange, reflexively, so do reason and nature.

Rarely is so concisely reasoned an explanation of this still-venerated piety put so pithily, and Lillo, with the force of religious certainty, puts it into the mouth of the purest of its proponents, the Thorowgood who in his conduct lives up to the precepts of basic Christian doctrine in its most humane form. In our hindsight, it may be difficult to empathize entirely with the virtue of his intent, but his behavior in the play, and the sincerity of his accomodation of Christian principle to the uses of commerce, marks Thorowgood as one of the very first, and perhaps the very last, of the international merchants of the last three centuries who live wholly and genuinely the imitation of Christ.

(Enter Thorowgood and Trueman.)

THOROWGOOD
Methinks I would not have you only learn the method of merchandize and practice it hereafter merely as a means of getting wealth. 'Twill be well worth your pains to study it as a science. See how it is founded in reason and the nature of things. How it has promoted humanity, as it has opened and yet keeps up an intercourse between nations far remote from one another in situation, customs, and religion; promoting arts, industry, peace and plenty, by mutual benefits diffusing mutual love from pole to pole.

Those countries where trade is promoted and encouraged do not make discoveries to destroy, but to improve mankind by love and friendship, to tame the fierce, and polish the most savage, to teach them the advantages of honest traffic by taking from them with their own consent their useless superfluities, and giving them in return what, from their ignorance in manual arts, their situation, or some other accident they stand in need of. The populous east, luxuriant, abounds with glittering gems, bright pearls, aromatic spices, and health-restoring drugs. The late found western world glows with unnumbered veins of gold and silver ore. On every climate, and on every country, heaven had bestowed some good peculiar to itself. It is the industrious merchant's business to collect the various blessings of each soil and climate, and, with the product of the whole, to enrich his native country.

53

WALLENSTEIN INVEIGHS AGAINST CHANCE, NOT HIS OWN WILL, GOVERNING HIS ACTS

(1799) FRIEDRICH SCHILLER, Wallenstein's Death, *tr. Jeanne Wilson, Act 1, Sc. 4*

Wallenstein, the great general of the Catholic forces in the Thirty Years' War, loses favor with the Holy Roman Emperor, under whose command he is ostensibly fighting against the Protestant alliance. But his victories and his personal magnetism win him such devotion among his armies that he is felt to be a growing threat to the Emperor's authority. When he develops doubts about the righteousness of the war, he plans to make peace with the Protestants and establish an independent, peaceful kingdom in Bohemia with himself as king. Before he can do so, he is assassinated, betrayed by his closest friend, Octavio Piccolomini, who has been secretly in alliance with the party at the Emperor's court.

That is, in brief, the overriding historical event of the Wallenstein trilogy. At the particular juncture when this speech is uttered, at the beginning of its third play, *Wallenstein's Death,* the General has secretly sent an emissary to the Protestant Swedish forces in anticipation—without as yet having come to any decision—of a possible separate peace. But the emissary has been followed and captured, and is being taken to the Emperor's court. Thus before he is ready for decision, Wallenstein is trapped into the necessity of making one. He is waiting now for the Swedish emissary to enter—"I want to know what he has to say to me"—which is the factor now to be considered on the other side. The new danger: he might be trapped from both directions.

The speech is governed then by a consideration of one of the major themes of the trilogy as a whole: What are the boundaries of constraint within which one has the freedom to come to any decision, and what, within those boundaries, is it possible to decide in freedom? Wallenstein's "boundaries" have been, until this moment, only his own sense of the moral propriety of cutting ties with the Emperor to end a by now futile and immoral war on the one hand, and on the other his practical certainty of the loyalty of his generals and his troops if he does. But his hesitancy on that score is suddenly overbalanced by the accident of his messenger being captured, giving accident itself a factor of control, a boundary unbidden. But—worst of all—the notion of a separate peace with the Protestant forces was not a "plan" but a "game," a thought that was free to dance about in his mind with neither reality nor constraint nor consequence. But suddenly, this "accident" gives it, so to speak, a retroactive meaning, a reality it had never possessed until this purely irrelevant factor provided it, and gives him himself a definition: traitor to his Emperor.

He argues further: "While in my breast, my deed was only mine," but once it was "released [and]... delivered to the foreign realm of life," it belongs now to Fate, "those malicious powers" that we have no way of understanding. That can bring what was originally only a "game" in one's head to any real, fateful, and uncontrollable consequence.

And then—perhaps the most subtle and profound part of Wallenstein's and Schiller's argument—there is the most fixed, the most immovable "boundary" of all: the "commonsense" judgment of the world in general that will call him traitor. That judgment is built into the world's "cradle custom" of beliefs, and though they are irrelevant and uncomprehending of the nature of his non-deed, or of its meaning should it have become a real deed, "woe betide" the man who "touches," goes counter to, those rooted beliefs. Willy-nilly, his action is finally defined, made "real," by them—the irrelevant judges of the world and their irrelevant beliefs.

The Swedish emmisary is announced. Wallenstein waits anxiously—the "crime" of his "treachery" has not yet become known. The Swedish factor may yet come into play, and he may yet escape from the "net" he has made—by "deeds of violence." And so the contraction of his freedom of decision is confirmed: his choice has already been made for him: not "peace," but inevitably, "deeds of violence."

WALLENSTEIN

(talking to himself)
Could this be true? Can I no longer act
As I would choose? no longer can turn back?
I must *complete* the deed because I *thought* it—
By that great God of Heaven! I was not
In earnest, it was never my resolve.
The fancy pleased me only in my mind;
'Twas freedom charmed me, possibility.
Then where am I so suddenly conveyed?
My tracks are gone behind me, and a wall
Has been created by what I have done
That, towering, prevents my turning 'round.
I seem so guilty and I cannot shift
The guilt away, no matter how I try.
While in my breast, my deed was only mine;
But once released from that safeguarded nook
Within my heart that was its native soil,
Delivered to the foreign realm of life,
It then belonged to those malicious powers
That no man's skill can make him privy to.
And what was the beginning? Do you know
In honesty yourself? You want to shake
That might that safely and securely rules,
That in deep-rooted, sanctified possession
Rests firmly anchored in the common use.
That is attached with myriad stubborn roots
To what the people have believed since childhood.

This is not strength here striving against strength,
That would not frighten me. I'd challenge each
Opponent I can fix my eyes upon,
Who, full of courage, makes me bolder yet.
I fear the enemy I cannot see,
That can oppose me from within the breast
Of men where cowards' fears make me afraid.
Not what proclaims itself as powerful
Is dangerous and fearful, but instead
That which is common, the eternity
Of yesterday, which always was and will
Tomorrow be because it was today!
For from the commonplace mankind is made,
And in his cradle custom is his nursemaid;
So woe betide him who would touch those things
His ancestors have left behind for him!
The *years* exert a sanctifying strength;
As gray is for old age, so it is holy.
Be in possession and you're in the right ,
And solemnly the crowd will guard it for you.

(to the page who enters)
The Swedish colonel? Well, let him come in!

(The page exits. Wallenstein fixes his gaze reflectively on the door.)
It is still pure. The crime has not gone past
This doorstep—yet.—The border that divides
The two paths that a life can take is fine.

54

WALLENSTEIN INTERPRETS A DREAM AS A PREDESTINED SAVIOR OF HIS LIFE

(1799) FRIEDRICH SCHILLER, Wallenstein's Death, *tr. Jeanne Wilson, Act 2, Sc. 3*

In contrast to his ambition, megalomania, paternalism, courage, steadfastness, and other such qualities that make for a great general and leader of men, Wallenstein is also credulous, and it's this quality that proves his undoing [see II, #53]. He believes in, and follows, astrological and dream portents, and when his followers have already become certain of the imminent treachery of Octavio Piccolomini, who had been Wallenstein's most trusted ally, he rejects the possibility out of hand because of certain portents. His unshakable faith in these signs makes him invulnerable to the pleas of his lieutenants not to send Piccolomini to command the French and Spanish troops, a command which will give him the potential strength to undermine Wallenstein's command. Ultimately it does, but when his lieutenants' pleas become importunate, Wallenstein replies confidently that he has a "pledge" from fate itself that Octavio is his most faithful friend. To the rejoinder, "Have you a pledge [that] the pledge is not a lie?" Wallenstein treats his lieutenants to the whole story behind his absolute trust in his friend—his recollection of the dream in which Octavio rescued him from certain death, and from which he woke to find Octavio over him, rescuing him in reality as the dream foretold.

For Wallenstein, it was a pivotal moment in his life, not only for the proof it offered of an ally's loyalty, but for its confirmation of his own proximity to "the spirit of the world" which in that magical moment left no room for doubt. As he concludes, "There's no such thing as chance," and that it was "the deepest source" that "sealed and certified" Octavio as his "good angel."

He speaks his evidence with the confident, not to say smug, assurance of the religious believer; he brooks no argument to counter it.

WALLENSTEIN
The life of man has in it certain moments
In which he comes close to the spirit of
The world, and to one question fate will answer.
Just such a moment was it in the night
Before the fight at Lutzen, when I had
Been leaning on a tree in deepest thought
And looked across the plain. So mournfully
The campfire flickered through the bank of fog,
The muffled sound of weapons and the call
Of a patrol were all that broke the silence.
And in this single moment my whole life,
Both what had happened and what was to come,
Passed through the vision of my inner eye.
And that portentous spirit was to link
The next day's fortune to the distant future.

Then I said to myself; "You have command
Of many men! They're guided by your star
And wager everything on your lone head
Like on a number in a game of chance.
They all have boarded fortune's ship with you.
But there will come the day when all of them
Are once more scattered distantly by fate,
And but a few will keep their faith with you.
I want to know who is most faithful of
All those who are within this camp's confines.
Give me a sign, O fate, and let it be
That one who first shall come to greet me in
The morning with a token of his love."
And as I fancied this, I fell asleep.

And then my spirit was propelled into
The battle. Great was the distress. My steed
Was shot from under me, I sank, while horses
And riders passed above me unconcerned.
I lay there gasping like a dying man,
Crushed underneath the trampling of the hooves.
Then someone grabbed my arm to help me up.
It was Octavio—and I awoke,
The day had come—Octavio stood there.
He said, "My brother, do not ride today
Upon your piebald horse, but rather mount
A safer animal I've found for you!
Do this for me because of what I dreamed."
The swiftness of this animal allowed
Me to escape Bannier's pursuing band.
My cousin rode the piebald on that day.
I never saw him or his horse again.

Just chance?
There's no such thing as chance;
What seems to us to be blind accident,
Just that comes to us from the deepest source.
I have it sealed and certified that he
Is my good angel. Not another word!

Lutzen: one of the great battles of the Thirty Years' War in which Wallenstein was defeated but his nemesis Gustavus Adolphus was killed **Bannier**: almost certainly Duke Bernhard of Saxe-Weimar who pursued Wallenstein at the end of the battle **piebald**: a horse whose coat is black and white

XIX CENTURY FRENCH/GERMAN

55

AN OLD MAN BRINGS NEWS OF DEATH TO A
FAMILY, AND WONDERS HOW
TO APPROACH THEM

(1896) MAURICE MAETERLINCK, *Home*, *tr. Richard Hovey*, 1-act

There are three windows facing the garden in the rear of a house. A family is visible in the windows, sitting silently, hardly moving, at peace, untroubled by sinister expectation. But hovering over their tranquility is news they have not yet learned: a daughter was found floating in the river, and her body is soon to be borne along the road up to the house. The only intrusion in this motionless scene, of which the family is not yet aware, is the entrance of an old man accompanied by a stranger, waiting in the shadows of the garden, bearing the terrible news of the daughter's death. The scene remains otherwise still, the family and the place undisturbed by the anxious ruminations of the old man. He is sensitive to the fragility of the moment, the scene, and the family's peace, and deliberates on how, in what posture, from what vantage point, with what words, to destroy the family's ignorance and plunge them into the knowledge of their tragedy. Over the stillness hovers the dread: the scene is breathless with expectation.

Stillness and words on the edge of silence are the signature of Maeterlinck's poetry. What hovers is the transcendant, the unknowable that can be intimated, if at all, only in meditation and silence. The design, or the intent, or the pattern, beyond the known is the subject of his scenes' curiosity; but their revelation can be hinted at more in the silences between words and the motionlessness between gestures, than in either words or gestures themselves. So tenuous, so fragile, are the hushed atmospherics of Maeterlinck's theatre; it is as though the slightest intrusive motion, the slightest sneeze, could explode its shrouded substance.

The Old Man is ruminating here in a painfully extended duration of time—usually existent in the mind alone, and not measurable as here in real time—between his intent and his act. It is the distending beyond the bearable of the normally brief hiatus between the two that gives to the whole play what this passage only samples: growing suspense, growing dread, a growing fear of the overwhelming impact the news will finally effect. But true to the aesthetic of Maeterlinck's Theatre of Silence, when the impact comes, it is little visible on the outside: the family moves and gestures a bit this way and that. The impact on them is entirely internal.

> **OLD MAN**
> We are in the part of the garden behind the house. They never come here. The doors are on the other side.—They are closed, and the shutters are up. But there are no shutters on this side, and I saw a light... Yes; they are sitting up still under the light. It is fortunate they have not heard us; the mother or the young girls would have come out, perhaps, and then what should we have done?...
>
> I should like to see, first, if they are all in the room. Yes, I see the father sitting in the chimney-corner. He waits, with his hands on his knees;... the mother is resting her elbow on the table. Is she looking at us? No; she doesn't know where she is looking: her eyes do not wink. She cannot see us; we are in the shade of great trees. But do not go any nearer... The two sisters of the dead girl are in the room too. They are embroidering slowly; and the little child is asleep. It is nine by the clock in the corner... They suspect nothing, and they do not speak.
>
> Which one should be told before the others? I don't know which one to choose... We must take great precautions... The father is old and ailing... So is the mother; and the sisters are too young... And they all loved her with such love as will never be again... I never saw a happier household... No, no, do not go near the window; that would be worse than anything else... It is better to announce it as simply as possible,—as if it were an ordinary event,—and not to look too sad; for otherwise

their grief will wish to be greater than ours and will know of nothing more that it can do... Let us go on the other side of the garden. We will knock at the door and go in as if nothing had happened. I will go in first: they will not be surprised to see me; I come sometimes in the evening, to bring them flowers or fruit, and pass a few hours with them.

Will you go in with me? It is better not to be alone. A sorrow that one does not bring alone is not so unmixed nor so heavy... I was thinking of that as we were coming here... If I go in alone, I shall have to be speaking from the first minute; in a few words they will know everything, and I shall have nothing more to say; and I am afraid of the silence following the last words that announce a woe... It is then the heart is rent... If we go in together, I shall tell them, for example, after going a long way about, "She was found so... She was floating in the river, and her hands were clasped."... Ah, no! Her hands were not clasped; her arms were hanging down along her body.

You see, one speaks in spite of oneself... And the sorrow is lost in the details;... but otherwise, if I go in alone, at the first words, knowing them as I do, it would be dreadful, and God knows what might happen... But if we speak in turn, they will listen to us and not think to look the ill news in the face... Do not forget the mother will be there, and that her life hangs by a thread... It is good that the first wave break on some unnecessary words... There should be a little talk around the unhappy, and they should have people about them... The most indifferent bear unwittingly a part of the grief... So, without noise or effort, it divides, like air or light...

An angel even would not see what should be seen; and man only understands when it is too late... Yesterday evening she was there, under the lamp like her sisters, and you would not see them as they should be seen, if this had not occurred... I seem to see her now for the first time... Something must be added to common life before we can understand it... They are beside you day and night, and you perceive them only at the moment when they depart forever... And yet the strange little soul she must have had; the poor, naive, exhaustless little soul she had, my son, if she said what she must have said, if she did what she must have done!

Just now they are smiling in silence in the room... They are at peace... They did not expect her tonight... They think themselves in safety... They have shut the doors; and the windows have iron bars... They have mended the walls of the old house; they have put bolts upon the oaken doors... They have foreseen all that can be foreseen...

We must end by telling them...

56

CYRANO DEFENDS HIS NOSE AGAINST INSULT, AND RUNS THE INSULTING CULPRIT THROUGH

(1897) EDMOND ROSTAND, Cyrano de Bergerac, *tr. Brian Hooker, Act 1*

For sheer theatrical and rhetorical bravura, it's not likely that anyone ever has or ever will surpass Rostand's Cyrano when he replies to the studied insult about the size of his nose offered by a certain Valvert. The scene is the interior of a 17th century Parisian theatre. While waiting for the play to begin, the talk of the cavaliers is the guardsman Cyrano, who they're hoping doesn't show up; he's forbidden the actor billed for the afternoon, Montfleury, to step on the stage for a month. An affront to the swaggering Cyrano isn't easily forgiven.

A much romanticised version of his historical counterpart, still, like him, de Bergerac is a brilliant swordsman, a splenetic poet, a bookish scholar, even a somewhat admired playwright (the original strongly influenced Moliere). What's not so much admired but feared is his tongue and his sword.

Cyrano, famously, is hard-pressed to carry his blemish—an extra-ordinarily large nose—very visibly before him; it is (to stand metaphor on its head) his Achilles' heel. A mere reference to it swells his wrath; direct insult to its prominence might possibly mean death. A fool-hardy nobody, a Vicomte de Valvert, musters the courage to challenge him, and breathes, "Your nose is... very large."

Cyrano, not stooping to precipitate revenge, goes the long way round to accomplish a worthy and thoroughly torturing retribution: first, he offers the tongue-tied Vicomte a dazzling repertoire of possi-ble insults that might have encompassed the enormity of such an insult's challenge. Then, using his poet's and his swordsman's skill in sync, suiting action to word, he improvises a Ballade in exact stanzaic form. He dances his sword, cued stanza by stanza, around the now quaking Vicomte, and finishes his action and words in tandem with a final refrain and a final sword-thrust struck home.

While the wounded Vicomte is borne off stage by his friends, the followers of the powerful Duc de Guiche, Cyrano is cheered by the assembled crowd, but in his triumph, he's added to his roster another dangerous enemy. They accumulate until the play's end.

> **CYRANO**
> Take notice, all
> Who find this feature of my countenance
> A theme for comedy! When the humorist
> Is noble, then my custom is to show
> Appreciation proper to his rank—
> More heartfelt... and more pointed...
> Ah, no, young sir!
> You are too simple. Why, you might have said,
> Oh, a great many things! Mon dieu, why waste
> Your opportunity? For example, thus:—
> Aggressive: I, sir, if that nose were mine,
> I'd have it amputated—on the spot!

Friendly: How do you drink with such a nose?
You ought to have a cup made specially.
Descriptive: 'Tis a rock—a crag—a cape—
A cape? say rather, a peninsula!
Inquisitive: What is that receptacle—
A razor-case or a portfolio?
Kindly: Ah, do you love the little birds
So much that when they come and sing to you,
You give them this to perch on? Insolent:
Sir, when you smoke, the neighbors must suppose
Your chimney is on fire. Cautious: Take Care—
A weight like that might make you topheavy.
Thoughtful: Somebody fetch my parasol—
Those delicate colors fade so in the sun!
Pedantic: Does not Aristophanes
Mention a mythologic monster called
Hippocampelephantocamelos?
Surely we have here the original!
Familiar: Well, old torchlight! Hang your hat
Over that chandelier—it hurts my eyes.
Eloquent: When it blows, the typhoon howls,
And the clouds darken. Dramatic: When it bleeds—
The Red Sea! Enterprising: What a sign
For some perfumer! Lyric: Hark—the horn
Of Roland calls to summon Charlemagne!—
Simple: When do they unveil the monument?
Respectful: Sir, I recognize in you
A man of parts, a man of prominence—
Rustic: Hey? What? Call that a nose? Na na—
I be no fool like what you think I be—
That there's a blue cucumber! Military:
Point against cavalry! Practical: Why not
A lottery with this for the grand prize?
Or—parodying Faustus in the play—
"Was this the nose that launched a thousand ships
And burned the topless towers of Ilium?"
These, my dear sir, are things you might have said

Had you some tinge of letters, or of wit
To color your discourse. But wit,—not so,
You never had an atom—and of letters,
Yon need but three to write you down—an Ass.
Moreover,—if you had the invention, here
Before these folks to make a jest of me—
Be sure you would not then articulate
The twentieth part of half a syllable
Of the beginning! For I say these things
Lightly enough myself, about myself,
But I allow none else to utter them.
So while we fence, I'll make you a Ballade Extempore.

The Ballade, sir, is formed
Of three stanzas of eight lines each—
And a refrain of four. I'll compose
One, while I fight with you; and at the end
Of the last line—thrust home!

(Closes his eyes for an instant)
Stop... Let me choose my, rimes... Now!
Here we go—
(He suits the action to the word, throughout the following:)
Lightly I toss my hat away,
Languidly over my arm let fall
The cloak that covers my bright array—
Then out swords, and to work withal!—.
A Launcelot, in his Lady's hall...
A Spartacus, at the Hippodrome! ...
I dally awhile with you, dear jackal,
Then, as I end the refrain, thrust home!

(The swords cross—the fight is on.)
Where shall I skewer my peacock?... Nay,
Better for you to have shunned this brawl!—
Here, in the heart, thro' your ribbons gay?

—In the belly, under your silken shawl?
Hark, how the steel rings musical!
Mark how my point floats, light as the foam,
Ready to drive you back to the wall,
Then, as I end the refrain, thrust home!

Ho, for a rime! ... You are white as whey—
You break, you cower, you cringe, you ... crawl!
Tac!—and I parry your last essay:
So may the turn of a hand forestall
Life with its honey, death with its gall;
So may the turn of my fancy roam
Free, for a time, till the rimes recall,
Then, as I end the refrain, thrust home!

(He announces solemnly.)

Refrain:
Prince! Pray God, that is Lord of all,
Pardon your soul, for your time has come!
Beat—pass—fling you aslant, asprawl—
Then, as I end the reftain ...

(He lunges)

Thrust home!

hippocampelephantocamelos: a portmanteau word combining hippocampus, elephant, and a camel; hippocampus is a mythological sea animal that drew the car of Neptune **the horn of Roland**: in the French epic *The Song of Roland*, Roland, caught by the Caracins in the rear guard of Charlemaigne's retreating army during the battle of Roncevaux, heroically alone among his dead troops blew his horn for Charlemagne's return, which won the battle **parodying Faustus... Ilium**: the parody is of Marlowe's Faust who when he sees Helen cries in wonder "Was this the face that launched a thousand ships/And burned the topless towers of Ilium?" **Lancelot**: one of the Knights of the Round Table, lover of King Arthur's wife, Gwinevere **Spartacus... Hippodrome**: a gladiator (fought in the Hippodrome), and led the most successful rebellion against Rome **whey**: in the separation of milk, whey becomes liquid and the curds become solid

57

CYRANO BRAGS OF HIS CREDO: I BEND THE KNEE TO NO ONE

(1897) EDMOND ROSTAND, Cyrano de Bergerac, *tr. Brian Hooker, Act 2*

The Duc de Guiche, the nephew of Cardinal Richelieu and one of the most powerful men in France, has his own way of neutralizing his enemies [see II, #56]. At the very moment when his men are scouring Paris streets for Cyrano's Gascon Cadets to destroy them for their damaging exploit of the night before, he visits Cyrano in Ragueneau's shop—a vast kitchen furnished with mountains of food and implements (Rostand's play is reputed to call for a greater number of props than any play ever produced)—and offers him the poet's patronage of Richelieu himself. There's a caveat: Richelieu takes the liberty of "altering a passage here and there" of poet's works under his patronage. At the mere suggestion of such a liberty, Cyrano at once declines de Guiche's dazzling offer—just as, that very morning, he declined a multitude of offers that came in the wake of his newfound fame as swordsman-cum-poet [see II, #56]. The Duc is doubly enraged when Cyrano's men return with a swordful of hats from the deceased heads of the Duc's henchmen—they were themselves defeated in their morning's mission of assassinating Cyrano's unruly Gascons.

Le Bret, Cyrano's devoted ally, stunned at his "cutting the throat of opportunity" so cavalierly, admonishes him: Couldn't you for once leave aside your musketeer's integrity of soul for a bit of fame and fortune? At this, Cyrano rises to the height of his integrity's eloquence, and explains with fervor the credo that defines not only him but Rostand's own generation at the end of the century; a generation that responded to Ibsen's "The strongest man in the world is he who stands most alone," to Nietzsche's Zarathustra, and to the host of intellectual credos that found their residue of integrity in either aesthetic or political proud loneliness.

> **CYRANO**
> What would you have me do?
> Seek for the patronage of some great man,
> And like a creeping vine on a tall tree
> Crawl upward, where I cannot stand alone?
> No thank you! Dedicate, as others do,
> Poems to pawnbrokers? Be a buffoon
> In the vile hope of teasing out a smile
> On some cold face? No thank you! Eat a toad
> For breakfast every morning? Make my knees
> Callous, and cultivate a supple spine,—
> Wear out my belly groveling in the dust?
> No thank you! Scratch the back of any swine
> That roots up gold for me? Tickle the horns
> Of Mammon with my left hand, while my right
> Too proud to know his partner's business,
> Takes in the fee? No thank you! Use the fire
> God gave me to burn incense all day long
> Under the nose of wood and stone? No thank you!
> Shall I go leaping into ladies' laps
> And licking lingers?—or—to change the form—
> Navigating with madrigals for oars,
> My sails full of the sighs of dowagers?
> No thank you! Publish verses at my own
> Expense? No thank you! Be the patron saint
> Of a small group of literary souls
> Who dine together every Tuesday? No
> I thank you! Shall I labor night and day
> To build a reputation on one song,
> And never write another? Shall I find
> True genius only among Geniuses,

Palpitate over little paragraphs,
And struggle to insinuate my name
In the columns of the *Mercury?*
No thank you! Calculate, scheme, be afraid,
Love more to make a visit than a poem,
Seek introductions, favors, influences?—
No thank you! No, I thank you! And again
I thank you!—But...
To sing, to laugh, to dream,
To walk in my own way and be alone,
Free, with an eye to see things as they are,
A voice that means manhood—to cock my hat
Where I choose—At a word, a *Yes;* a *No,*
To fight—or write. To travel any road
Under the sun, under the stars, nor doubt
If fame or fortune lie beyond the bourne—
Never to make a line I have not heard
In my own heart; yet, with all modesty
To say: "My soul, be satisfied with flowers,
With fruit, with weeds even; but gather them
In the one garden you may call your own."
So, when I win some triumph, by some chance,
Render no share to Caesar—in a word,
I am too proud to be a parasite,
And if my nature wants the germ that grows
Towering to heaven like the mountain pine,
Or like the oak, sheltering multitudes—
I stand, not high it may be—but alone!

Mammon: a personification of riches as an evil spirit or deity **wood and stone**: idols **dowager**: a wealthy widow **Mercury**: a Parisian newspaper/journal published during the 17th century

58

CYRANO, TOTTERING BUT UPRIGHT, SWORD DRAWN, MEETS DEATH

(1897) EDMOND ROSTAND, Cyrano de Bergerac, *tr. Brian Hooker, Act 5*

In this art of expressing love," the beautiful Roxanne once told her confidential friend Cyrano, her lover Christian "is a master." Cyrano affects to belittle her claim, though he knows better: he had himself written all of the letters to Roxanne for the inept and tongue-tied but enormously good-looking Christian. His act of friendship toward Christian concealed his own love for Roxanne—he of the ugly nose who hadn't the (how should one say?) face to advance his own cause. But the letters permitted him to woo her incognito, and—in the most celebrated scene of the play—to woo her from the shadows by ventriloquizing for the lover Christian who stood tongue-tied below Roxanne's window.

Fifteen years later, after the wooing, marriage and death of Christian, his mourning widow Roxanne, retired to a nunnery, welcomes visits from her confidant, Cyrano. But in the intervening years, "philosopher, scientist, poet, musician, duellist" Cyrano, forever castigating cowardice and compromise, has gained enemies and lost income; he's impoverished and alone. On this day, on his way to his regular meeting with Roxanne, he's mortally wounded in the street; arriving nevertheless, he conceals from her his oncoming death. But his guard is down, and Roxanne discovers for the first time who her most genuine lover was. Then despite his increasing delirium, he remembers at the last to stand erect to meet his moment. (The whole episode reaches triumphantly the ultimate of operatic theatrical bravura—Puccini, Verdi and Rostand in one.)

CYRANO

Do you remember that night Christian spoke
Under your window? It was always so!
While I stood in the darkness underneath,
Others climbed up to win the applause—the kiss!—
Well—that seems only justice—I still say;
Even now, on the threshold of my tomb—
"Moliere has genius—Christian had good looks—"

> *(The chapel bell is ringing. Along the avenue of trees
> above the stairway, the Nuns pass in procession to their
> prayers.)*

They are going to pray now; there is the bell.
 No,—do not go away—
I may not still be here when you return...

> *(The Nuns have gone into the chapel. The organ begins
> to play.)*

A little harmony is all I need—
Listen...
I had never known
Womanhood and its sweetness but for you.
My mother did not love to look at me—
I never had a sister—Later on,
I feared the mistress with a mockery
Behind her smile. But you—because of you
I have had one friend, not quite all a friend—
Across my life, one whispering silken gown!...
The moon—yes, that would be the place for me—
My kind of paradise! I shall find there
Those other souls who should be friends of mine—
Socrates—Galileo—

> *(Half raises himself, his eye wanders.)*

The Cadets of Gascoyne,
The Defenders... The elementary mass—
On the other hand,
We have Copernicus—

(More and more delirious)

"Very well,
But what the devil was he doing there?—
What the devil was he doing there, up there?"...

(He declaims)

Philosopher and scientist,
Poet, musician, duellist—
He flew high, and fell back again!
A pretty wit—whose like we lack—
A lover... not like other men...
Here lies Hercule-Savinien
De Cyrano de Bergerac—
Who was all things—and all in vain!
Well, I must go—pardon—I cannot stay!
My moonbeam comes to carry me away...

> *(He falls back into the chair, half fainting. The sobbing of Roxane recalls him to reality. Gradually his mind comes back to him. He looks at her, stroking the veil that hides her hair.)*

I would not have you mourn any the less
That good, brave, noble Christian; but perhaps—
I ask yon only this—when the great cold
Gathers around my bones, that you may give
A double meaning to your widow's weeds
And the tears you let fall for him may be
For a little—my tears...

> *(Suddenly shaken as with a fever fit, he raises himself erect and pushes her away.)*

—Not here!—
Not lying down!...

> *(They spring forward to help him: he motions them back.)*

Let no one help me—no one!
Only the tree

(He sets his back against the trunk. Pause.)

It is coming... I feel
Already shod with marble... gloved with lead...

(Joyously)

Let the old fellow come now! He shall find me
On my feet—sword in hand—*(Draws his sword.)*
I can see him there—he grins—
He is looking at my nose—that skeleton
—What's that you say? Hopeless?—Why, very well!—
But a man does not fight merely to win!
No—no—better to know one fights in vain!...
You there—Who are you? A hundred against one—
I know them now, my ancient enemies—

(He lunges at the empty air.)

Falsehood!... There! There! Prejudice—Compromise—
Cowardice—*(Thrusting)*
What's that? No! Surrender? No!
Never—never!...
Ah, you too, Vanity!
I knew you would overthrow me in the end—
No! I fight on! I fight on! I fight on!

*(He swings the blade in great circles, then pauses, gasp-
ing. When he speaks again, it is in another tone.)*

Yes, all my laurels you have riven away
And all my roses; yet in spite of you,
There is one crown I bear away with me,
And to-night, when I enter before God,
My salute shall sweep all the stars away
From. the blue threshold! One thing without stain,
Unspotted from the world, is spite of doom
Mine own!—

(He springs forward, his sword aloft.)

And that is...

> *(The sword escapes from his hand; he totters, and opens his eyes and smiles up at her.)*

My white plume...

Copernicus (1473-1543): a Polish astronomer who introduced the concept of the earth's circulation around the Sun as opposed to the medieval concept of the earth as the center of the universe **white plum** decorating his hat

59

ROBESPIERRE CONCLUDES: IN HIMSELF "THE SON OF MAN IS CRUCIFIED"

(1835) GEORG BUCHNER, Danton's Death, *tr. C. R. Mueller, Act 1, Sc. 6*

It's laughable how each thought of mine suspects the other." Robespierre is undergoing—rare for him—momentary confusion. The "Incorruptible" has just undergone a painful session with his adversary Danton, who has mocked him for his moral rigidity and condemned him for inflicting wholesale punishment on "the enemies of Virtue" by guillotine; the dour Christian uprightness of Robespierre as against the easy epicurean tolerance of Danton. What lies behind their confrontation, and what they are genuinely addressing, is Danton's growing sense of futility concerning the future of the revolution. It is time, Danton is suggesting, to call a halt; human nature will never and should never respond to Robespierre's brutal imperatives.

Robespierre, left alone, considers. There are two questions to be resolved. The practical one first: that Danton must be got rid of, "drag[ged]...to the guillotine," is a given. But how to avoid the accusation that he is pushing Danton aside out of fear of his "gigantic" stature? Refutation: it's not out of fear or envy, but for the sake of "the Republic." And Robespierre counters Danton's implied notion that the Revolution is not worth pursuing with a significant—not argument but—image: the Revolution's ongoing is not a matter of debate; it's a moving mass, an unstoppable momentum. And the man who tries to stop its motion will be "trampled underfoot."

It's the argument of the fundamentalist and the fanatic: unrelentingly, he's fostering history's unstoppable forward and upward motion. But paradoxically enough, it's equally the argument of the skeptic like Danton who also sees history as unstoppable, but in no way harnessed to worthy ends, and in no way related to human good. It's humanity's irrelevance to "history's" momentum that makes, for Danton, the criminality and inhumanity of Robespierre's assuming the role of self-sacrificing pilot and brutal safeguard of human destiny.

This is essentially the point that for Robespierre, for all his contempt for Danton's wallowing in brothels and clinging to the leprosy of aristocracy, now troubles him. He is the Revolution's charioteer and scourge, but is that his merit or his guilt ? He picks up the newspaper *Le Vieux Cordelier* and reads in it a scathing condemnation of himself as "the Bloody Messiah." Enraged, he dismisses it: "Away with them!" But then, carefully considering, he finds his resolution, and his justification, in that very characterization: "the Bloody Messiah." Playing the game of Christ on the Cross as the symbol of the identity shared by all the flock, with the determined logic given preeminently to the viciously pious, he equates those who scourge the Christ with the Sufferer himself.

(alone)

ROBESPIERRE

Go on! He thinks he can halt the horses of the Revolution outside a brothel, like a coachman with his jaded nags; but they'll have enough strength to drag him to the guillotine.—To take me down, he said! According to my own notions!—But wait! Wait! Is it really that?— They'll say that his gigantic figure cast too great a shadow across me, and for that reason I had to order him from the sun.—And what if they were right? Is it so necessary? Yes, yes! The Republic! He must be got out of the light.—It's laughable how each thought of mine suspects the other.—He must be got out of the light. A man who stands still in a crowd pressing forward is as much an obstacle as if he opposed it: that man will be trampled under foot. We will not permit the Ship of Revolution to founder on the shallow notions and mudbanks of these people; the hand must be hacked away that would hold it back—and if he grasps at it with his teeth…Down with the class that has stolen the clothes of the dead aristocracy and inherited their sores!—No Virtue! Take me down! My own notions!—It keeps coming back to me. Why can't I rid myself of these thoughts? He points his bloody finger at me here, here! I can wrap it in as many bandages as I like, but the blood will always come through. *(After a pause.)* I don't know which part of me is lying to the other.

(He goes to the window.)

Night snores over the earth and tosses itself about in dreamful dreams. Thoughts, desires, scarcely imagined, confused and formless, that crept timidly from the light of day, take shape now and steal into the silent house of dreams. They push open the doors, they look out of the windows, they become half flesh and blood, their limbs stretch in sleep, their lips murmur.—And is our waking anything but a dream, a clear dream? Are we not all sleepwalkers? What are our actions but the actions of a dream, only more clear, more definite, more complete? Who will blame us for that? The mind in a single hour accomplishes more deeds of thought than the sluggish organism of our body can imitate in a year. Sin is in our thoughts. Whether the thought will grow into deed, or the body imitate it—is a matter of chance.

Le vieux Cordelier. (reading) "This bloody Messiah Robespierre on his calvary between the two thieves—where be sacrifices but will not himself be sacrificed. The prayerful sisters of the guillotine stand at his feet like Mary and the Magdalene. Are we to believe that the immaculate frockcoat of the Messiah is the winding sheet of France, and that his fingers twitching on the tribune are the knives of the guillotine? He's a widow with already half a dozen husbands, whom he has helped bury. But what can we do? It's a gift of his: like Hippocrates he can see the livid aspects of death in a man's face six months in advance. And who would want to sit with corpses and smell their putrefying odors?" — Away with them! Only the dead cannot return. No long death agonies! I've grown sensitive these last few days. Yes, the bloody Messiah who sacrifices but will not himself be sacrificed.—*He* redeemed them with *His* blood, and I will redeem them with their own. He created them sinners, and I take the sin on myself. He suffered the ecstasy of pain, and I the torment of the executioner. Who denied himself, He or I?—And yet there's something foolish in the thought—Why do we always look to *Him* as an example? Truly the Son of Man is crucified in us all; we all wrestle in bloody agony in our own Gardens of Gethsemane; but not one of us redeems the other with his wounds. —O Camille!—They are all leaving me—the world is empty and void —I am alone.

prayerful sisters of the quillotine: the women who religiously watched the beheadings **Hippocrates** (460?-357 BC): Greek physician, known as the father of medicine

60

DANTON, BORED AND DISENCHANTED, DELAYS FLIGHT FROM ARREST

(1835) GEORG BUCHNER, Danton's Death, *tr. C. R. Mueller, Act 2, Sc. 1*

Like Leonce in his unreal world [see I, #124], Danton in his real world likes to maintain a certain detachment from the moment's particulars. At this moment he is surrounded by his followers urging him desperately to get a move on, so that he and they might escape arrest and certain guillotine.

Their situation is, in fact, desperate. Robespierre, just weeks ago, has eliminated the Hebertists, one of the three factions—the others Dantonists and Robespierrists—warring among themselves in the National Convention, the ruling government. Robespierre's next move is grimly predictable. But Danton's response to his followers' urgency is to speculate, while he's unhurriedly dressing, on the boredom of dressing. On the boredom, in fact, of living.

In Buchner's version of Danton's revolutionary career, his collapse into indifference, following a remarkable rise to power and prestige as the representative of the revolution's moderates, was confirmed by the ongoing obscenity of the Reign of Terror, now in progress for a year. Danton, by his own definition of himself an Epicurean, is constitutionally incapable of dividing Virtue from Vice, or of regarding Vice as appropriate moral food for the guillotine. But his detachment goes beyond the issue of the guillotine; he's lost faith in dogma, and therefore in Revolution, both of which are defined for him by Robespierre's righteousness.

It's only a step from these defections to loss of faith in life itself. And Danton begins, in his unhurried rumination while dressing, and while his followers are on tenterhooks for him to flee France altogether, to quash distinctions between life-defining causes ("Why must men fight one another? We should sit down and be at peace together,") and between one kind of dying (by guillotine while healthy) and another (feverish old age), and between a large, ambitious, empty life (drinking spoonfuls out of a vast tub) and a tiny, tasteful life (sipping the whole contents of liqueur glasses). And he concludes finally, "Life isn't worth the effort."

But is fleeing necessary? First, there's little point in living outside one's country; and as for arrest and execution, he reasons, "they wouldn't dare." He was wrong.

Beside the emptiness and despair Danton professes, there's a redeeming posture that goes with it: the pleasure of the rumination itself, the pleasure of winning a victory over the Robespierres that passes their understanding—their lack of understanding distinctly part of the pleasure. Danton, in meditation, wins that quiet victory of the resigned skeptic's restraint over the headlong brutality of the grim believer. It's a victory belonging to the inner self alone; otherwise, beyond the self, meaningless, not noticed, not credited.

DANTON

How tedious it is always to have to put one's shirt on first and then pull up one's trousers; to spend the night in bed and then in the morning have to crawl out again and always place one foot in front of the other—and no one even imagines it could be otherwise. It's very sad; millions have already done so and millions more are destined to do so; and besides that we consist of two halves, each doing the same thing, so everything happens twice—it's very sad. Always to go about in the same coat and make the same kind of face! It's pitiable. To be a miserable instrument on which each string gives out only a single note!—I couldn't stand it any longer. I wanted to make myself comfortable. And I've succeeded; the Revolution is retiring me, but not in the way I had expected.— Besides, on what can we support ourselves? Our whores might still find a place with the prayerful sisters of the guillotine; otherwise I can think of nothing else. You can figure it all out on your fingers: the jacobins have declared Virtue the order of the day. Robespierre is the dogma of the Revolution that can't be stricken. But that wouldn't work either. We didn't make the Revolution, the Revolution made us.—And even if it could work—I'd rather suffer the guillotine myself than make others suffer it. I'm disgusted with it all; why must men fight one another? We should sit down and be at peace together. I think there was a mistake in the creation of us; there's something missing in us that I haven't a name for—but we'll never find it by burrowing in one another's entrails, so why break open our bodies? We're a miserable lot of alchemists! What does it matter whether they die on he guillotine or of fever or of old age! But there's still something to be said for leaving the stage with a good spring in your step and a fine gesture and hearing the applause of the spectators behind you. It's an agreeable way to go and it also suits us: we stand on the stage all our lives, even though in the end we are finally stabbed in earnest.—It's not so terrible to have our life's span cut down a bit; especially since the coat was too long, and our limbs never quite filled it out. Life becomes an epigram; that makes it bearable. Who has either breath or imagination for an epic in fifty or sixty cantos? It's time we started drinking our little bottle of elixir out of liqueur glasses instead of tubs; that way at least we'd get a mouthful, rather than have the few drops lost in the bottom of the clumsy vessel.—Finally—my

God, I can't hold it in any longer!—finally it isn't worth the trouble,
life isn't worth the effort it costs us to keep it going.

Escape, then, Danton? If I could take my country with me on the
soles of my shoes, yes.—But finally—and this is the main point—they
wouldn't dare lay a hand on me. Good-bye! Good-bye!

(Danton and Camille leave.)

Jacobins: the revolutionary party led by Robespierre

61

DANTON RECONCILES HIMSELF TO DESPAIR AND TO IMMINENT DEATH

(1835) GEORG BUCHNER, Danton's Death, *tr. C. R. Mueller, Act 4, Sc. 1*

In the prison in which Danton and his party are awaiting
Robespierre's guillotine, Danton suffers the frightening feeling that
the shriveling of the time left to him is producing a vise-like shriveling of the space around him [see II, #60]. He is already, he imagines,
enclosed in his coffin, he's already a mere body, already a corpse.
Making the best of it, he tries to imagine that the "smelly corpse" he's
become is a perspiring woman. "Death mimicks birth," he concludes,
and, in imagery close to Beckett's vision of birth as "astride the grave,"
he stares at the image of the dying, as naked as newborn babes, with
"a shroud for swaddling clothes." There's an incredibly transcendent
Danton, though, who yearns for a death that obliterates from imagination the smelly corpse he knows he will become tomorrow, one that
slips past, so to speak, that stinking residue: it would be a death that
slides smoothly and silently into non-being. And the vast difference
between such a death and the one meted out to human being pro-

vokes his final judgment: the stars (tears) looking down on the human plight as it inevitably is, must be full of great sorrow.

(The Conciergerie, Lacroix and Herault sitting on one, Danton and Camille sitting on another bed.)

DANTON

Will the clock never stop! Every tick pushes the walls closer around me, till they're narrow as a coffin.—I read a story like that once when I was a child, it made my hair stand on end. Yes, when I was a child! It wasn't worth the trouble to fatten me up and keep me warm. Just another job for the gravediggers!—I feel as if I'd already begun to stink. My dear body, I shall hold my nose closed and imagine that you are a lovely woman, sweating and stinking a bit after a dance, and pay you compliments. We've had better times than this with one another. Tomorrow you'll be nothing but a broken fiddle with no more tunes to play. Tomorrow you'll be an empty bottle; I've emptied all the wine but I'm still not drunk and go sober to bed—they're lucky people who can still get drunk. Tomorrow you'll be a worn-out pair of pants; you'll be thrown in the wardrobe, and be eaten by moths, and then you can stink as much as you like.—Yes, it's useless! Of course it's miserable having to die. What does death do but mimic birth? We die as helpless and naked as newborn babes. And of course we get a shroud for swaddling clothes. What good will it do! We can whimper just as well in the grave as in the cradle.—Camille! He's sleeping. *(While bending over him.)* There's a dream between his lashes. I mustn't wipe that golden dew of sleep from his eyes.

(He rises and goes to the window.)

I won't be going alone: thank you, Julie! Still, I wish I could have died differently, without effort, like a star failing, or a note of music that breathes itself out, kissing itself with its own lips, like a ray of light burying itself in a sea of clear water.—The stars are scattered through the night like glistening teardrops; what a terrible grief must be behind the eyes that dropped them.

Tragedy/Drama
XIX/XX CENTURY ENGLISH

62

CENCI CRIES CURSES ON BEATRICE AND PRAYS FOR HER DESTRUCTION

(1819) PERCY SHELLEY, The Cenci, *Act 4, Sc. 1*

Count Francesco Cenci, on hearing that his daughter Beatrice, whom he has violated, refuses to come once again at his bidding, falls to his knees, and in a paroxysm of rage, prays to God to become His accomplice in her punishment. But the doom he begs to have visited on her recalcitrance outdoes even the grotesque. Shelley's portrait of Count Cenci emulates but also goes beyond the villainy depicted in Elizabethan and Jacobean tragedy. There, the villain's motive was born in the pursuit of policy that might be pushed, if unrestrained, to the point of madness (Barrabas in *The Jew of Malta,* Francesco in *The White Devil).* In Shelley's 19th century version, power in itself is the villain's disease; in itself it generates his evil. His frustration lies only in the limits of his power's possibilities. Like the villains of melodrama, concurrently and similarly disporting themselves, the maximum of power's pleasure is to be found in its total unobstruction.

Count Cenci has that maximal pleasure: in his domain, he is law, subject only to the restraint of overriding papal law, but happily, papal law is not given, in Clement's papacy, to exercising its prerogatives over the Italian nobility. So Count Cenci's harnessing of God as his accomplice in destroying and even mangling Beatrice as well as her possible future issue is well within the bounds of his reality. And within Shelley's as well. The paranoia of the passionate fighters for liberty throughout the century constructed their image of power as the exact counter to unobstructed liberty. But the devastation power wrought in political life was measured, compared to its devastations in literary and theatrical imagination. Shelley's libertarian passion created Count Cenci; on the other hand, the popular playwright for the bourgoisie,

Scribe, with his class's infinitely slighter devotion to untrammeled liberty, created in Tosca a much more tempered, a far less terrifying, portrait of villainy in Scarpia.

But nowhere but in de Sade is the untrammeled appetite for the absolute of evil more fully accomplished than in Count Cenci. In the course of the play, he violates most of the taboos endemic to civilized life. His credo is to pursue them joyously: "All men delight in sensual luxury,/ All men enjoy revenge; and most exult / over the tortures they can never feel... I delight in nothing else. I love/ The sight of agony, and the sense of joy,/ When this shall be another's." After his multiple crimes and murders, both done before the play begins and within it (the murder of his two sons, the torment of his wife, the rape of his daughter), he overwhelms the hopelessly patient submissiveness of wife and daughter, and even the greed of the corrupt Papacy from whom he "buys impunity with gold." But ironically, before the papal mission arrives to "investigate" the Count, mother and daughter accomplish his murder, for which—they having won no such immunity for multiple crimes as had the murdered father and husband—they are executed for their single, and somewhat more justifiable, crime.

> **CENCI**
> *(kneeling)* God!
> Hear me! If this most specious mass of flesh,
> Which Thou hast made my daughter; this my blood,
> This particle of my divided being;
> Or rather, this my bane and my disease,
> Whose sight infects and poisons me; this devil
> Which sprung from me as from a hell, was meant
> To aught good use; if her bright loveliness
> Was kindled to illumine this dark world;
> If nursed by Thy selectest dew of love
> Such virtues blossom in her as should make
> The peace of life, I pray Thee for my sake,

As Thou the common God and Father art
Of her, and me, and all; reverse that doom!
Earth, in the name of God, let her food be
Poison, until she be encrusted round
With leprous stains! Heaven, rain upon her head
The blistering drops of the Maremma's dew,
Till she be speckled like a toad; parch up
Those love-enkindled lips, warp those fine limbs
To loathed lameness! All-beholding sun,
Strike in thine envy those life-darting eyes
With thine own blinding beams!

> (Leaping up, and throwing his right hand towards
> Heaven)

This in addition, that if she have a child...
That if she ever have a child; and thou,
Quick Nature! I adjure thee by thy God,
That thou be fruitful in her, and increase
And multiply, fulfilling his command,
And my deep imprecation! May it be
A hideous likeness of herself, that as
From a distorting mirror, she may see
Her image mixed with what she most abhors,
Smiling upon her from her nursing breast.
And that the child may from its infancy
Grow, day by day, more wicked and deformed,
Turning her mother's love to misery:
And that both she and it may live until
It shall repay her care and pain with hate,
Or what may else be more unnatural.
So he may hunt her through the clamorous scoffs
Of the loud world to a dishonoured grave.
Shall I revoke this curse? Go, bid her come,
Before my words are chronicled in Heaven.

Maremma: a marshy, unhealthy region near the seashore; miasma and malaria
are associated with it

63

VIRGINIUS, HAVING KILLED HIS DAUGHTER TO PREVENT HER ENSLAVEMENT AND RUIN, RUNS MAD AND SEARCHES FOR HER

(1820) AMOS SHERIDAN KNOWLES, *Virginius, Act 5, Sc. 3*

To encompass the 19th century runaway madness of Virginius, one must forget madness and think theatre. Also opera. The persuasiveness of his madness is not so much in his text, which is banal and repetitious, but in his vocal range, exhibiting feats of lung power at the top and bottom of his register. Why? Because the idea of madness in 19th century theatre had more to do with demonstrating its inherently enthralled commitment to one of the purities—virtue, honor, patriotism, godliness, etc.—totally outraged by circumstance. Madness in Victorian theatre was essentially a lesson in how the grip of the virtues in the soul is so absolute that all—villains, heroes, and heroines—are in their greatest moments of adversity, and in the greatest moments of their recognition of their own sinful acts (whether advertent or inadvertent), so inwardly seized by virtue's stranglehold, and so strenuously held in virtue's clutch that it causes screams of remorse in the sinners or wild untutored ravings in their victims. The core of madness is virtue's inner pummeling of soul, heart and mind; the response to so lacerating a punishment is maximal howl. No one escapes the grip of the good; madness is one of its retributions.

Virginius, in his madness, is fixed in the monomania of his paternal love. His fixity, absolute, makes it possible for him to deny, or at least overlook, the terror that lurks for him: the recognition that his daughter Virginia is gone, and that he himself killed her. The intent of his madness is fixed entirely on staving off that double recognition. It is no comfort to him after her death that he murdered her for the sake of her honor; to save her from enslavement by the tyrant Appius, who, under the false testimony that Virginius was in fact born a slave to his nephew Claudius—his ally in the plot—was on the verge of possessing her. And so the strategy of his madness is to suppose that his daughter has possibly, or merely, been abducted, and that what is needed for her recovery is simply his demanding from tyrant, from citizen, from anyone, her return. He roars, he pleads, he bellows, he asks contritely. But then he passes, in his mad quest, to another stage. Having stormed into the cell where the Roman tyrant has now become Rome's prisoner, he imagines he sees his daughter behind the head of Appius, and supposes he's discovered his villainy: Appius, he imagines, has already despoiled her in his cell. And with the strength of madness, his fingers "turned to steel," Virginius strangles her supposed defiler, crying to his daughter to look on, to "keep her eye fixed, let it not wink," as he perpetrates her revenge.

His friends arrive, and find him beside the corpse of Appius, professing to feel "Lighter!…Ten times lighter!" for his act, but when confronted by the urn holding his daughter's ashes, and it is named, his sense of the real is restored, and "in a passion of tears," recognizes the terrors he's avoided, screams his daughter's name, and collapses.

VIRGINIUS
Call my daughter to me.
What keeps her thus? I never stept within
The threshold yet, without her meeting me
With a kiss. She's very long coming. Call her!
Come, come, make ready. Brother, you and he
Go on before: I'll bring her after you.

Justice will be defeated?
Who says that?
He lies in the face of the gods! Justice is immutable,
Immaculate and immortal! And though all

The guilty globe should blaze, she will spring up
Through the fire, and soar above the crackling pile,
With not a downy feather ruffled by
Its fierceness!

Will she come or not?
I'll call myself! She will not dare! O when
Did my Virginia dare—Virginia!
Is it a voice, or nothing answers me?
I hear a sound so fine—there's nothing lives
'Twixt it and silence. Aha! She is not here!
They told me she was here: they have deceiv'd me;
And Appius was not made to give her up,
But keeps her, and effects his wicked purpose
While I stand talking here, and ask you if
My daughter is my daughter! Though a legion
Sentried that brothel, which he calls his palace,
I'd tear her from him! Ha!
Apius is now in prison!
With my daughter!
He has secur'd her here! Has he so?
Gay office for a dungeon! Hold me not,
Or I will dash you down, and spoil you for
My keeper. My Virginia, struggle with him!
Appall him with thy shrieks; ne'er faint, ne'er faint!
I am coming to thee! I am coming to thee!

(Enters Appius' dungeon.)

Give me my daughter!
My child, my daughter!
Give her me!
Ay! Deny that she is mine
And I will strangle thee, unless the lie
Should choke thee first.
Play not with me!
Thou sport'st with fire. I am wild, distracted, mad!
I am all a flame—a flame! I tell thee once

For all, I want my child, and I will have her;
So give her to me.
Not a step thou stirr'st from hence,
Till I have found my child.

Do you say, indeed
She is not here? You nothing know of her?
How if I thrust my hand into your breast,
And tore your heart out, and confronted it
With your tongue? I'd like it. Shall we try it? Fool!
Are not the ruffians leagued? The one would swear
To the tale o' the other.
Then I must seek her elsewhere. I did dream
That I had murder'd her. 'Tis false! 'twas but
A dream. She isn't here, you say. Well, well!
Then I must go and seek her elsewhere. Yet
She's not at home—and where else should I seek her
But there or here? Here, here, here! Yes, I say,
But there or here—I tell you I must find her—
She must be here, or what do you here? What
But such a wonder of rich beauty could
Deck out a dungeon so as to despoil
A palace of its tenant? Art thou not
The tyrant Appius?
Have you not secur'd her here
To compass her dishonour, ere her father
Arrives to claim her?

Vile tyrant! Think you, shall I not believe
My own eyes before your tongue? Why, there she is!
There at your back—her locks dishevell'd and
Her vestment torn! Her cheeks all faded with
Her pouring tears, as flowers with too much rain!
Her form no longer kept and treasur'd up.
Villain! Is this a sight to show a father?
And have I not a weapon to requite thee?

(Searches about his clothes, holds up his hands.)

Ha, here are ten!
No other look but that! Look on, look on!
It turns my very flesh to steel. Brave girl!
Keep thine eye fix'd—let it not wink. Look on!

(He strangles Appius.)

64

LUKE EXPLAINS THE JUSTIFICATION FOR HIS REVENGE: HIS WIFE'S DEATH BY STARVATION
(1826) JOHN BALDWIN BUCKSTON, *Luke the Laborer, Act 1, Sc. 2*

Sometimes even early melodrama's voice is raised several cuts above "Avaunt!" and "Belay there!" and speaks in the middle register in text that is simple, direct, and convincing. Luke speaks quietly to Farmer Wakefield, once his employer, now a ruined and broken old man. He is offering explanation for his years' long hostility to the old man, but offering it in the tone of a man spelling out facts, letting their weight alone bear the weight of his argument. Old Wakefield, a moment before, called Luke a scoundrel for tricking him into taking a loan which he knew the old man could not repay, and then throwing him into debtor's prison for defaulting. The old man, sneering at Luke's explanation that he loaned the money "out of pity," and then supposed that the farmer might be holding out on him for repayment, is moving toward wrath when Luke cuts him short with his quiet recall of his real explanation, never before spoken, for his duplicity.

What gives the speech its power is the white-hot rage in Luke that has lasted for years, that has never abated, and that he never allows to surface during his recitation. He's lived with the pain of his tragedy ever since it occurred; it's now the motive that informs every moment of his life. It's a rare villain in melodrama who articulates so persuasively the motive that impels his villainies, both those that he is fostering now, and those that have informed the devastating villainies he's already accomplished (and surface later in the play.) Quietly, he informs his victim—I'll have my [full] revenge yet.

LUKE

I ha' summut to say, summut at my tongue's end—it must come out. Farmer, do you recollect when you sent me away fra' your sarvice? Do you recollect when I were starving for want o' work, and, because I were at times given to drink, you turn'd your back upon me? I ha' never been a man since that time.

If it had been gone by a hundred years, and I alive, I should never ha' forgotten it; and I must and I will tell thee on't. I never had the chance 'afore; but now it do all come fresh upon my brain, my heart do seem ready to burst wi' summut buried in it, and I cannot keep it down. You turn'd me away, and I had no character, because you said I were a drunkard. I were out o' work week after week, till I had not a penny in the world, nor a bit o' bread to put in mine nor my wife's mouth. I then had a wife, but she sicken'd and died—yes, died—all—all along o' you.

She wouldn't let me go to parish, because she were daughter of as good a man as you were then; so we crept on little by little, and bad enough it were—but at last all things went cross; and at one time, when a bit hadn't been in my mouth for two days, I sat thinking, wi' my wife in my arms—she were ill, very ill—I saw her look at me wi' such a look as I shall never forget—she laid hold o' this hand, and, putting her long thin fingers all round it, said, "Luke, would na' the farmer give you sixpence if he thought I were dying o' want?" I said I'd try once more—I got up, to put her in a chair, when she fell, stone dead, down at my feet.

(After a pause) I were then quite ruin'd. I felt alone in the world. I stood looking on her white face near an hour, and did not move from

the spot an inch; but, when I did move, it were wi' my fist clench'd in the air, while my tongue, all parch'd and dry, curs'd a curse, and swore that, if I had not my revenge, I wish'd I might fall as stiff and as dead as she that lay before me.

I'll have it yet—if I die for't, I'll have it.

summut: something **fra'**: from **'afore**: before **would na'**: wouldn't

65

THE DUKE OF FERRARA EXPLAINS TO A VISITOR THE SMILE ON HIS LATE DUCHESS'S FACE
(1842) ROBERT BROWNING, *My Last Duchess*

The Duke of Ferrara is receiving the emissary of the Count for whose daughter's hand he is negotiating. Playing proud host, he brings the emissary to his gallery and seats him before the portrait of his late Duchess, who, he explains, was affable toward everyone, smiling the same smile on everyone, including her husband. The Duke recalls that this uniformity of agreeableness disgusted him, but prevented him too from mentioning his annoyance to the Duchess, since even hearing out her apologies meant he was, to some degree, "stooping" to hear her, "and," he explains, "I choose never to stoop." The consequence? In the most famous lines of the monologue, notable for their succinctness, the Duke explains: "I gave commands;/ Then all smiles stopped together." The Duke, carrying his villainy at his fingertips, conducts the emissary out, reminding him of his suggestion of the dowry to be settled on him in this new marriage.

Browning, like other Victorian poets, carried the idea of drama out of the theatre where poetic drama was generally not welcomed, and brought it to the poetic genre alone. The dramatic monologues of Browning were remarkable for their character studies in little, their revealing the drama of a lifetime in a single incident, and expressing the whole of it through a single voice.

FERRARA

That's my last Duchess painted on the wall,
Looking as if she were alive. I call
That piece a wonder, now: Fra Pandolf's hands
Worked busily a day, and there she stands.
Will 't please you sit and look at her? I said
"Fra Pandolf" by design, for never read
Strangers like you that pictured countenance,
The depth and passion of its earnest glance,
But to myself they turned (since none puts by
The curtain I have drawn for you, but I)
And seemed as they would ask me, if they durst,
How such a glance came there; so, not the first
Are you to turn and ask thus. Sir, 'twas not
Her husband's presence only, called that spot
Of joy into the Duchess' cheek: perhaps
Fra Pandolf chanced to say, "Her mantle laps
Over my lady's wrist too much," or "Paint
Must never hope to reproduce the faint
Half-flush that dies along her throat": such stuff
Was courtesy, she thought, and cause enough
For calling up that spot of joy. She had
A heart—how shall I say?—too soon made glad,
Too easily impressed: she liked whate'er
She looked on, and her looks went everywhere.
Sir, 'twas all one! My favor at her breast,
The dropping of the daylight in the West,
The bough of cherries some officious fool
Broke in the orchard for her, the white mule
She rode with round the terrace—all and each
Would draw from her alike the approving speech,

Or blush, at least. She thanked men—good! but thanked
Somehow—I know not how—as if she ranked
My gift of a nine-hundred-years-old name
With anybody's gift. Who'd stoop to blame
This sort of trifling? Even had you skill
In speech—(which I have not)—to make your will
Quite clear to such an one, and say, "Just this
Or that in you disgusts me; here you miss,
Or there exceed the mark"—and if she let
Herself be lessoned so, nor plainly set
Her wits to yours, forsooth, and made excuse,
—E'en then would be some stooping; and I choose
Never to stoop. Oh sir, she smiled, no doubt,
Whene'er I passed her; but who passed without
Much the same smile? This grew; I gave commands;
Then all smiles stopped together. There she stands
As if alive. Will 't please you rise? We'll meet
The company below, then. I repeat
The Count your master's known munificence
Is ample warrant that no just pretense
Of mine for dowry will be disallowed;
Though his fair daughter's self, as I avowed
At starting, is my object. Nay, we'll go
Together down, sir. Notice Neptune, though,
Taming a sea-horse, thought a rarity,
Which Claus of Innsbruck cast in bronze for me!

Fra Pendalf: a painter invented by Browning

66

MATHIAS, HAVING SUCCESSFULLY CONCEALED HIS THEFT AND MURDER FOR YEARS, IS TROUBLED ONLY BY THE SOUND OF BELLS
(1871) LEOPOLD LEWIS, *The Bells*, *Act 2*

Fifteen years ago, the innkeeper Mathias, on the verge of ruin, wel-comed a traveler, a Polish Jew, who before retiring inadvertently displayed his money-belt filled with gold. The next morning, Mathias followed his sledge with its tinkling bells to the bridge crossing, mur-dered the traveler, stole his gold, and dropped his body into the lime kiln which consumed his remains. The Polish Jew's disappearance remained an unsolved mystery.

Now Mathias, with a fortune built on his theft and murder, is suc-cessfully marrying his daughter Annette, with a dowry of 30,000 francs, to Christian, a young gendarme, with the expectation that the young officer, should the murder ever come to light, would be his willing defender. The guilty past is buried for Mathias, but unac-countably, from time to time, he hears the distant tinkling of bells.

It happens again—in the First Act—when, in the midst of his tri-umph over his daughter's betrothal, the sounds mysteriously recur. When his guests are gone, he is suddenly terrified by the vision—an upstage tableau—of the man on the bridge, who turns and faces him accusingly, at which moment Mathias understandably "utters a pro-longed cry of terror, and falls senseless." Hurry music, end of Act.

In the Second Act, restored to calm, he puts the incident behind him, cheers himself by counting over the money he's saved for his daughter's dowry, dwells on his wife Catherine's knowing nothing of his crime—and sure enough, the bells sound again [for the conclu-sion, see II, #67].

MATHIAS

(taking pinch of snuff)

All goes well! Luckily all is over. But what a lesson, Mathias,—what a lesson! Would anyone believe that the mere talk about the Jew could bring on such a fit? Fortunately the people about here are such idiots they suspect nothing.

(Seats himself in chair by table.)

But it was that Parisian fellow at the fair who was the real cause of all. The rascal had really made me nervous. When he wanted to send me to sleep as well as the others, I said to myself, 'Stop, stop, Mathias— this sending you
to sleep may be an invention of the devil, you might relate certain incidents in your past life! You must be cleverer than that, Mathias; you mustn't run your neck into a halter; you must be cleverer than that—ah! you must be cleverer than that.'

(Starting up and crossing to R.)

You will die an old man yet, Mathias, and the most respected in the Province—*(takes snuff)*—only this, since you dream and are apt to talk in your dreams, for the future you will sleep alone in the room above, the door locked, and the key safe in your pocket. They say walls have ears—let them hear me as much as they please.

(Music. Takes bunch of keys out of his pocket.)

And now to count the dowry of Annette, to be given to our dear son-in-law, in order that our dear son-in-law may love us.

(He crosses to L., unlocks the escritoire, takes out a large leather bag, unties it and empties the contents, consisting of gold pieces and rouleaux, upon the table.)

Thirty thousand francs.

(He sits at table, front to the audience, and commences to count the money.)

Thirty thousand francs—a fine dowry for Annette. Ah ! it is pleasant to hear the sound of gold! A fine dowry for the husband of Annette.

He's a clever fellow, is Christian. He's not a Kelz—half deaf and half
blind; no, no—he's a clever fellow is Christian, and quite capable of
getting on a right track. *(A pause.)* The first time I saw him I said to
myself, 'You shall be my son-in-law, and if any thing should be discovered, you will defend me.'

> *(Continues to count, weighing piece upon his finger—*
> *takes up a piece and examines it.)*

A piece of old gold! *(Looks at it more closely—starts.)* Ah! that came from
the girdle of the Jew; not for them—no, no, not for them, for me.

> *(Places the piece of gold in his waistcoat pocket—he goes*
> *to the escritoire, opens a drawer, takes out another piece*
> *of gold and throws it upon the table in substitution.)*

That girdle did us a good turn—without it—without it we were
ruined. If Catherine only knew—poor, poor Catherine.

> *(He sobs—his head sinks on his breast. Music ceases—*
> *the Bells heard off L., he starts.)*

The Bells! the Bells again! They must come from the mill.

> *(Rushes across to door R., calling.)*

Sozel! Sozel, I say, Sozel !

> *(Enter Sozel.)*

Don't you hear the sound of Bells?

> *(The Bells cease.)*

(aside) Strange—strange. Enough, enough! There, go—go!

> *(Exit Sozel, door R. Seats himself at the table and puts*
> *remaining money into the bag.)*

SD *escritoir*, Fr: writing desk *rouleaux*, Fr: a number of coins put up in cylindrical
form in a paper wrapping

67

MATHIAS, IN NIGHTMARE, DREAMS HE IS UNDER HYPNOSIS, AND OVERCOME BY HIS CONFESSION OF MURDEROUS GUILT, DIES

(1871) LEOPOLD LEWIS, The Bells, *Act 3*

The play's ending, the celebrated *tour de force* of *The Bells,* has Mathias in his bed—alcove, dreaming [see II, #66]. At the rear of the stage, a gauze curtain rises, and reveals a sitting court with three ominous judges seated center, a courtroom crowd, and Mathias on a low stool before them, dressed as he was on the night of the murder. He denies the Court's accusation, refuses to answer its questions, until, to Mathias' horror, the Court orders a Mesmerist "who will read the inmost secrets of your heart" to be brought in to examine him under hypnosis.

In his dream, Mathias comforts himself with the thought that he *is* only in a dream. Nevertheless, when the Mesmerist begins his proce- dure, Mathias is determined not to fall asleep. But he does, and under hypnotic spell, within the setting of the Courtroom, he recounts and performs the events of that fatal night. (The style and horrific effect of the scene's recitation and mime looked forward to a genre that was to come later: Grand Guignol.) Finishing his account, he imagines a hangman's rope is tied around his neck, and waking—both within the dream and in fact—he struggles to pull the rope loose, but fails. The imaginary rope strangles him, and he falls dead.

The play has a dark lineage: Poe, the Gothic novel, and German "Fate" tragedy of a century before. In all of them, the guilty past hov- ers over the present, once in a while making chilling signs, until the fateful moment when the past accomplishes its horrifying retribution. The play made theatre history. Henry Irving's performance of the guilty man's guile and terror made him famous overnight, and established him as England's leading actor-manager for three decades. Among a very few other critics, Bernard Shaw was never impressed. He regarded Irving's style of acting and taste in repertory, for all its immense popularity and prestige, as the nadir of theatrical art. The attractions of *The Bells* are different from Shaw's.

MATHIAS

(striking the table)

It is abominable! It is in defiance of all justice! Who can believe in the follies of the Mesmerist? They merely perform the tricks of conjurers. I will not be made the subject of this conjurer's experiments.

(to himself) Mathias, if you sleep you are lost. *(His eyes are fixed as if struck with horror—in a hollow voice.)* No—no—I will not sleep—I—will—*(in a hesitating voice)* I will—not—no—

(Falls asleep. Music ceases. Still in the same attitude, speaking as if he were describing a vision presented to his sight.)

The people are leaving the inn—Catherine and little Annette have gone to rest. Our man Kasper comes in. He tells me the lime-kiln is lighted. I answer him, it is well; go to bed, I will see to the kiln. He leaves me; I am alone with the Jew, who warms himself at the stove. Outside, everything sleeps. Nothing is heard, except from time to time the Jew's horse under the shed, when he shakes his bells.

I am thinking that I must have money—that if I have not three thousand francs by the 31st, the inn will be taken from me. I am thinking that no one is stirring; that it is night; that there are two feet of snow upon the ground, and that the Jew will follow the high road quite alone!

(after a short silence) That man is strong. He has broad shoulders. I am thinking that he would defend himself well, should any one attack him.

(He makes a movement; in a low voice)

He looks at me. He has grey eyes. *(As if speaking to himself.)* I must strike the blow! Yes—yes; I will strike the blow! I will risk it! I must, however, look round. I go out; all is dark! It still snows; no one will trace my footsteps in the snow.

(He raises his hand as if feeling for something.)

I am feeling in the sledge—should he carry pistols! There is nothing— I will strike the blow! *(listens)* All is silent in the village! Little Annette is crying; a goat bleats in the stable; the Jew is walking in his room! Yes. The Jew has placed six francs upon the table; I return him his money; he fixes his eyes steadily upon me! The night of the 24th December, 1818. Half-past eleven. He asks me how far it is to Mutzig? Four leagues. I wish him well on his journey! He answers— 'God bless you!' He goes out—He is gone!

(Mathias, with body bent, takes several steps forward as if following and watching his victim, he extends his hands.)

The axe! Where is the axe? Ah, here, behind the door! How cold it is! *(He trembles.)* The snow falls—not a star! Courage, Mathias, you shall possess the girdle—courage! I have crossed the fields! *(Pointing.)* Here is the old bridge, and there below, the frozen rivulet! How the dogs howl at Daniel's farm—how they howl! *(Low, as if speaking to himself.)* Kill a man:—kill a man! You will not do that, Mathias—you will not do that! Heaven forbids it. *(Proceeding to walk with measured steps and bent body.)* You are a fool! Listen, you will be rich, your wife and child will no longer want for anything! The Jew came; so much the worse— so much the worse. He ought not to have come! You will pay all you owe; you will no more be in debt. *(Loud, in a broken tone.)* It must be, Mathias, that you kill him! *(He listens.)* No one on the road—no one! *(With an expression of terror.)* What dreadful silence! *(He wipes his forehead with his hand.)* One o'clock strikes, and the moon shines. Ah! The Jew has already passed! Thank God! thank God!

(He kneels—a pause—he listens—the Bells heard with-
out as before.)

No! The Bells! The Bells! He comes!

(He bends down in a watching attitude, and remains
still—a pause—in a low voice.)

You will be rich—you will be rich—you will be rich!

(The noise of the Bells increase—all at once Mathias
springs forward, and with a species of savage roar, strikes
a terrible blow with his right hand.)

Ah! ah! I have you now, Jew!

(He strikes again—leans forward and gazes anxiously on
the ground—he extends his hand as if to touch some-
thing, but draws it back in horror.)

He does not move! *(He raises himself, utters a deep sigh of relief and*
looks round.) The horse has fled with the sledge! *(The Bells ease—kneel-*
ing down.) Quick, quick! The girdle! I have it. Ha! *(He performs the*
action in saying this of taking it from the Jew's body and buckling it
round his own.) It is full of gold, quite full. Be quick, Mathias, be
quick! Carry him away.

(He bends low down and appears to lift the body upon
his back; then he walks across stage, his body bent, his
step slow as a man who carries a heavy load.)

To the lime-kiln. I am there. *(He appears to throw the body upon the*
kiln.) How heavy he was! *(He breathes with force, then he again bends*
down to take up a pole—in a hoarse voice.) Go into the fire, Jew, go
into the fire! *(He appears to push the body with tire pole, using his whole*
force, suddenly he utters a cry of horror and staggers away, his face covered
with his hands.) Those eyes, oh, those eyes! How he glares at me.

(He sinks on to stool, and takes the same attitude as
when first thrown into sleep. Awakes gradually—he
appears bewildered)

Where am I? *(He looks round.)* Ah! Yes; what is going on? *(aside)*
Wretched, wretched—fool! I have told all; I am lost! *(in a voice of*
strangulation) The rope! the rope! Take the rope from my neck!

(He falls suddenly, the Bells heard off. His hands clutch at his throat as if to remove something that strangles him—he looks pitifully round as if trying to recognize those about him, and then his head falls on his breast.)

lime-kiln: a furnace where matter, including human bodies, can be dissolved
four leagues: approx. 12 miles

68

JOKANAAN CRIES ABOMINATION ON HEROD, HERODIAS, AND THEIR DAUGHTER SALOME
(1893) OSCAR WILDE, Salome

The Herod of Oscar Wilde's play (Herod Antipas) was historically the son of the Herod (called the Great) who caused the family of Jesus to take flight into Egypt at his birth. Herod Antipas divorced his first wife, the daughter of an Arabian king, in order to marry Herodias, the wife of his half-brother. It is this marriage—and the abandoned character of Herodias' previous life—that John the Baptist (Wilde's Jokanaan) denounced so bitterly that at Herodias' request Herod ordered him executed. It is out of these circumstances—not unusual in ancient Palestine—that Wilde weaves a kind of Klimt tapestry overlaid with heavily scented text.

Even Jokanaan's denunciations of the rulers' abominations share in the lush sensuality of the play's language. The incantatory style of its rhetoric is a kind of tongue's massage of words and rhythms and sounds that takes precedence over their substance. The thunder of Jokanaan's message is countered by the musical coursing of his sentences. Jokanaan sings with the *basso* rumble of a Chaliapin, and the resonance of his sound subsumes his meaning more than do his words.

It is Herodias' daughter Salome who greets Jokanaan when he rises out of the cistern into which Herod has had him thrown. But at first, it is not Salome against whom Jokanaan fulminates, but against his particular anathema, Herodias, and her consort in sin, Herod. But as Salome insinuates her temptation with more and more overt insistence ("I will kiss your mouth, Jokanaan, I will kiss your mouth") with no change in the pitch of his intensity, Jokanaan's condemning of the monarchs gives way to repelling the young temptress.

(In reducing this scene to a monologue, what's lost is the musical alternation of the major key fulminations of the prophet and the minor key wooing of the temptress. Truncating the cadensed duologue of the original, with Salome's chant lost, leaves only half—but a characteristically powerful half—of the original so-to-speak musical score.)

(The prophet comes out of the cistern. Salome looks at him and steps slowly back.)

JOKANAAN
Where is he whose cup of abominations is now full ? Where is he, who in a robe of silver shall one day die in the face of all the people ? Bid him come forth, that he may hear the voice of him who had cried in the waste places and in the houses of kings.

Where is she who, having seen the images of men painted on the walls, the images of the Chaldeans limned in colours, gave herself up unto the lust of her eyes, and sent ambassadors into Chaldea?

Where is she who gave herself unto the Captains of Assyria, who have baldricks on their loins, and tiaras of divers colours on their heads? Where is she who hath given herself to the young men of Egypt, who are clothed in fine linen and purple, whose shields are of gold, whose helmets are of silver, whose bodies are mighty? Bid her rise up from the bed of her abominations, from the bed of her incestuousness, that she may hear the words of him who prepareth the way of the Lord, that she may repent her of her iniquities. Though she will never repent, but will stick fast in her abominations; bid her come, for the fan of the Lord is in His hand.

Who is this woman who is looking at me? I will not have her look at me. Wherefore doth she look at me with her gold eyes, under her gilded eyelids ? I know not who she is. I do not wish to know who she is. Bid her begone. It is not to her that I would speak.

Back! Daughter of Babylon! Come not near the chosen of the Lord. Thy mother hath filled the earth with the wine of her iniquities, and the cry of her sins hath come up to the ears of God.

Daughter of Sodom, come not near me! But cover thy face with a veil, and scatter ashes upon thy head, and get thee to the desert and seek out the Son of Man. Get thee behind me! I hear in the palace the beating of the wings of the angel of death.

Angel of the Lord God, what lost thou here with thy sword? Whom seekest thou in this foul palace? The day of him who shall die in a robe of silver has not yet come.

Back! Daughter of Babylon! By woman came evil into the world. Speak not to me. I will not listen to thee. I listen but to the voice of the Lord God.

Chaldeans, Assyrians, Egyptians: Jokanaan recounts Herodias's endless sexual exploits; Chaldea was a region is S. Babylonia, Chaldeans were one of the ancient Semitic people that formed the dominant element in Babylonia **baldric**: an ornamented belt supporting a sword, horn, etc.

69

HEROD OFFERS SALOME ANY TREASURE TO RELIEVE HIM OF HIS OATH TO GRANT HER THE HEAD OF JOKANAAN

(1893) OSCAR WILDE, Salome

With quivering lust, Herod begged his wife's daughter Salome to dance for him, and promised that if she would, she might "ask of me what you will... even to the half of my kingdom." [see II, #68] She, inflamed by the perverse longing she'd conceived for the Prophet Jokanaan, dances, and then asks for her reward: the head of Jokanaan. Terrified at the sacrilege this would entail, Herod begs her to ask for anything else; she's adamant, and he makes his last offer: every treasure in his possession that might tempt her appetite.

The catalogue of Herod's offerings is inspired by the same source Wilde used in *The Portrait of Dorian Gray,* the novel by the Belgian Huysmans, *Against the Grain.* It offered Wilde an incredible cornucopia of sensuous extravagances: jewels, stuffs, a multitude of beautiful objects, a multitude of scents, even strange fruits. The catalogue, enhanced, is poured into Herod's final exhortation to the perverse Salome to give up her demand.

The strategy of the speech is, on the face of it, merely enumerative; but in reality it's a rising arc of tortured supplication that reaches its apogee laying before the feet of Salome what is exquisite beyond exquisite, moved by Herod's deadly urgency to escape the trap of his doom. At the top of his urging, he gives out and gives up: "Let her be given what she asks!"

It is one of the memorable moments of modern theatre—Salome dancing with and kissing the lips of the severed head of Jokanaan. The repletion of her sexual pleasure lasts only till the moment when Herod cries to his guards: "Kill that woman!" The play is probably as close to the brutal matter of Renaissance tragedy as it is to the effete poetizing of the 1890's.

> **HEROD**
>
> I slipped in blood when I entered. Also, I heard a beating of wings in the air, a beating of mighty wings. These are very evil omens, and there were others. I am sure there were others, though I did not see them. Well, Salome, you do not wish a misfortune to happen to me ? You do not wish that. Listen to me, then.
>
> Ah! you are not listening to me. Be calm. I—I am calm. I am quite calm. Listen. I have jewels hidden in this place—jewels that your mother even has never seen; jewels that are marvellous. I have a collar of pearls, set in four rows. They are like unto moons chained with rays of silver. They are like fifty moons caught in a golden net. On the ivory of her breast a queen has worn it. Thou shalt be as fair as a queen when thou wearest it. I have amethysts of two kinds, one that is black like wine, and one that is red like wine which has been coloured with water. I have topazes, yellow as are the eyes of tigers, and topazes that are pink as the eyes of a woodpigeon, and green topazes that are as the eyes of cats. I have opals that burn always with an ice-like flame, opals that make sad men's minds, and are fearful of the shadows. I have onyxes like the eyeballs of a dead woman. I have moonstones that change when the moon changes, and are wan when they see the sun. I have sapphires big like eggs, and as blue as blue flowers. The sea wanders within them and the moon comes never to trouble the blue of their waves. I have chrysolites and beryls and chrysoprases and rubies. I have sardonyx and hyacinth stones, and stones of chalcedony, and I will give them all to you, all, and other things will I add to them. The King of the Indies has but even now sent me four fans fashioned from the feathers of parrots, and the King of Numidia a garment of ostrich feathers. I have a crystal, into which it is not lawful for a woman to look, nor may young men behold it until they have been beaten with rods. In a coffer of nacre I have three wondrous turquoises. He who wears them on his forehead can imagine things which are not, and he who carries them in his hand can make women sterile.

These are great treasures above all price. They are treasures without price. But this is not all. In an ebony coffer I have two cups of amber, that are like apples of gold. If an enemy pour poison into these cups, they become like an apple of silver. In a coffer incrusted with amber I have sandals incrusted with glass. I have mantles that have been brought from the land of the Seres, and bracelets decked about with carbuncles and with jade that come from the city of Euphrates... What desirest thou more than this, Salome? Tell me the thing that thou desirest, and I will give it thee. All that thou askest I will give thee save one thing. I will give thee all that is mine, save one life. I will give thee the mantle of the high priest. I will give thee the veil of the sanctuary.

(sinking back in his seat)
Let her be given what she asks!

70

SHERLOCK HOLMES, WHILE ENJOYING HIS SEVEN-PERCENT SOLUTION, ANTICIPATES THE ARREST AND DEMISE OF MORIARTY

(1899) WILLIAM H. GILLETTE, Sherlock Holmes, *Act 2, Sc. 2*

The complacency of Sherlock Holmes is thoroughly earned. From out of the corner of his eye, from hardly noticed details, he can resurrect identities, habits, motives, even consequences still belonging to the future. From the models originated by Edgar Allen Poe, Conan Doyle perfected not only the detective story genre, but the most celebrated detective of the genre: Holmes, the ultimate sleuth, the unfailing discerner of the hidden, the perfect ratiocinating machine, the impeccable gentleman, the stern moralist (when it suits his case), and in distinct but only apparent contradiction, the restrained sybarite who indulges in only two private gratifications—the violin, and the seven-percent solution (cocaine). And one other smaller gratification: the amiable baffling of his close—only?—friend, the indefatigably obliging Dr. Watson.

Gillette played Sherlock Holmes in this immensely popular stage version of a Conan Doyle story on and off for over 30 years. In this scene with Dr. Watson, he exhibits signature Holmes attributes: baffling Watson with his preternatural deductions from near-invisible hints, his languid enjoyment of his cocaine fix, and his relish for confronting, and possibly overcoming his perpetual criminal adversary, "The Napoleon of Crime," Professor Moriarty.

HOLMES

(extending left hand to Watson) Ah, Watson, my dear fellow! I'm delighted to see you—perfectly delighted, upon my word—but—I'm sorry to observe that your wife has left you in this way!

> *(Goes to chemical table and puts spirit lamp out, then turns up piano lamp.)*

How do I know. How do I know anything?

> *(Comes down a little way; gives a very little sniff an instant, smelling something.)*

How do I know that you've opened an office and resumed the practice of medicine—without letting me hear a word of it? How do I know you've been getting yourself very wet lately? That you have an extremely careless servant girl—and that you've moved your dressing table to the other side of your room?

Too simple to talk about. *(Points at WATSON's shoes.)* Scratches and clumsy cuts—on the side of shoe there just where the fire strikes it, somebody scraped away crusted mud—and did it badly—badly! There's your wet feet and your careless servant all in one. Face badly shaved on right side—used to be on left—light must come from other side—couldn't very well move your window—must have moved your dressing table. And, Watson! How perfectly absurd of you to come

marching in here fairly reeking with the odor of iodiform, and with
the black mark of nitrate of silver on the inner side of your right fore-
finger—Ah, and how the deuce did I know your wife was away? Well,
where the deuce is your waistcoat button—and what the deuce is yesterday's boutonniere doing in today's lapel—and why the deuce do
you wear the expression of a lost child?

Elementary! The child's play of deduction!

> *(He turns to mantel, takes a neat morocco case and a
> phial, which he brings to the table and lays carefully
> upon it. He opens the case and takes therefrom a hypo-
> dermic syringe. Carefully adjusts the delicate needle. Fills
> from the phial, then rolls back left cuff of shirt a little.
> Pauses, looking at arm or wrist a moment. Inserts needle;
> presses piston home.)*

Cocaine, my dear fellow, I'm back to my old love! A seven percent
solution.

> *(Offers syringe and phial.)*

Would you like to try some? Oh! I'm sorry!

> *(Draws hypo and phial back and replaces them on the
> mantel.)*

Quite right, my dear Watson—quite right—

> *(Throws himself languidly into sofa, leaning back in lux-
> urious enjoyment of the drug.)*

But kindly don't tell me again that these drugs are poisons, and that
they involve tissue changes of a most serious character. Because that's
just what I want! I'm bored to death with my present tissues and am
after a brand new lot! No, no! Don't try to save me, my dear Watson!
You can't do it, old fellow—so don't waste your time.

(They look at one another an instant.)

Watson—in the enthusiasm which has prompted you to chronicle, and—if you will excuse my saying so, to somewhat embellish—a few of my little—adventures, you have occasionally committed the error—or—indiscretion—of giving them a certain tinge of romance—which struck me as being just a trifle—out of place! Something like working an elopement into the fifth proposition of Euclid. I merely refer to this in case you should see fit at some future time—to chronicle the most important and far-reaching case in my entire career—one upon which I have laboured for nearly fourteen months, and which is now rapidly approaching a singularly diverting climax;—the case of Professor Robert Moriarty. The Napoleon of crime! Sitting motionless like an ugly venomous spider in the center of his web—but that web having a thousand radiations and the spider knowing every quiver of every one of them!

But the real interest will come when the Professor begins to realize his position—which he cannot fail to do shortly. By ten o'clock tomorrow night the time will be ripe for the arrests. Then the greatest criminal trial of the century! The clearing up of over forty mysteries... and the rope for every one! But then—what will he do when he sees that I have him? He will do me the honor, my dear Watson, of turning every resource of his wonderful organization of criminals to the purpose of my destruction! Oh, my dear Watson, it's perfectly delightful! It saves me any number of doses of those deadly drugs upon which you occasionally favor me with your medical views! My whole life is spent in a series of frantic endeavors to escape from the dreary commonplaces of existence! For a brief period I escape! Congratulate me!

fifth proposition of Euclid: in Euclid's *Geometry*

71

MR. O'CONNELL, A CATHOLIC OF CONSCIENCE, IS ASKED FOR POLITICAL REASONS NOT TO DENOUNCE HIS WIFE'S ADULTERER

(1907) HARLEY GRANVILLE BARKER, Waste, *Act 3*

An election has just been held and the Conservatives are back in power but have not yet taken the reins of government. Lord Horsham is assembling his future Cabinet, and one man would, he thinks, prove a particular asset to it: a Mr. Trebell, who has a scheme for church disestablishment that would unlock considerable funds for overhauling British free education. But a difficulty has arisen: Mr. Trebell has had an unfortunate liaison with a Mrs. O'Connell which lasted only a single night, but its consequences would prove more than an embarrassment to the new government should Mr. Trebell be named. Mrs. O'Connell became pregnant, and after a cold interview with Trebell in which it was clear to her that he would not support her in her difficulty, she went to a back-street abortionist who effectively killed her.

Mrs. O'Connell, a Catholic herself, was the wife of a staunch practicing Irish Catholic from whom she lived apart for the very reason that she wanted to bear him no children. Mr. O'Connell's learning of his wife's affair, pregnancy, abortion and death was accompanied by the politically understandable request of the newly elected party chiefs for him to refrain from mentioning Mr. Trebell's name at the impending inquest. He's arrived now for an interview with the newly elected.

At the interview, his irony is muted, polite, but acid. He dismisses his wife from his consideration. "She was a worthless woman" is the opinion of her that he offers to Trebell, and has by her action put a burden on him that he shares, he ventures, with Trebell himself. The standing and reputation of both have been entrapped by a woman on whom neither, in retrospect, placed any value. As to sparing Trebell exposure, he feels that the threat of it is itself revenge enough, and (eventually, later in the play) spares him out of indifference.

What is so extraordinarily and succinctly defined in the portrait of the man is Mr. O'Connell's bitter integrity. As a Catholic, he implicitly condemns his wife's actions on every count. As an Irishman, he dismisses as of no interest to him the fate of the newly elected British Party. As a thoroughgoing Conservative (his scholarly specialty is the 13th Century, whose politics he esteems), he holds democracy and its illusory procedures in contempt. Over and above these narrow, irrelevant, and (for the party hacks) unpromising attitudes, Mr. O'Connell views and judges these political matters from an astonishing height, as though observing with utter consistency such temporal events from the perspective of what are for him eternal values. To bring such considerations into the arena of the moment's politics puts Mr. O'Connell, whatever one might think of his opinions in the aggregate, in the position of making the whole matter of the politician's concerns trivial, even unworthy of serious reflection. His parting comment to Trebell sums it up: "You value your work more than anything else in the world, do you not? Then I am sorry for you."

Granville Barker's sober and subtle intelligence in examining Edwardian life and the welter of moral perspectives it exhibited, not blessed with the addition of Shavian hijinks, prevented his plays from reaching the ears, and certainly the minds, of his contemporaries. But none of the playwrights of their time was closer to Shaw in the quality and depth of dramatic writing and political understanding.

O'CONNELL
You have sent for me, Lord Horsham?

I am always in some doubt as to by what person or persons in or out
of power this country is governed. But from all I hear you are at the
present moment approximately entitled to send for me.

>   *(The level music of his Irish tongue seems to give finer
>   edge to his sarcasm.)*

I understand that if the fact of Mr. Trebell's adultery with my wife
were made as public as its consequences to her must be tomorrow,
public opinion would make it difficult for you to include him in your
cabinet.

And you are asking me to consider the particular circumstances and
forget the man in the statesman. My wife is dead, Lord Horsham.
What have I to do at all with Mr. Trebell as a man? As a statesman I
am in any case uninterested in him.

I suppose my point of view must be an unusual one. I notice, at least,
that twenty four hours and more has not enabled you gentlemen to
grasp it. Now you say I have the life or death of a man's reputation to
decide on. *(with a cold flash of contempt)* That's a petty enough thing
nowadays it seems to me. There are so many clever men... and they
are all so alike... surely one will not be missed.

Will you please to make an allowance, Lord Charles, for a medieval
scholar's contempt of modern government? *You* at least will partly
understand his horror as a Catholic at the modern superstitions in
favour of popular opinion and control which it encourages. You see,
Lord Horsham, I am not a party man, only a little less enthusiastic for
the opposite cries than for his own. You appealed very strangely to my
feelings of patriotism for this country; but you see even my own is—
in the twentieth century—foreign to me. From my point of view
neither Mr. Trebell, nor you, nor the men you have just defeated, nor
any discoverable man or body of men will make laws which matter...

or differ in the slightest. You are all part of your age and you all voice—though in separate keys, or even tunes they may be—only the greed and follies of your age. That you should do this and nothing more is, of course, the democratic ideal. You will forgive my thinking tenderly of the statesmanship of the *first* Edward, king so many centuries ago.

And you are as far from me in your code of personal morals as in your politics. In neither do you seem to realize that such a thing as passion can exist. No doubt you use the words Love and Hatred; but do you know that love and hatred for principles or persons should come from beyond a man? I notice you speak of forgiveness as if it were a penny in my pocket. You have been endeavoring for these two days to rouse me from my indifference towards Mr. Trebell. Perhaps you are on the point of succeeding... but I do not know what you may rouse.

Again... have I been wrong to shrink from personal relations with Mr. Trebell? Hatred is as sacred a responsibility as love. And you will not agree with me when I say that punishment can be the salvation of a man's soul. You have said we have some authority for thinking that the punishment of a secret sin is awarded by God secretly.

We have very poor authority, sir, for using God's name merely to fill up the gaps in an argument, though we may thus have our way easily with men who fear God more than they know him. I am not one of those. Yes, Farrant, you and your like have left little room in this world except for the dusty roads on which I notice you beginning once more to travel. The rule of them is the same for all, is it not... from the tramp and the labourer to the plutocrat in his car? This is the age of equality; and it's a fine practical equality... the equality of the road. But you've fenced the fields of human joy and turned the very hillsides into hillboards. Commercial opportunity is painted on them, I think.

And do they still think it worth while to administer an oath to your witness?

(by this time Trebell is in the room)

I am Justin O'Connell. There's a dead woman between us, Mr. Trebell. I am called upon by your friends to save you from the consequences of her death.

Yes... If I wanted revenge I have it. She was a worthless woman. First my life and now yours! Dead because she was afraid to bear your child, isn't she? Not the shame... not the wrong she had done me... but just fear—fear of the burden of her womanhood. And because of her my children are bastards and cannot inherit my name. And I must live in sin against my Church, as—God help me—I can't against my nature. What are men to do when this is how women use the freedom we have given them? Is the curse of barrenness to be nothing to a man? And that's the death in life to which you gentlemen with your free civilization are bringing us. I think we are brothers in misfortune, Mr. Trebell.

And by which shall I help you to a solution... telling lies or the truth tomorrow? You value your work more than anything else in the world, do you not? *(with grim ambiguity)* Then I am sorry for you, Mr. Trebell, Lord Horsham, by all means, let us go.

Edward I: an implied comparison between staunchly religious Edward I and the contemporary Edward VII (which caused the play to be banned) **Farrant**: the only other Catholic in the room at whom O'Connell levels ironic criticism

72

DICAEOPOLIS SPEAKS HIS MIND ABOUT THE STUPID REASONS FOR THE CURRENT WAR

(425 BC) ARISTOPHANES, The Acharnians, tr. Jack Flavin

Four years before he wrote *Peace* (when the likelihood of it coming about was small) [see I, #77], Aristophanes was faced with a desperate situation: the Athenians had been fighting the Lacedaemonians (the Spartans) for ten years, the farmlands and rural areas outside of Athens had been devastated, and the populace crowded into the walled city suffered from illness and hunger. But the Athenian demagogues refused to negotiate with the Spartans, who were ready for truce. Of Aristophanes' three Peace plays, *The Acharnians* is the most bitter, and aims its satire directly and contemptuously at the Athenian political and military hawks.

At the beginning of the play, Dicaeopolis, the rustic "good citizen" who shares entirely Aristophanes' contempt for Athenian self-delusion and chauvinism, tries to speak out for peace at the Assembly; the fatuousness of its general proceedings silences him, and he determines to conclude a truce with the Spartans on his own. His "envoy" returns with a packet of proposals, but when the super-patriotic charcoal burners, the Acharnae, get wind of this, they are ready to stone him.

Dicaeopolis faces either convincing them or being stoned by them. He knocks at Euripides' door to get suitable beggar's paraphernalia to gain sympathy for his plea, which the tragic poet gives him unwillingly ("You're stealing a whole tragedy!"), puts his head on the block, as agreed, in readiness for demise in case he loses, and speaks.

His plea is a parody of Athens' and Sparta's reasons for going to war in the first place, and an attack on the sheer inhumanity of Athens' treatment of its foreign neighbors and minor adversaries (the

Megarians). Though he is careful, before these supercharged patriotic hardhats, to "hate the Spartans" and put no blame on "the state" but only on "a few" of our own "wicked men," his argument appeases only half the (chorus of) Acharnians, and they fall into scuffling among themselves.

The victory in principle that Dicaeopolis wins at the end of the play contrasts with the fate of the army's General Lamachus, who is crippled *almost* in the line of duty, by falling into a ditch on the way to the battle. Dicaeopolis, on the other hand, is also "crippled," but only sexually, at his orgiastic banquet celebrating his victorious truce. His victory satisfies entirely the needs of comedy, if not of then-current Athenian politics.

Note: A joke explained dies as a joke. But unexplained, it may never even qualify as the memory of a joke. To preserve at least the memory of what was for Aristophanes' Athens brilliant joking, the details of the political environment of *The Acharnians's* humor and wit has to be explained at length, and so, with apologies, the footnotes to this monologue labor to tell the whole relevant story.

DICAEOPOLIS

All of you who are watching, do not hold it against me that I, a mere beggar, should dare to address the Athenian people in a comic play. For even comedy can discern truth. I may say some things that startle you, but this year Cleon cannot slander me by claiming that I defame the State with strangers present. This is the Lenaean Festival and no strangers are present. We citizens are quite alone here now. Make no mistake, I too am filled with hatred for the Spartans. May Poseidon, Lord of Earthquakes, bring all their houses down around their ears. Because I, like you, have had my vines cut down. But after all—and we are all friends here today—how can we blame the Spartans for this? It was some of our own people and not the State—remember that I say it was not the State—but some of our own, a few wicked little men, worthless fellows with no scruples and less character, who began spreading rumors that the Megarans were importing contraband produce to the City. Before long, not so much as a cucumber or a rabbit, a suckling pig or a bit of garlic or salt could come in without it being whispered that it was Megaran and then promptly confiscated. But the real trouble began when a few tipsy young men went over to Megara one night and kidnaped the courtesan, Simaetha. The Megarans were cut to the quick and, in return, stole two girls from the house of Aspasia. So all of Greece went to war over three whores. As we all know, Aspasia has Friends in High Places. Pericles, from on high in Olympus, unlimbered his heavy missiles. He thundered and lightened, and befuddled all of Hellas. He enacted laws. The Megarians, dying of hunger, beseeched their Spartan friends to get the Law of the Three Whores rendered null and void. When the Spartans failed, the instant clash of shields was heard. But who among us can say that they were in the wrong? Do you mean to say that if the Spartans had.stolen so much as a small dog from one of our islands we would have stood aside and said, "Be our guests!" No, by heaven, we would have launched three hundred ships of war, and the whole City would have been infested with brawling troops and uproar over the election of a Trierarch, the distribution of pay, the gilding of figureheads, and the measurement of rations. The navy dockyard would have rung with the sounds of ships being built, of boatswains' pipes and flutes, trills and whistles. Oh, yes, we would have done all these things.

(shaking the beggar's staff)
Even the beggar, Telephus, thinks so. Anyone who doesn't is witless.

Cleon: the tyrant of Athens whom Aristophanes loathed, and whom he satirized mercilessly in his comedy *The Babylonians*. Cleon was so outraged that he sued the playwright, but lost his case. Aristophanes responded with a withering parody in *The Knights*, in which Cleon is portrayed as a reprobate foreign slave. **Lenaean Festival**, held in winter when few foreigners were in Athens or in the theatre **Spartans...vines cut down**: in the early years of the Peloponnesian wars the Spartans' annual siege of Athens forced the farmers in the suburbs to take shelter within the walled city, at which time the Spartan soldiers would despoil their crops and homes; the siege was intermittent, lasting only several months each year because of the Spartans' anxiety lest a rebellion of their slaves at home take advantage of a more extended absence **...the Megarians...contraband**: The Athenians alleged that the city-state of Megara, bordering on Athens, had encroached on its sacred land, and so instituted economic sanctions and a blockade against Megara, which had been under the protection of Sparta. Pericles' refusal of Sparta's ultimatum to revoke the Megara Decree tipped the scales in the developing conflict between the two strongest Greek powers, and led to the beginning of hostilities **the real trouble...kidnapped the courtesan Simaetha**: Aristophanes parodies what he regarded as the triviality of the contentions over Megara that led to the outbreak of war **house of Aspasia**: the hetaera, or courtesan, of ruler Pericles, whose devotion to her was the provocation for Athenian/Clintonian scandal. To designate her as one of the instigators of a mythical "Law of the Three Whores" was close to the limit of Athenian political tolerance for comic poets **Trierarch**: a title of the wealthy persons in Athens upon whom, once or twice in a lifetime, fell the onerous public duty of underwriting the equipment and manpower of a trireme (the biggest battleship of ancient times) **even the beggar Telephus**: before launching this defense, Aristophanes dressed as Telephus (who in myth disguises as a beggar in order to sneak inside Agamemnon's palace, take his son hostage, and then trade him for a cure for his mortal wound) to extract sympathy from his auditor-judges

73

ARISTOPHANES ARGUES THE CASE FOR HIS COMEDY'S WINNNG FIRST PRIZE

(421 BC) ARISTOPHANES, *Peace, tr. Fred Beake*

The *parabasis* of an Aristophanic comedy comes roughly halfway through the play; it follows the first resolution of the plot's demented action, in this case, Trigaeus having actually dug Peace out of the deep pit in which she's been buried, is ready to return to earth to enjoy her resurrection [see I, #77; II, #72]. Then the Chorus steps forward and speaks, and sings, the parabasis, i.e., the editorial.

The *parabasis* can vary in its relevance to the play's subject. In this case, the Chorus sings a plea to the Muse to bring actual peace, an attack on a rival poet and his sons. But—for our pleasure, at any rate—they sing, or speak, the playwright's plea to win first prize. Why shouldn't he? He's the most honest, the most illustrious; he's banished the stale jokes about poverty; about lice; about clumsy Heracles gorging his fat face; and aims instead at the toughest targets of all—public figures. When the show is over, virtuously he goes straight home, and doesn't waste his time running to the gym to diddle young boys. In general, a very convincing appeal. Sadly, it didn't work—he got second prize.

ARISTOPHANES

It's for the umpire to strike hard if any poet in the comedy context should praise himself to the audience. But if ever, Daughter of Zeus, it is reasonable, it is Aristophanes, myself, this best of chorus trainers and finest born of men who should be called wise and our teacher. For he alone put a stop to the ceaseless battles of wit, and puns on minute matters, and interesting struggles with lice. He removed this load of stupidity, these jokes of lesser men. He made for us a great art, a city, and a citadel of great thoughts and purposes, and jokes not guffawed in the fields. None of the idiotic portrayals of the semblance of men and women, but with the passion of Heracles assailed great matters, passed through the fearsome smells of the tannery, and crossed through the minds of mud.

My first competitor was the sharpest-toothed monster of all. The light of his eyes was dreadful, like the prostitution of Cynna. A hundred flatterers moaned in a circle of serpents around his head. And he had the voice of a mountain stream, begetting destruction. And the scent of a seal, and the unwashed balls of a goblin, and the ass-end of an oven. I was not afraid at this wondrous sight but fought for You, and fought for the Islands. I was your bastion. I did this first. I did not cruise the gymnasium on the lookout for boys, but picked up my clobber and went home, having done little harm, and given much fun, and done what was needed.

And you men, and you boys, must be of my party, and baldheaded men must especially exert themselves for my victory. And all shall speak of my victory at the concluding party: "Take baldy, give baldy his nuts, and take them not away from the man that has the brow of the poets of nobility."

But if Crabby comes and asks if his boys can dance, harken not nor succor them, but regard them as housebred quails, dancers with necks like a soldier's knapsack, cousins of dwarves, hammer chippings, stage machinery makers. And if the father says, "the play went as good as could be expected," let the polecat strangle him at midnight.

And these are the songs of the Muses of bright hair that the wisehearted poet should sing, just as the swallow sits and shrieks his Spring noise. And no chorus for Morsimos, my competitor, the gratings of whose words I have heard. He, he and his brother had the chorus of the tragedy: gorgons of vegetarian tendency, desirers of skates and harpies, pursuers of ancient women. Unclean! Armpits with the foetor of goats, bringers of fish to a dark end. Let them be spat upon from head to toe, and then my Muse, my Goddess, let You and me enjoy the holiday.

daughter of Zeus and Mnemosyne (Memory): the Muse of Poetry **this best of chorus trainers**: Aristophanes trained his own choruses **Cynna**: one of the best-known courtesans in Athens **fought for the Islands** in the Peloponesian Wars between Athens and Sparta **bald-headed men** who automatically belong to the party of Aristophanes, who was also bald **polecat**: a skunk **gorgons of vegetarian tendency**: from the mythic Gorgons, monster-women with hairs of snakes and petrifying stares **skate**: a fish-ray with a poisonous sting **Harpies**: the feared swift-winged women-birds who snatched up criminals for punishment by the Furies **foetor**: as in fetid, stench

74

MNESILOCHUS, IN DRAG AT THE WOMEN'S FESTIVAL, DEFENDS HIS NEPHEW EURIPIDES' ATTACKS ON WOMEN

(411 BC) ARISTOPHANES, Thesmaphoriazusae, *tr. Anonymous*

Euripides is terrified that the women in their Assembly at the festival of Thesmaphoria will condemn him to death for the insults to their sex in his plays, he whom they loathe for his misogyny. When Agathon, the effeminate poet, refuses him the favor of defending him at the Festival in convincing drag, Euripides' burly father-in-law, Mnesilochus, volunteers. He is shaved above and below, dressed in a lady's wardrobe loaned by Agathon, and goes to the Festival. Sure enough, there's a motion made to put Euripides to death, and Mnesilochus, his barrel-tones squeezed into a dulcet key, rises to defend him.

His defense is badly calculated. Starting off circumspectly by voicing the hate he shares with the ladies for Euripides, he argues for gentler treatment of the poet because—his deadly mistake—misogynist though he is, his plays hardly mention some of the really awful sins the ladies know—and do—all too well. As the catalogue grows and Mnesilochus gets totally into the spirit of male rage, the ladies lunge for him. The free-for-all continues until Clisthenes, the ladylike pederast, rushes in to tell them that there's a disguised male in their midst.

The rest of Mnesilochus' troubles—his being unmasked to the skin, his grabbing a babe and threatening to cut open its veins, his being lashed to a post—etc., escalate Aristophanically until Euripides contrives his escape.

MNESILOCHUS

Oh, women! I am not astonished at these outbursts of fiery rage; how could your bile not get inflamed against Euripides, who has spoken so ill of you? As for myself, I hate the man, I swear it by my children; 'twould be madness not to hate him! Yet, let us reflect a little; we are alone and our words will not be repeated outside. Why be so bent on his ruin? Because he has known and shown up two or three of our faults, when we have a thousand? As for myself, not to speak of other women, I have more than one great sin upon my conscience, but this is the blackest of them. I had been married three days and my husband was asleep by my side; I had a lover, who had seduced me when I was seven years old; impelled by his passion, he came scratching at the door; I understood at once he was there and was going down noiselessly. "Where are you going?" asked my husband. "I am suffering terribly with colic," I told him, "and am going to the closet." "Go," he replied, and started pounding together juniper berries, aniseed, and sage. As for myself, I moistened the door-hinge and went to find my lover, who embraced me, half-reclining upon Apollo's altar and holding on to the sacred laurel with one hand. Well now! Consider! that is a thing of which Euripides has never spoken. And when we bestow our favours on slaves and muleteers for want of better, does he mention this? And when we eat garlic early in the morning after a night of wantonness, so that our husband, who has been keeping guard on the city wall, may be reassured by the smell and suspect nothing, has Euripides ever breathed a word of this? Tell me. Neither has he spoken of the woman who spreads open a large cloak before her husband's eyes to make him admire it in full daylight to conceal her lover by so doing and afford him the means of making his escape. I know another who for ten whole days pretended to be suffering the pains of labour until she had secured a child; the husband hurried in all directions to buy drugs to hasten her deliverance, and meanwhile an old woman brought the infant in a stew-pot; to prevent its crying she had stopped up its mouth with honey. With a sign she told the wife that she was bringing a child for her, who at once began exclaiming, "Go away, friend, go away, I think I am going to be delivered; I can feel him kicking his heels in the belly... of the stew-pot." The husband goes off full of joy, and the old wretch quickly picks the honey out of the child's mouth, which sets a-crying; then she seizes the babe, runs to the father and tells him with a smile on her face, "'Tis a lion, a lion, that is born to you; 'tis your very image. Everything about it is like you, even to its pistle, which is all twisty like a fir-cone." Are these not our everyday tricks? Why certainly, by Artemis, and we are angry with Euripides, who assuredly treats us no worse than we deserve! And Heaven knows, I have not said all that I know. Do you want any more? Why, I haven't told the thousandth part of what we women do. Have I said how we use the hollow handles of our brooms to draw up wine unbeknownst to our husbands? And how we give meats to our pimps at the feast of Apaturia and then accuse the cat. Have I mentioned the woman who killed her husband with a hatchet? Or another, who caused her husband to lose his reason with her potions? And of the Acharnian woman who buried her father beneath the bath? Have I told you how you attributed to yourself the male child your slave girl had just borne and gave her your little daughter? By Zeus, don't touch me!—There!—Tit for tat!—Come on, then, and by Demeter, I'll make you crap forth the sesame cake you've just eaten!

juniper berries, aniseed, and sage: as remedies for colic **Apollo's altar**: an altar in the form of a column in the front vestibule of houses **...and suspect nothing**: because the smell of garlic is not inviting to gallants **Go away...of the stew-pot**: the thoughts of the woman who pretends to be in child-bed; she is, however, careful not to utter them to her husband **the feast of Apaturia**: at which fathers brought their children born since the last festival, to inscribe their names in the rolls of the *phratrie* (the extended family association)

75

BLEPYRUS, NEEDING TO TAKE A CRAP IN THE DEAD OF NIGHT, HAS NO CHOICE BUT TO WEAR HIS WIFE'S CLOTHING

(392 BC) ARISTOPHANES, Ecclesiazusae, *tr. Anonymous*

From each according to his ability, to each according to his need is a principle not far from the one established by the women in *Ecclesiazusae* who take over the Athenian Assembly. Blepyrus, the old and not too able husband of their beautiful young leader Praxagora, finds his wife gone in the morning—she's at the Assembly—and needing desperately to take a crap, he has no choice but to grab her clothes and slippers, and stumble out of doors to do it.

But he can't. He squats and tries. He squeezes and thinks of remedies. He may need a doctor. Ruminating, trying, wondering—at last, ahhh…

The episode has no bearing on the progress of the play. A friend comes by, tells him what the women have accomplished at the Assembly, and Blepyrus is delighted that now he can be at leisure while his wife runs things. But it is not to be so easy for the men. By the end of the play, the principle of shared and common property, and to each according to his/her need, lead to one of Aristophanes' most hilarious scenes. A young man spots a lovely girl, and on the way to her is intercepted by an old crone who claims first privilege. Then the old one is intercepted by an older one, and she by an inconceivably ancient one, and the last two go off with the helpless stud at play's end, still contending for who's first. The same principles were later contemplated by Plato in *The Republic,* but he ignored the lesson of the young man in Aristophanes' play.

(BLEPYRUS appears in the doorway of his house, wearing PRAXAGORA'S Persian sandals and, saffron robe.)

BLEPYRUS

What does this mean? My wife has vanished! it is nearly daybreak and she does not return! I had to take a crap! I woke up and hunted in the darkness for my shoes and my cloak; but grope where I would, I couldn't find them. Meanwhile Mr. O'Shit was already knocking on the door and I had only just time to seize my wife's little mantle and her Persian slippers. But where shall I find a place where I can take a crap? Bah! One place is as good as another at night-time; no one will see me. Ah! what a damned fool I was to take a wife at my age, and how I could thrash myself for having acted so stupidly! It's certainty she's not gone out for any honest purpose. But the thing to do now is to take a crap.

(He squats.)

Oh! oh! oh! how stopped up I am! Whatever am I to do? It's not merely for the present that I am frightened; but when I have eaten, where is my crap to find an outlet now? This damned McPear fellow has bolted the door. Call a doctor; but who is the cleverest in this branch of the science? Amynon? Perhaps he would not come. Ah! Antisthenes! Let him be brought to me, cost what it will. To judge by his noisy sighs, that man knows what an arse wants, when it needs to crap. Oh! venerated Ilithyia! I shall burst unless the door gives way. Have pity! pity! Let me not become a thunder-mug for the comic poets.

(finding relief at last)

Oh! there! it is over and I can get up again.

Amynon was not a physician, according to the Scholiast, but one of the orators called laticuli (wide-assed), because addicted to anal reception, and was invoked by Blepyrus for that reason **Antisthenes**: a doctor notorious for his dissolute life **Ilithyia**: the goddess who presides over childbirth

76

FRA TIMOTEO PERSUADES LUCREZIA THAT IT IS PIOUS TO COMMIT ADULTERY

(c1515-20) MACHIAVELLI, Mandragola, *tr. Kenneth and Laura Richards, Act 3, Sc. 11*

The monk Timoteo speaks with forked tongue, but does it so well that he's become the classic prototype of the hypocrite, a place he holds in Western literature beside Moliere's Tartuffe. The final obstacle in Callimaco's journey to Lucrezia's bed [see I, #78] is the wife's virtue, and the task of overcoming that is given, appropriately, to her father confessor. He accomplishes his task with the aid of sacred doctrine: the word of God, the teachings of the Church. Each principle is accurately expounded, and yet bent jesuitically toward its opposite intent. His arguments retire one after the other the implicit objections of a virtuous wife, for whom adultery is adultery. Out of the mouth of Timoteo, adultery itself becomes a blessing, and its avoidance almost a sin.

The monologue is a parody of classical rhetoric's speech of persuasion, but in no sense is parody evident in Timoteo's delivery; he is, in style, the very model of religion's sincere and compassionate conservative. But unlike Tartruffe, engaged in much the same doctrinal persuasion, Timoteo is entirely successful.

TIMOTEO
Madonna Lucrezia, you've known me a long time. There are many things which seen at a distance appear terrible, unbearable and strange. But close up they're human, acceptable and quite ordinary. That's why we say that fear of evil is worse than evil itself. This is just such a case. As far as your conscience is concerned you must keep in mind this general rule: if you are confronted with an action which will result on the one hand in a certain good and on the other in an uncertain evil,

then you must never, for fear of that evil, sacrifice the certain good. As far as this case is concerned, the fact that you will become pregnant is a certain good, because you will gain a soul for our Savior. The uncertain evil is that the man who sleeps with you after you've taken the potion may well die. But there have been cases when it was not an inevitable consequence. However, as death is a possibility it is good that Messer Nicia should not run the danger. As far as the act itself is concerned, it is absolute nonsense that it should be construed a sin, for it is the will that sins and not the body. The cause of sin would lie in displeasing your husband, but by doing this you would be pleasing him. It would be a sin if you derived pleasure from the act, but it will not give you pleasure. In addition, particular consideration must be given to the purpose of an act; your purpose is to fill a seat in Paradise and satisfy the wish of your husband. It is written in the Bible that the daughters of Lot, thinking themselves to be the only women left in the world, had relations with their father. But because their intention was good, they did not sin.

Know that a woman without children is a woman without a home. If her husband dies she's nothing but an animal, nobody wants her. Madonna, I swear, by this consecrated breast, that to do as your husband wishes in this matter need worry your conscience no more than eating meat on a Wednesday. A little holy water will just wash the sin away. I'm leading you to things that will cause you to thank God for me. And you'll be even more grateful a year from now.

Why, for a chance like this there are fifty women in this town who'd raise their hands to Heaven. Don't be afraid, my daughter. I shall pray to God for you. I'll repeat the prayer of the Archangel Raphael, so that he'll be by your side.

Go and prepare yourself in good time to perform this mystery. Peace be with you.

77

SIMON EYRE PREPARES A FEAST FOR HIS KING
(1599) THOMAS DEKKER, The Shoemaker's Holiday, Act 5, Sc. 4

The Shoemaker Simon Eyre (who is to become the Mayor of London) is the Old King Cole of Elizabethan comedy: supremely jolly, but also supremely overbearing. Both the play and its principle character are tributes to the London shopkeeper citizenry who supported and applauded with vim their prosperous England and their Virgin Queen. Bursting with patriotic zeal and jollity, Simon Eyre rules his shop-kingdom's bustling apprentices with a merry, iron hand.

With apoplectic vivacity, he is preparing a feast to welcome the King who has advanced him to the office of Lord Mayor.

(Enter Eyre, Hodge, Firk, Rafe, and other Shoemakers, all with napkins on their shoulders.)

EYRE

Come, my fine Hodge, my jolly gentlemen shoemakers! soft, where be these cannibals, these varlets, my officers? Let them all walk and wait upon my brethren; for my meaning is, that none but shoemakers, none but the livery of my company shall in their satin hoods wait upon the trencher of my sovereign.

No more, Firk; come, lively! Let your fellow-prentices want no cheer; let wine be plentiful as beer, and beer as water. Hang these penny-pinching fathers, that cram wealth in innocent lamb-skins. Rip, knaves, avaunt! Look to my guests!

Cover me those hundred tables again, and again, till all my jolly prentices be feasted. Avoid, Hodge! Run, Rafe! Frisk about, my nimble Firk! Carouse me fadom-healths to the honour of the shoemakers. Do they drink lively, Hodge? Do they tickle it, Firk? Want they meat? Where's this swag-belly, this greasy kitchen-stuff cook? Call the varlet

to me! Want meat? Firk, Hodge, lame Rafe, run, my tall men, belea-
guer the shambles, beggar all Eastcheap, serve me whole oxen in
chargers, and let sheep whine upon the tables like pigs for want of
good fellows to eat them. Want meat? Vanish, Firk! Avaunt, Hodge!

Is my sovereign come? Vanish, my tall shoemakers, my nimble
brethren; look to my guests, the prentices. Away, you Islington
whitepot! hence, you hopper-arse! hence, you barley-pudding, full of
maggots! you broiled carbonado! avaunt, avaunt, avoid,
Mephistophilus! Shall Sim Eyre learn to speak of you, Lady Madgy?
Vanish, Mother Miniver-cap; vanish, go, trip and go; meddle with
your partlets and your pishery-pashery, your flewes and your
whirligigs; go, rub, out of mine alley! Sim Eyre knows how to speak to
a Pope, to Sultan Soliman, to Tamburlaine, an he were here, and shall
I melt, shall I droop before my sovereign? No, come, my Lady Madgy!
Follow me, Hans! About your business, my frolic free booters! Firk,
frisk about, and about, and about, for the honour of mad Simon Eyre,
lord mayor of London.

trencher: food **lamb-skin**s: parchment bags, purses **fadom-healths**: healths a
fathom deep **beleager the shambles**: surround the slaughterhouses **chargers**:
large, shallow platters **Islington**: district in northern London; **whitepot**: concoc-
tion of milk, eggs, raisins and sugar **hopper-arse**: a funnel-shaped chamber, in
which materials stored in it were discharged through the narrower opening at
the bottom, hence "arse" **carbonado**: steak **Mother Miniver-cap**: a cap lined
with white or spotted grey-and-white fur **partlets**: neckbands **pishery-pashery**:
depreciatory talk **flewes**: flapping skirts **whirligigs**: something that whirls,
revolves

78

CAPTAIN SEAGULL PEDDLES THE GLORIES OF VIRGINIA TO DUPES

(1604) MARSTON, CHAPMAN, AND JONSON, Eastward Ho!, *Act 3, Sc. 3*

Captain Seagull is a worthy forerunner of the more aggressive pitchmen on TV commercials, or more accurately, the more unscrupulous "travel agents" shepherding immigrants to America in the 1890s. A grin, a slap on the back, and a spiel of promised blessings wrapped the imagination of the Elizabethan dupe-colonist in a kind of gold-ecstasy. Seagull is the original agent-pied-piper, and his pitch the model for later centuries' brochures. But his was the earliest, when ships' captains were accosting passengers to make the voyage to England's touted Shangri-la of the 17th century, Virginia.

In this instance, it's not the impoverished for whom Seagull is trawling; it's two of the well-heeled, who are deep in their cups. But more than these have booked passage; about half the cast, in fact, some absconding, some merely fleeing, but all doomed by the storm that subsequently shipwrecks the voyage altogether before the ship has passed the Thames, and still later dooms the characters on board to their just retribution [see I, #83; II, #79].

> *(Blue Anchor Tavern, Billingsgate. Enter Seagull, Spendall, and Scapethrift, in the Tavern, with a Drawer.)*

SEAGULL
Come, boys, Virginia longs till we share the rest of her maidenhead. A whole country of English is there, man, bred of those that were left there in `79. They have married with the Indians, and make `em bring forth as beautiful faces as any we have in England; and therefore the Indians are so in love with `em, that all the treasure they have they lay at their feet.

I tell thee, gold is more plentiful there than copper is with us; and for as much red copper as I can bring, I'll have thrice the weight in gold. Why, man, all their dripping-pans and their chamber-pots are pure gold; and all the chains with which they chain up their streets are massy gold; all the prisoners they take are fettered in gold; and for rubies and diamonds, they go forth on holidays and gather `em by the sea-shore to hang on their children's coats and stick in their caps, as commonly as our children wear saffron-gilt brooches and groats with holes in `em. Wild boar is as common there as our tamest bacon is here; venison, as mutton. And then, you shall live freely there, without sergeants, or courtiers, or lawyers, or intelligencers; only a few industrious Scots, perhaps, who, indeed, are dispersed over the face of the whole earth. But as for them, there are no greater friends to Englishmen and England, when they are out on't, in the world than they are. And for my part, I would a hundred thousand of `em were there, for we are all one-countrymen now, ye know; and we should find ten times more comfort of them there than we do here. Then for your means to advancement there, it is simple, and not preposterously mixed. You may be an alderman there, and never be scavenger: you may be a noble man, and never be a slave. You may come to preferment enough, and never be a pandar; to riches and fortune enough, and have never the more villainy nor the less wit.

Some six weeks' sail, no more, with any indifferent good wind. And if I get to any part of the coast of Africa, I'll sail thither with any wind; or when I come to Cape Finisterre, there's a foreright wind continually wafts us till we come at Virginia.

---

rest of her maidenhead: pun on the continuation of the 'Virgin' colony's settling **left there in '79**: the "lost colony" was left on Roanoke Island in 1587. No English had arrived until 1583. The 'natives' were uniformly hostile, the colonists uniformly inept. By this date (1604), efforts to colonize Virginia had failed repeatedly. Seagull's pitch is total sham (9-15) closely imitated from More's *Utopia* **saffron-gilt**: false gold **groat**: a silver English coin worth fourpence **we are all one-countrymen now**: with the accession of James of Scotland to the English throne in 1603 **scavenger**: street cleaner **preferment**: advancement, promotion **pandar**: in this context, low servant, lackey, flatterer **Cape Finisterre**: on the northwestern coast of France

79

TOUCHSTONE REVEALS THE SINS OF THE SHIPWRECKED TO THE CONSTABLE

(1604) MARSTON, CHAPMAN, AND JONSON, Eastward Ho!, Act 4, Sc. 2

The plot convolutions of *Eastward Ho!* are a little daunting, but here's a summary of the facts relevant to this episode: Touchstone, a worthy goldsmith, has two apprentices: Golding, an upright man like himself, and Quicksilver, an idler and debauchee. He has two correspondingly antithetical daughters: Mildred, virtuous and worthy, and Gertrude, proud, ambitious and wanton. Gertrude, in her ambition to rise to Ladyship, marries Sir Petronel Flash, a knight. But he's an impoverished knight, who absconds with her money aboard the ship to Virginia, and with another man's wife as well. And it's the debauched Quicksilver who is bringing her aboard for him (as it happens, he's bringing the *wrong* other wife in disguise, but that's another story).

The ship gets no farther than the Thames; it's wrecked in a storm off Cuckold's Haven [see I, #83]. After their rescue, Sir Petronel and Quicksilver are arrested and charged by Touchstone with "suspicion of felony" (Sir Petronel's absconding) and "accessory in the receipt of stolen goods" (Quicksilver's assistance with the alternate wife). Ironically, they have to appear before Golding, the newly elected alderman's deputy, who is to examine them and will subsequently send them off to prison. Gertrude, back from her journey to her "country castle"—"in air," as her father points out—is bitter and undone.

Touchstone, with the wrath of vengeance in his heart but the satisfaction of seeing his revenge accomplished, makes his case with both bitterness and pleasure to his former apprentice and now friendly arm of the law, while the two culprits stand hangdog before the Golding they formerly despised.

TOUCHSTONE

Yes, Master Deputy; I had a small venture with them in the voyage—a thing called a son-in-law, or so. Officers, you may let 'em stand alone, they will not run away; I'll give my word for them. A couple of very honest gentlemen. One of 'em was my prentice, Master Quicksilver here; and when he had two year to serve, kept his whore and his hunting nag, would play his hundred pound at gresco, or primero, as familiarly (and all o' my purse) as any bright piece of crimson on 'em all; had his changeable trunks of apparel standing at livery, with his mare, his chest of perfumed linen, and his bathing-tubs: which when I told him of, why he—he was a gentleman and I a poor Cheapside groom! The remedy was, we must part. Since when, he hath had the gift of gathering up some small parcels of mine, to the value of five hundred pound, dispersed among my customers, to furnish this his Virginian venture; wherein this knight was the chief, Sir Flash—one that married a daughter of mine, ladyfied her, turned two thousand pounds' worth of good land of hers into cash within the first week, bought her a new gown and a coach, sent her to seek her fortune by land, whilst himself prepared for his fortune by sea; took in fresh flesh at Billingsgate, for his own diet, to serve him the whole voyage—the wife of a certain usurer called Security, who hath been the broker for 'em in all this business. Please, Master Deputy, work upon that now!

gresco: a card game **primero**: a card game fashionable in England in 16th and 17th centuries **Cheapside**: the poor section of London **Billingsgate**: a fish market in London

80

VOLPONE WELCOMES THE MORNING SUN AND HIS GOLD

(1606) BEN JONSON, Volpone, *Act I, Sc.1*

Roman satirists mocked the legacy-hunters who made gifts to wealthy acquaintances in the hope of winning reward in their wills. Jonson adapted the custom to contemporary Venice—one of England's synonyms for vice—and set in it the ultimate worshipper of gold, the Magnifico Volpone, who reveled not only in his wealth but in his cynically delicious way of accumulating it. In his opening monologue, he throws wide his "shrine," and salutes his gold with rapture: "Hail the world's soul, and mine!" And with even greater rapture ("I glory more in the cunning purchase.../Than in the glad possession)" describes his strategem for gaining it in "no common way."

Jonson's satiric portraits of desire operating *in extremis* are among the most arresting and profound creations of Elizabethan/Jacobean drama. His men in the outer reaches of obsession reach for the ultimate limits of ingenuity in their pursuit of satiation. Volpone, in the course of the play, building on the credo of this opening profession and prayer, reaches for that limit. But because of Mosca, his parasite who turns nemesis, he never grasps it, cut off finally from his soul's repletion—which is, more than imprisonment, his true retribution.

> **VOLPONE**
> Good morning to the day; and next, my gold!—
> Open the shrine, that I may see my saint.
>
> *(Mosca draws a curtain and reveals a hea of gold)*
> Hail the world's soul, and mine! More glad than is
> The teeming earth to see the longed-for sun

Peep through the horns of the celestial Ram,
Am I, to view thy splendor darkening his;
That lying here, amongst my other hoards,
Show'st like a flame by night, or like the day
Struck out of chaos, when all darkness fled
Unto the center. O thou son of Sol,
But brighter than thy father, let me kiss,
With adoration, thee, and every relic
Of sacred treasure in this blessed room.
Well did wise poets, by thy glorious name,
Title that age which they would have the best;
Thou being the best of things, and far transcending
All style of joy, in children, parents, friends,
Or any other waking dream on earth.
Thy looks when they to Venus did ascribe,
They should have giv'n her twenty thousand Cupids;
Such are thy beauties and our loves!
Dear saint, Riches, the dumb god, that giv'st all men tongues,
That canst do nought, and yet mak'st men do all things.
The price of souls! Even hell, with thee to boot,
Is made worth heaven. Thou art virtue, fame,
Honor, and all things else. Who can get thee,
He shall be noble, valiant, honest, wise—

Yet I glory
More in the cunning purchase of my wealth
Than in the glad possession, since I gain
No common way. I use no trade, no venture;
I wound no earth with plowshares, fat no beasts
To feed the shambles; have no mills for iron,
Oil, corn, or men to grind 'em into powder;
What should I do
But cocker up my genius, and live free
To all delights my fortune calls me to?
1 have no wife, no parent, child, ally,
To give my substance to; but whom I make
Must be my heir, and this makes men observe me.

This draws new clients daily to my house,
Women and men of every sex and age,
That bring me presents, send me plate, coin, jewels,
With hope that when I die—which they expect
Each greedy minute—it shall then return
Tenfold upon them; whilst some, covetous
Above the rest, seek to engross me whole,
And counter-work the one unto the other,
Contend in gifts, as they would seem, in love.
All which I suffer, playing with their hopes,
And am content to coin' em into profit,
And look upon their kindness, and take more,
And look on that; still bearing them in hand,
Letting the cherry knock against their lips,
And draw it by their mouths, and back again.

horns of the celestial Ram: in the zodiac the constellation of Aries as represented by the ram (the male sheep) **center**: i.e., of the earth **that age**: i.e., the
Golden Age **purchase**: acquisition **venture**: investment or speculation **shambles**: slaughterhouse **cocker up**: pamper **observe**: pay obsequious court to
engross: monopolize **suffer**: allow **bearing them in hand**: manipulating them

81

VOLPONE, DISGUISED AS A MOUNTEBANK, HAWKS QUACK REMEDIES
(1606) BEN JOHNSON, Volpone, *Act 2, Sc. 1*

Volpone, intent on seducing the wife of Corvino, one of the palpitating would-be heirs of Volpone's estate, disguises himself as
the mountebank Scoto of Mantuo, and sets up a bench below Celia's
window ostensibly to sell medicines and unguents.

Here, Jonson pays tribute to the tradition of Italian street vending
out of which *commedia dell'arte* was born: the merchant on his bench

or platform in the piazza, with the aid of his clutch of performers—mountebanks ("tumblers on the bench"), singers, dancers, jugglers and so on—hawking his wares to a crowd seduced by the entertainment. As with television, the show alternates with the pitch.

Merchant Volpone has two products to sell: a flask of oil and a paper of powders. The first is pitched to the rabble. Having caught the lady's attention at her window above the square, and she having tossed down a handkerchief—a signal of readiness to purchase the oil—Volpone offers her the addition of the powders under cover of which he makes his initial advances.

Unhappily for Volpone, Corvino at first puts an end to the ruse before Volpone reaches his object. But subseqently, in his eagerness for the inheritance, the greedy husband becomes the willing procurer for Volpone's seduction of his wife.

> **VOLPONE**
>
> Gentlemen, honorable gentlemen, know that for the time our bank, being thus removed from the clamor of the *canaglia,* shall be the scene of pleasure and delight; for I have nothing to sell, little or nothing to sell.
>
> I protest, I and my six servants are notable to make this precious liquor so fast as it is fetched away from my lodging by gentlemen of your city, worshipful merchants, ay, and senators too, who, ever since my arrival, have detained me to their uses, by their splendidous liberalities. Oh health! Health! The blessing of the rich! The riches of the poor! Who can buy thee at too dear a rate; since there is no enjoying this world without thee? Be not then so sparing of your purses, honorable gentlemen, as to abridge the natural course of life.
>
> You all know, honorable gentlemen, I never valued this *ampulla,* or vial, at less than eight crowns; but for this time, I am content to be deprived of it for six. Six crowns is the price, and less, in courtesy, I know you cannot offer me. Take it or leave it, howsoever, both it an I am at your service. I ask you not as the value of the thing, for then I

should demand of you two thousand crowns; but I despise money. Only to show my affection for you, honorable gentlemen, and your illustrious state here, I have framed my journey hither only to present you with the fruits of my travels.

Well, I am in a humor this time to make a present of the small quantity my coffer contains. Wherefore, now mark: I have asked you six crowns, and six crowns, at other times, you have paid me. You shall not give me six crowns, nor five, nor four, nor three, not two, nor half a ducat. Sixpence it will cost you—expect no lower price, for the banner of my front, I will not bate a *bagatine;* that I will have, only, a pledge of your loves, to carry something from amongst you to show I am not contemned by you. Therefore now, toss your handkerchiefs, cheerfully, cheerfully; and be advertised that the first heroic spirit that deigns to grace me with a handkerchief, I will give it a little remembrance of something beside, shall please it better than if 1 had presented it with a double pistolet.

> *(Celia, at the window, throws down her handkerchief)*

Lady, I kiss your bounty, and for this timely grace you have done your poor Scoto of Mantua, I will return you, over and above my oil, a secret of that high and inestimable nature, shall make you forever enamored of that minute where your eye first descended on so mean, and yet not altogether despised, an object. Here is a powder concealed in this paper, of which, if I should speak to the worth, it is the powder that made Venus a goddess—given her by Apollo—that kept her perpetually young, cleared her wrinkles, firmed her gums, filled her skin, colored her hair; from her derived to Helen, and at the sack of Troy unfortunately lost; till now, in this our age, it was as happily recovered by a studious antiquary, out of some ruins of Asia; who sent a moiety of it to the court of France—but much sophisticated—wherewith the ladies there now color their hair. The rest, at this present, remains with me extracted to a quintessence, so that, wherever it but touches, in youth it perpetually preserves, in age restores the complexion; sets your teeth, did they dance like virginal jacks, firm as a wall.

And as to the unguent, to fortify the most indigent stomach, ay, were it of one that, through extreme weakness, vomited blood, putting but a drop into your nostrils, likewise behined the ears, a most sovereign and approved remedy; the cramps, convulsions, paralyses, epilepsies, retired nerves, ill vapors of the spleen, stoppings of the liver, the stone, the strangury; stops a *dysinteria* immediately; easeth the torsion of the small gut; and cures *melancholia hypochondriaca,* being taken and applied, according to my printed receipt.

(Pointing to his bill and his glass.)

For this is the physician, this the medicine; this counsels, this cures; this gives the direction, this works the effect; and, in sum, both together may be termed the abstract of the theoric and practic in the Aesculapian art. `Twill cost you eight crowns.

canaglia, It: rabble **coffer**: a box or chest, especially for valuables **bagatine**, It: a small coin **pistolet**: a Spanish gold piece **Scoto of Mantua**: an Italian juggler, then in England; Volpone is assuming his identity **moiety**: an indefinite portion, part **virginal jacks**: pieces of wood which made quills pluck the strings of a virginal (a musical instrument) **unguent**: ointment or salve **stone**: kidney stone **strangury**: painful urination **bill**: prescriptions **esculapian**: the art of Esculapus, the father of Greek medicine

82

MOROSE, WHO CAN BEAR NO NOISE, INSTRUCTS HIS SERVANT MUTE
(1609) BEN JOHNSON, Epicoene, or The Silent Woman, *Act 2, Sc. 1*

Morose is a miser who hates every kind of noise. He is—or should be, according to the definition of Jonsonian "humours"—an example of a humours character exhibiting the eccentricities and affectations of a distinct social type. But he is not that, or at least he is a great deal more.

His hatred of noise is not a characteristic of a social prototype as humours characters are supposed to be; his is an intensely private obsession. In these later comedies of Jonson's, "humours" go far beyond formula—the phlegmatic (excess of phlegm), the melancholic (of black bile), the sanguine (of blood), the choleric (of green bile). The "tendency toward excess" in one of these characters becomes excess to the point of mania and like Molière's obsessed characters, veers as much toward the tragic as toward the comic. As with Molière, what is judged—and the judgment of both their comedies is harsh— is the inapplicability of such manias to serve possible, or even conceivable, social ends.

Molière's monomaniacs arrive at their obsession by rational self-justification. But Jonson's Morose becomes ridiculous another way: not as the victim of his own rationality or fixed belief, but of uncontrollable urgencies that have nothing to do with reason or justification. They are not arrived at, they are willy-nilly *givens, there;* premises, not conclusions. As with Marlowe's tragic supermen, Jonson's equally out-of-scale comic supermen—Morose, Volpone, Epicure Mammon—dream at the edge of possibility, and though ravenous in their longing to reach the absolute of their desire, that desire evokes for them only its celebration, not its logical justification.

And so Morose, chained to his pursuit of absolute silence, is in this scene an engineer arranging for a smoothly functioning lifelong condition. In the play, he may end in torment, but he begins here to make his arrangements with punctilious exactitude, with precision, with anxious care. The tragic—or comic—hopelessness of those arrangements is previsioned by the blast of noise outside his house at the soliloquy's conclusion, a noise massively indifferent to his impeccable arrangements for his noiseless life within.

(Morose, Mute.)

MOROSE

Cannot I, yet, find out a more compendious method, than by this trunk, to save my servants the labour of speech, and mine ears the discord of sounds? Let me see: all discourses but mine own afflict me; they seem harsh, impertinent, and irksome. Is it not possible, that thou should'st answer me by signs, and I apprehend thee, fellow? Speak not, though I question you. You have taken the ring off from the street door, as I bade you? Answer me not by speech, but by silence; unless it be otherwise

(Mute makes a leg.)

Very good. And you have fastened on a thick quilt, or flock-bed, on the outside of the door; that if they knock with their daggers, or with brick-bats, they can make no noise?—But with your leg, your answer, unless it be otherwise

(makes a leg)

Very good. This is not only fit modesty in a servant, but good state and discretion in a master. And you have been with Cutbeard the barber, to have him come to me?

(makes a leg.)

Good. And, he will come presently? Answer me not but with your leg, unless it be otherwise; if it be otherwise, shake your head, or shrug

(makes a leg)

So! Your Italian and Spaniard are wise in these: and it is a frugal and comely gravity. How long will it be ere Cutbeard come? Stay; if an hour, hold up your whole hand, if half an hour, two fingers; if a quarter, one;

(holds up a finger bent)

Good: half a quarter? 'tis well. And have you given him a key, to come it without knocking?

(makes a leg)
Good. And is the lock oil'd, and the hinges, to-day?

(makes a leg)
Good. And the quilting of the stairs no where worn out and bare?

(makes a leg.)
Very good. I see, by much doctrine, and impulsion, it may be effected; stand by. The Turk, in this divine discipline, is admirable, exceeding all the potentates of the earth; still waited on by mutes; and all his commands so executed; yea, even in the war, as I have heard, and in his marches, most of his charges and directions given by signs, and with silence: an exquisite art! and I am heartily asham'd, and angry oftentimes, that the princes of Christendom should suffer a barbarian to transcend 'em so high a point of felicity. I will practise it hereafter.

(One winds a horn without.)
How now? oh! oh! what villain, what prodigy of mankind is that? look.

(Exit Mute Again.)
Oh! cut his throat, cut his throat! what murderer, hell-hound, devil can this be? Pain of thy life, be silent!

compendious: concise SD **makes a leg**: bows **flock-bed**: mattress **doctrine**: discipline **impulsion**: force **potentate**: ruler, monarch

83

MOROSE INTERVIEWS A
POTENTIALLY SILENT WIFE
(1609) BEN JOHNSON, Epicoene, or The Silent Woman, *Act 2, Sc. 5*

M orose's dread of garrulous females has kept him a bachelor, but spitefully, he is anxious to disinherit his nephew Dauphine by marrying and begetting an heir [see II, #82]. He fastens on Epicoene, a young gentlewoman whom he is assured is of a "divine softness." Cutbeard, a barber playing matchmaker, brings the lady to him. Wooing her, she answers in the fewest, most modest, most nearly inaudible words, and Morose has the happy feeling that he has found his perfect helpmate.

Unhappily—tragically or farcically—Morose is unaware that his Epicoene is a boy in disguise foisted on him by his impoverished but ingenious nephew. After the wedding, the lulling, lisping Epicoene finds his voice with a vengeance. Morose, driven by the roaring clamor of the wedding party and of his wife, climbs to a crossbeam over his house to escape, and is rescued by Dauphine only after he extracts from his uncle an immediate financial settlement.

In this scene, the final pathos has not yet visited Morose. He is still in pursuit of that sole perfection which he craves, and testing the putative bride from one vantage point, then from another, closing all avenues of doubt, he finds at last, without equivocation, that—she is the one.

MOROSE

(Epicoene, Cutbeard, Mute)

Very well done, Cutbeard. Give aside now a little, and leave me to examine her condition, and aptitude to my affection.

(He goes about her and views her.)

She is exceeding fair, and of 'a special good favour; a sweet composition or harmony of limbs; her temper of beauty has the true height of my blood. The knave hath exceedingly well fitted me without: I will now try her within.—Come near, fair gentlewoman; let not my behaviour seem rude, though unto you, being rare, it may haply appear strange.

(She curtsies.)

Nay, lady, you may speak, though Cutbeard and my man might not; for of all sounds, only the sweet voice of a fair lady has the just length of mine ears. I beseech you, say, lady; out of the first fire of meeting eyes, they say, love is stricken: do you feel any such motion, suddenly shot into you, from any part you see in me? ha, lady?

(Curtsy.)

Alas, lady, these answers by silent curtsies from you are too courtless and simple. I have ever had my breeding in court; and she that shall be my wife, must be accomplished with courtly and audacious ornaments. Can you speak, lady?

(She speaks softly)

What say you, lady? Speak out, I beseech you.

(He cups his ear.)

O' my judgment, a divine softness! But can you naturally, lady, as I enjoin these by doctrine and industry, refer yourself to the search of my judgment, and, not taking pleasure in your tongue; which is a woman's chiefest pleasure, think it plausible to answer me by silent gestures, so long as my speeches jump right with what you conceive?

(Curtsy.)

Excellent! divine! if it were possible she should hold out thus!—Peace, Cutbeard, thou art made for ever, as thou hast made me, if this felicity have lasting: but I will try her further. Dear lady, I am courtly, I tell you; and I must have mine ears banqueted with pleasant and witty conferences, pretty girds, scoffs, and dalliance in her that I mean to choose for my bed-pheere. The ladies in court think it a most desperate impair to their quickness of wit, and good carriage, if they cannot give occasion for a man to court'em; and when an amorous discourse is set on foot, minister as good matter to continue it, as himself. And do you alone so much differ from all them, that what they, with so much circumstance, affect and toil for, to seem learn'd to seem judicious, to seem sharp and conceited, you can bury in yourself with silence, and rather trust your graces to the fair conscience of virtue, than to the world's or your own proclamation?

(He cups his ear again)

O Morose, thou art happy above mankind! Pray that thou mayest contain thyself. I will only put her to it once more, and it shall be with the utmost touch and test of their sex. But hear me, fair lady; I do also love to see her whom I shall choose for my heifer, to be the first and principal in all fashions, precede all the dames at court by a fortnight, have her council of tailors, lineners, lace-women, embroiderers: and sit with 'em sometimes twice a day upon French intelligences, and then come forth varied like nature, or oftener than she, and better by the help of art, her emulous servant. This do I affect: and how wilt you be able, lady, with this frugality of speech, to give the manifold but necessary instructions, for that bodice, these sleeves, those skirts, this cut, that stitch, this embroidery, that lace, this wire, those knots, that ruff, those roses, this girdle, that fan, the t' other scarf, these gloves? Ha! what say you, lady? How, lady? pray you, rise a note. Admirable creature! I will trouble you no more: I will not sin against so sweet a simplicity. Let me now be bold to print on those divine lips the seal of being mine.

favour: appearance **motion**: impulse, influence **girds**: gibes **bed-pheere**: bedfellow **carriage**: manner **circumstance**: effort, ceremony **conceited**: sophisticated **touch**: trial **intelligences**: news **emulous**: trying to

84

SIR EPICURE MAMMON PREPARES FOR PROJECTION'S SUCCESS

(1610) BEN JOHNSON, The Alchemist, *Act 2, Sc. 2*

Subtle the quack alchemist, his slut Dol Common, and Face their colleague gull a string of dupes into supplying them with money to turn base metal into gold. Of all of them, Sir Epicure Mammon is duped on the most grandiose scale. Awaiting the prospect of his investment returning infinite wealth, Sir Epicure, stretching his fancy beyond limit, dilates on the sensual delights in store for him with the success of the alchemist's "projection." His dream is voracious, a swelling list of sheer accumulation. But note how remarkably like the catalogue of Sir Epicure's invention is to Faustus's similarly swelling list of delights in anticipation of his elixir: satanic knowledge [see I, #16, 17]. The afflatus of Sir Epicure's imagination is no less than Faustus's, different only in that one dreams of omnipotence and the other of sybaritic repletion. The method of storing-up is the same; the imagined prowess is the same; the dream of ultimate accumulation is the same. As Sir Epicure enlarges on his theme, piling image on image and dream on dream, again like Faustus, he becomes ecstatic over his own imagination's largesse.

No less than Marlowe's Faustus or Tamburlaine [see I, #13], Jonson's Sir Epicure is the icon of Renaissance and later Western dreams of endless accumulation. The three are among the great pied pipers of Western dreams of all the mythical forms of life's bounty. Jonson, less seduced than later Sir Mammons by the glittering prospect, brings his Sir Epicure along with his other dupes to their moment of truth: that there's nothing lying in wait but the bubbles of their own invention. Before that dark moment, though, Sir Epicure basks gleefully, fulsomely, ecstatically, in utopian sensual fulfillment.

SIR EPICURE

Do we succeed? Is our day come?
And holds it? Pertinax, my Surly,
Again I say to thee aloud, *be rich.*
This day thou shalt have ingots; and tomorrow
Give lords th' affront.—Is it, my Zephyrus, right?
Blushes the bolt's-head?—My only care is
Where to get stuff enough now, to project on;
This town will not half serve me. And lastly,
Thou hast descried the flower, the *sanguis agni?*

Lungs, I will set a period
To all thy labours; thou shalt be the master
Of my seraglio. But do you hear?
I'll geld you, Lungs. For I do mean
To have a list of wives and concubines
Equal with Salomon, who had the stone
Alike with me; and I will make me a back
With the elixir, that shall be as tough
As Hercules, to encounter fifty a night.—
I will have all my beds blown up, not stuff'd;
Down is too hard: and then, mine oval room
Fill'd with such pictures as Tiberius took
From Elephantis, and dull Aretine
But coldly imitated. Then, my glasses
Cut in more subtle angles, to disperse
And multiply the figures, as I walk
Naked between my succubae. My mists
I'll have of perfume, vapour'd 'bout the room,
To lose our selves in; and my baths, like pits
To fall into; from whence we will come forth,
And roll us dry in gossamer and roses.—
Where I spy
A wealthy citizen, or rich lawyer,
Have a sublim'd pure wife, unto this fellow
I'll send a thousand pound to be my cuckold.

I'll ha' no bawds
But fathers and mothers; they will do it best,
Best of all others. And my flatterers
Shall be the pure, and gravest of divines
That I can get for money. My mere fools,
Eloquent burgesses, and then my poets
The same that writ so subtly of the fart,
Whom I will entertain still for that subject.
The few that would give out themselves to be
Court- and town-stallions, and, each-where, bely
Ladies who are known most innocent, for them,—
Those will I beg, to make me eunuchs of:
And they shall fan me with ten estrich tails
Apiece, made in a plume to gather wind.
We will be brave, Puff, now we ha' the med'cine.
My meat shall all come in, in Indian shells,
Dishes of agate set in gold, and studded
With emeralds, sapphires, hyacints, and rubies.
The tongues of carps, dormice, and camels' heels,
Boil'd i' the spirit of Sol, and dissolv'd pearl.
And I will eat these broths with spoons of amber,
Headed with diamond and carbuncle.
My foot-boy shall eat pheasants, calver'd salmons,
Knots, godwits, lampreys: I myself will have
The beards of barbels serv'd, instead of salads;
Oil'd mushrooms; and the swelling unctuous paps
Of a fat pregnant sow, newly cut off,
Dress'd with an exquisite and poignant sauce;
For which, I'll say unto my cook, *There's gold;
Go forth, and be a knight.*—My shirts
I'll have of taffeta-sarsnet, soft and light
As cobwebs; and for all my other raiment
It shall be such as might provoke the Persian,
Were he to teach the world riot anew.
My gloves of fishes and birds' skins, perfum'd
With gums of paradise, and Eastern air—
And I do think t' have all this with the stone.

pertinax: persistently **Zephyrus**: west wind **bolt's-head**: flask **project**: projection is the alchemist's method of turning a base metal into gold *sanguis agni*, Lat: blood of the lamb **seraglio**: harem **geld**: to castrate the philosopher's **stone**: the key to alchemy's success **Tiberius**: by reputation the lewdest of all Roman emperors **Elephantis, Aretine**: both wrote verses to accompany lewd pictures **succubae**: female demons fabled to have intercourse with men in their sleep **burgesses**: townfolk **estrich**: ostrich **agate**: semi-precious stone **the spirit of Sol**: gold **calver'd**: elaborately prepared **knots, godwits**: kinds of snipe **lampreys**: eels **barbel**: fresh-water fish **taffeta-sarsnet**: fine silk

85

ALLWIT CONGRATULATES HIMSELF ON THE EASE AND PROFIT OF HIS CUCKOLD'S LIFE

(1612) THOMAS MIDDLETON, A Chaste Maid of Cheapside, *Act 1, Sc. 2*

For grossly cynical audacity there is nothing in Stuart drama that can outdo the speech ... in which Allwood glories in the advantages of being a cuckold," says F.S. Boas in *Stuart Drama*. There is considerably more audacity to be found in Stuart drama, but for the post-Victorianism of early 20th century drama histories, Middleton's speech is audacious enough. Regarded head on now, Allwit's argument is not merely casuistical; it makes solid sense, comparing favorably (in argument, not in stylistic brilliance) with the justification of the business of prostitution in Shaw's *Mrs. Warren's Profession*. Allwit's justification comes to this: there's little advantage for a middle-class London citizen in emulating knightly codes of honor when, if once relieved of them (especially in deference to one of those knights blessed with means), one enjoys at no cost or effort all the pleasures, comforts, and fruits of the labor of said knight.

His ease and contentment compare more than favorably with the situation of the laboring knight. Sir Walter Whorehound is not only the provider of goods and heirs for the Allwits; he also labors to maintain another mistress, the Welshwoman, pretending she is his "niece," and at the same time pursues the chaste maid Moll for purposes of marriage. "The founder," Allwit calls his benefactor, "founders" being the makers of metal objects, preeminently of gold.

At the moment, Mrs. Allwit is on the verge of lying-in again ("on the point of grunting," as Allwit puts it). Laid back, feet up, and grinning, he congratulates himself observing the difference between his own plight and Whorehound's, who's taken on himself the burden of husband-like care for the lying-in wife, as well as every-day-of-the-year husband-like jealousy. Allwit has reason to sing.

ALLWIT

> The founder's come to town! I am like a man
> Finding a table furnished to his hand,
> As mine is still to me, prays for the founder:
> 'Bless the right worshipful the good founder's life'.
> I thank him, h'as maintained my house this ten years;
> Not only keeps my wife, but 'a keeps me
> And all my family. I am at his table;
> He gets me all my children, and pays the nurse
> Monthly or weekly; puts me to nothing,
> Rent, nor church-duties, not so much as the scavenger.
> The happiest state that ever man was born to!
> I walk out in a morning; come to breakfast,
> Find excellent cheer; a good.fire in winter;
> Look in my coal-house about midsummer eve,
> That's full, five or six chaldron new laid up;
> Look in my back-yard, I shall find a steeple
> Made up with Kentish faggots, which o'erlooks
> The water-house and the windmills. I say nothing,
> But smile and pin the door. When she lies in,
> As now she's even upon the point of grunting,
> A lady lies not in like her. There's her embossings,

Embroid'rings, spanglings, and I know not what,
As if she lay with all the gaudy-shops
In Gresham's Burse about her; then her restoratives,
Able to set up a young pothecary,
And richly stock the foreman of a drug-shop;
Her sugar by whole loaves, her wines by runlets.
I see these things, but like a happy man
I pay for none at all; yet fools think 's mine.
I have the name, and in his gold I shine.
 And where some merchants would in soul kiss hell
To buy a paradise for their wives, and dye
Their conscience in the bloods of prodigal heirs
To deck their night-piece, yet all this being done,
Eaten with jealousy to the inmost bone
As what affliction nature more constrains
Than feed the wife plump for another's veins?
These torments stand I freed of; I am as clear
From jealousy of a wife as from the charge.
Oh, two miraculous blessings! 'Tis the knight
Hath took that labour all out of my hands.
I may sit still and play; he's jealous for me,
Watches her steps, sets spies. I live at ease;
He has both the cost and torment. When the strings
Of his heart frets, I feed, laugh, or sing:

                    (Sings)
La dildo, dodo la dildo, la dildo dildo de dodo.

---

chaldron: an English dry measure for coal, coke, lime, etc., 32-36 bushels **emboss**: to raise a design on a fabric by pressing **spanglings**: sparkling beads **gaudy shops in Gresham's Burse**: shops in the London Royal Exchange built in 1566 by Sir Thomas Gresham **restoratives**: medications **runnlets**: a great cask or vessel for wine **nightpiece**: a mistress

86

OVERREACH TUTORS HIS DAUGHTER IN MARITAL ENTRAPMENT

(1621-22) PHILIP MASSINGER, A New Way To Pay Old Debts, *Act 3, Sc. 2*

Sir Giles Overreach is a self-made man; he's frightened his victims out of land and revenues, reduced men to poverty, broken laws "as if they were cobwebs," and with the aid of useful henchmen like Justice Greedy, he's risen not only to fortune but to legal and social invulnerability. Not a new type, but an exaggeration of an old one who now, in the Jacobean age of declining landed wealth and rising capital, is displacing the old.

To cap his rise, his chief aim now is to marry his daughter Margaret to a title. She must, he resolves, "write honorable, right honorable, my right honorable daughter" before her name, "if all I have, or e'er shall get, will do it."

And so he offers Margaret (who is of course really in love with young and penniless Wellborn) paternal guidance in bringing title to its knees. It's an old trick, and Sir Giles is not above commanding his daughter to stoop low to win so high a station. Step by step, he outlines procedure, overriding, step by step, her "mincing modesty." The thing is assured: let him woo you, let him "kiss you close," let him have you, and once the thing is done and he has your "wounded honor," leave it to Sir Giles to "make you equals" and force Lord Lovell into marriage. For Sir Giles, the most straightforward way to produce a lady calls first for the most straightforward manner toward his daughter of an officer giving battle orders to his troops.

OVEREACH

As I said, Meg, this honourable lord, this colonel,
I would have thy husband:
Be thou no enemy to thyself, my wealth
Shall weight his titles down, and make you equals.
Now for the means to assure him thine, observe me:
Remember he's a courtier and a soldier,
And not to be trifled with; and, therefore, when
He comes to woo you, see you do not coy it:
This mincing modesty hath spoil'd many a match
By a first refusal, in vain after hop'd for.
And Virgin me no virgins!
I must have you lose that name, or you lose me.
I will have you private—start not—I say, private;
If thou art my true daughter, not a bastard,
Thou wilt venture alone with one man,
Though he came like Jupiter to Semele, and come off, too;
And therefore, when he kisses you, kiss close.
Or, if his blood grow hot, suppose he offer
Beyond this, do not you stay till it cool,
But meet his ardour; if a couch be near,
Sit down on't, and invite him.
Stand not on form;
Words are no substances.
And when to his lust you have given up your honor,
Fear not,—he will not forsake thee!
How! Forsake thee!
Do I wear a sword for fashion? Or is this arm
Shrunk up or wither'd? Does there live a man
Of that large list I have encounter'd with
Can truly say I e'er gave inch of ground
Not purchas'd with his blood that did oppose me?
Forsake thee when the thing is done! He dares not.
Give me but proof he has enjoy'd thy person,
Though all his captains, echoes to his will,
Stood arm'd by his side to justify the wrong,

And he himself in the head of his bold troop,
Spite of his lordship, and his colonelship,
Or the judge's favour, I will make him render
A bloody and a strict accompt, and force him,
By marrying thee, to cure thy wounded honour!
I have said it.

Jupiter to Semele: when Jupiter revealed his true face to Semele she was consumed by flames **and come off, too**: and survive (unlike Semele)

Comedy

XVII CENTURY FRENCH

87

ARNOLPHE EXPLAINS HIS PROCEDURE FOR RAISING A PERFECT WIFE IN PERFECT IGNORANCE

(1662) JEAN-BAPTISTE MOLIÈRE, The School for Wives, *tr. Morris Bishop, Act 1, Sc.1*

Arnolphe is, as described in II, #90, a careful French rationalist attempting to solve the general problem of marital infidelity, but is defeated in the end by the ways of nature. Like other of Molière's near-tragic fools, he is rational to the point of madness, contending, whether in nature or in society, with reason's irrelevance to the way things are. According to his logic, it should follow that the removal of a cause cancels its effect. And since it follows that the avoidance of the prime and inevitable cause of cuckoldry—a wife who has graces, knowledge and social opportunity—by raising a potential wife from infancy with no graces, no knowledge and no future opportunity, there is no possibility of one's becoming a cuckold.

Arnolphe is committed to the religion of his moment; he is a devotee of Reason, and in the course of the play, we watch the encroachments of irrational instinct—the successful wooing under his nose of his potential wife by a young lover—destroy the bulwark of his faith. He is left bereft of both a wife and a faith.

ARNOLPHE
No one is going to make a fool of me:
For I know all the tricks, all the devices
That ladies use to victimize their husbands,
And I know how they work their sleight-of-hand,
And so I've taken adequate precautions.
The girl I'll marry is an innocent,
And her simplicity is my protection.
And you imagine that simplicity—
One isn't simple to take a simple wife.

Of course I know your wife is virtuous,
But an intelligent woman isn't safe.
I know what certain friends of mine have suffered
For marrying women with too many talents.
I'll hardly pick an intellectual,
Whose talk is all of literary clubs,
Who writes seductively in prose and verse,
While I am just the lovely lady's husband,
A saint, of course, but one without worshipers.
No, I don't care for the blue-stocking type;
If she writes books, she knows a lot too much.
I want her so sublimely ignorant
That she won't even know that words can rhyme.
Everyone has his method.
I have my own; and it applies to marriage.
I'm rich enough to do without a dowry;
My wife will be dependent upon me.
She'll be in no position to allege
Her property rights, or her superior birth.
I noticed her when she was four years old,
And I was taken by her modest air.
Her mother was destitute, and so I had,
The idea of asking for her guardianship.
And the good peasant woman was delighted
To make provision for her daughter's welfare.
In a small convent, off the beaten track,
I had her educated by my system.
That is, I furnished them a set of rules
To cultivate her simple-mindedness.
And God be praised, the process was successful.
Now she is grown; and she's so innocent
That I bless heaven which has favored me,
Making a bride to fit my specifications.
Why, her naive remarks are my delight.
Some of them make me nearly die with laughing.
The other day—and this you'll hardly credit—
She was much troubled, and she came to ask me,
In absolute and perfect innocence,
If children are begotten through the ear!

88

DON JUAN'S FATHER CONDEMNS HIS SON FOR SHAMING HIS HERITAGE

(1665) JEAN-BAPTISTE MOLIÈRE, Don Juan, *tr. G. Graveley and I. Maclean, Act 4, Sc. 6*

Don Juan's father Don Luis bursts in on his son, only too aware of the welcome awaiting him. He doesn't wait to receive it; instead, acknowledging it before it is made, he launches with no preamble into the speech blazing in his heart. It is not only a speech of condemnation; it is a speech of mourning, and has much the same character it would have had if it were spoken over his son's grave. Note that there is little exhortation in it; Don Luis is beyond exhortation, mourning the very fact that his son is utterly beyond the reach of either correction or reproof. He laments the very fact that having prayed for a son, he was given the misery of having one such as this; that Don Juan's "baseness" has transgressed beyond the patience of either King or his own noble family; that Don Juan has—and this is the essential charge—besmirched the "escutcheon," the honorable reputation of the noble family into which he was born. Note too that it is not merely the personal disgrace visited on the father by the son's behavior, but on the renown of his ancestry, whose honor, as well as the father's honor, has been blackened.

It is, in other words, entirely within the legalisms of the honor-code that Don Luis condemns his son. And the principle he brings powerfully to bear is this: that no "honor" derives automatically from birth or station; it must be renewed by each descendant born into its legacy. The life of a scion of the nobility has no other meaning or reason for being than his devotion to that task. Don Luis has so thoroughly given up on hope for his son's redemption of honor that he has only the hope of a mere substitute, a sort of negative, redemption: through a punishment he himself would contribute to. "And by your punishment, wash away my dishonor in having been your father."

Later, Don Juan is to perpetrate the last of his "subversions" by fooling his father into supposing that he has reformed, that he's "reclaimed from all his errors." His father, uplifted by this about-face, is unaware that his son is adding to the list of his iniquities his last and best: pious hypocrisy [see I, #115].

(Enter DON LOUIS)

DON LOUIS

It is easy to see that my coming is unwelcome, and causes you more embarrassment than pleasure. Each of us is a thorn in the side of the other; and, if you are weary of me, I am equally weary of your bad behaviour. Alas! We little know what we are doing when, instead of leaving to God the choice of what is good for us, we try to be wiser than He, and pester Him with our blind and ill considered longings. To have a son was the dearest wish of my heart, for which I never ceased to pray. And this son, granted at last to my unwearying petition, has made my life a misery and a burden, instead of being, as I had hoped, its joy and consolation. Do you think I can see without shame and indignation this continued course of disgraceful actions? They are beyond any possibility of excuse; and are fast exhausting the patience of the King our master, and outweighing in his eyes both my past services and the credit of my friends. What baseness! Are you not ashamed to dishonour your family in this way? You have lost even the right to be proud of your descent, so little is your conduct worthy of a nobleman. Do you think it is enough to bear the name and the escutcheon, or that noble blood can confer honour on a man who lives in infamy? No, no. Birth is of no account unless accompanied by nobility of character. The measure of our share in our ancestors' renown is the measure of our efforts to resemble them; and the very lustre of their achievements, in whose reflected glory we shine, obliges us, by following in the same paths of virtue, to return the honour we have received; or we proclaim ourselves no true descendants of them.

You may no longer claim the consideration due to noble birth. Your
ancestors cast you out. The fame of their great deeds, which should
have brought you credit, is a beacon in whose light your dishonour
shows the blacker. A gentleman who lives an evil life is a freak of
nature. Virtue is the true title to nobility. I judge of a man, not by
who he is, but by what he does; and I would have more respect for the
son of a street-porter who was an honest man, than for the son of an
emperor who lived like you. I know well enough that nothing I can
say will ever touch your heart. But listen carefully. Your unworthy conduct has almost extinguished your father's love; and, sooner perhaps
than you think, I shall find a way to put a stop to your disorders; forestall the anger of Heaven; and, by your punishment, wash away my
dishonour in having been your father.

(He goes out)

escutcheon: the shield bearing the family insignia

89

HARPAGON, FEARING HIS TREASURE STOLEN, RUNS MAD
(1668) JEAN-BAPTISTE MOLIÈRE, The Miser, *tr. G. Graveley and I. Maclean Act 4, Sc. 7*

Harpagon has one love: his gold; and one way of protecting it:
concealment. The fear that it will be ravished, leads, as it would
for any truly possessed lover, to his suspecting everyone, son, daughter, servants, of coveting it. And, like any true votary, his own value is
indistinguishable from his possession. Its only function is to be his; it
has no other use, meaning or value.

He plans for his son Cleante to marry an elderly rich widow who
will bring him a dowry; for his daughter Elise, that she marry an elderly rich widower, provided he is relieved of providing her with a dowry;

for himself, that he marry the young sweet Mariane, provided she bring something of a dowry. The difficulty is that his son Cleante is in love with Mariane with or without a dowry, and the discovery leads to open enmity between them. But Cleante's servant, digging in the garden, comes across Harpagon's buried casket of gold, and Cleante sensibly plans to hold it hostage until his father relents.

Harpagon's discovery that his gold is gone brings him, in this scene, to the edge of madness. The scene is a surreal exhibition of a bereft lover's delirium, in which Harpagon accuses the world, even himself, even the audience, of having stolen his love. He swears vengeance on them all; he'll have the law hang the whole world, including himself. The miser reaches a pitch of frenzy that oversteps the boundaries of laughter; his frenzy, when that pitch is reached, becomes frightening.

> *(Harpagon's voice can be heard crying 'Thief' from the garden. He rushes in.)*

HARPAGON

Stop thief! Stop thief! After the villain! After the murderer! Justice, just Heaven! I am lost. I am killed. My throat is cut. My money is stolen. Who can it be? Where has he taken it? Where is he? Where is he hiding? What can I do to find him? Where can I go? Where can I not go? Is that him? Or that? Who's this? Stop!

> *(Catching himself by the arm)*

Give me back my money, thief... Ah, it is myself. My brain's in a whirl; and I don't know where I am, who I am or what I am doing. Oh, my beloved money, my beloved money, my kind friend, they have taken you from me, and with you is gone all my being, all my comfort, all my joy. My world is at an end. There is nothing left for me to do on earth. Without you it is impossible for me to go on living. Yes, I am finished. I am dying. I am dead. I am buried. Will no one give me back my life by giving me back my beloved money, or telling me who has taken it? Eh? What do you say? There's no one there. The rascal who has done this must have timed it to the very hour, and chosen the very moment I was talking to my traitor of a son. I'll go call the police, and have all my household put to the torture, maids, valets, son, daughter, even myself.

(Looking at the audience)

What a lot of people there are all round me! I suspect them all. Each one of them has the look of a thief. Eh? What's that they are saying there? Something about the man who has robbed me? What noise is that up there? Is it the thief?

(Addressing the audience)

For pity's sake, if any of you know anything about him, I beseech you to tell me. Is he not hidden there among you? Ah, they all stare at me and grin. You can see they are all part of the gang. Come quick, constables, guards, judges, racks, gallows, hangmen. I'll have every one in the world hanged for this; and, if I don't get back my money, I'll string myself up beside them.

RESTORATION

90

PINCHWIFE APPREHENDS HIS WIFE AUTHOR-ING A LETTER OF HER OWN INVENTION
(1675) WILLIAM WYCHERLEY, The Country Wife, *Act 4*

Pinchwife, to cheat the town's cuckold-makers, has gone into the country to buy a wife ignorant of men's uses of women and equally of women's wiles toward men. His aim is to keep her close, in fact imprisoned at home, out of reach of the town's seductions. Unhappily for him, his sister Alithea introduces wife Margery to the theatre, where at her first visit she exchanges glances with Horner, the prime cuckold-maker in London [see I, #91], and instantly falls in love with him, and he as instantly determines to have her.

At a second encounter between them, Pinchwife, bringing Margery outdoors disguised as a man, is convinced that Horner sees through the disguise when he showers her with kisses to "take to her sister." Determined to be finally rid of Horner's attentions to his wife, Pinchwife dictates the letter Margery is to send to Horner repulsing him. In his absence, she writes another more to her taste, and Pinchwife, returning, snatches the paper from her, and reads.

He, reading it, might well reach the apogee in Western comedy of Outraged-Apoplectic-Husband. Whereas his progenitor Arnolphe in the Molière comedy *The School for Wives* (from which *The Country Wife* derived) grew apoplectic at his wife-to-be's inevitable escape from his domination, his rage was more against himself at the failure of his strategy. In the case of Pinchwife, his anger results from the abomination of women's and the devil's wiles. One is a careful French rationalist experimentally attempting to solve the general problem of marital infidelity, but is defeated in the end by Nature's course. The other is an English Puritan attempting to cheat the conspiratorial alignment of Woman and the Devil, and is defeated by the surrogates of the Evil One. It's a more lugubrious world that Pinchwife is confronting; his enemies are age-old and terrifying, and his only resource is the patriarchal male's battered and ancient barricades and siege-weapons thrown up ever hopefully but ever feebly against them. That he loses to the Fiend in his wife and her libertine, as Arnolphe lost to Nature in his fiancée and her lover, is a foregone conclusion.

> *(Enter Mr. PINCHWIFE who seeing her writing steals softly behind her, and looking over her shoulder, snatches the paper from her.)*

PINCHWIFE
What, writing more Letters?

> *(She offers to run out: he stops her, and reads)*

How's this! nay you shall not stir Madam. Deare, Deare, deare, Mr Horner—very well—I have taught you to write Letters to good purpose—but let's see't.

> *(Reads)*

'First I am to beg your pardon for my boldness in writing to you, which I'de have you to know, I would not have done, had not you said first you lov'd me so extreamly, which if you doe, you will never suffer me to lye in the arms of another man, whom I loath, nauseate, and detest—[Now you can write these filthy words] but what follows—Therefore I hope you will speedily find some way to free me from this unfortunate match, which was never, I assure you, of my choice, but I'm afraid 'tis already too far gone; however if you love me, as I do you, you will try what you can do, but you must help me away before to morrow, or else alas! I shall be for ever out of your reach, for I can defer no longer our—our—

> *(The letter concludes.)*

what is to follow our—speak what? our journey into the Country, I suppose—Oh Woman, damn'd Woman, and Love, damn'd Love, their old Tempter, for this is one of his miracles, in a moment, he can make

those blind that cou'd see, and those see that were blind, those dumb
that could speak, and those prattle who were dumb before, nay what
is more than all, make these dough-bak'd senseless, indocile animals,
Women, too hard for us their Politick Lords and Rulers in a moment;
But make an end of your Letter, and then I'le make an end of you
thus, and all my plagues together.

(Draws his sword.)

91

SIR FEEBLE, WITH THE HELP OF HIS MAN
FRANCIS (HIS RIVAL IN DISGUISE), READIES
FOR BEDTIME WITH HIS NEW BRIDE
(1686) APHRA BEHN, The Lucky Chance, *Act 3. Sc. 1*

As luck would have it, the law banning duelling, making it a mortal offense, was passed into law a day or two before Bellmore
killed a man in a duel which, only the day before, was *de rigeur* for the
rescue of his honor. Solution: escape to the Continent, where he
remained unaware that his affianced one, Letitia, persuaded that he
was dead, had little choice—impoverished and defenseless as she
was—but to consent to marriage with the old man Sir Feeble.
Bellmore, eager to wed with her no matter what the risk, returns to
London on her wedding day.

The plot solution is standard—Bellmore assumes the identity of
Sir Feeble's nephew, the old man's presumed-to-be new employee, and
waits his moment to rescue Letitia. He succeeds only at the moment
of her imminent bedding by her lately reinvigorated, dangerously
eager, ancient husband. Sir Feeble's plot, the one that succeeded in
supplanting Bellmore, is inadvertently revealed to the young lover by

the gleeful husband during the very act of readying him for bed with his supposed new wife (but who is Bellmore's, we are carefully given to understand, in the eyes of God). Aphra Behn's mastery of hilarious farce is rarely demonstrated more perfectly than in this scene of Sir Feeble's great hurry to be pulled out of his clothes and hop into bed in the adjoining room, while he fills the palpitating moments by recounting to his presumed nephew and ally the entire story of his perfidy in winning her, and handing over to Bellmore the King's pardon for him to lock away "safe, Francis, safe." The King's pardon is the document that delivers Bellmore from the threat of the gallows.

In the later scene, Sir Feeble does in fact, as he promises here, "fright away" from the bedroom Letitia's women by flashing them, but servant Bellmore manages to prevent the bedding of his beloved Letitia by another ploy—again, conventional, but proven, in play after play, effective.

SIR FEEBLE

Come Francis, you shall have the the honour of undressing me for the encounter; but 'twill be a sweet one, Francis. But is the young rogue laid, Francis, is she stolen to bed? What tricks the young baggages have to whet a man's appetite! A piss of these bandstrings. The more haste, the less speed. Thy aid a little, Francis.

(BELLMOUR pinches him by the throat)

Oh, oh thou chok'st me! 'S bobs, what dost mean? Come, come, quick, good Francis. Adod, I'm as yare as a hawk at the young wanton. Nimbly, good Francis, untruss, untruss. So, so, my breeches, good Francis. But well, Francis, how dost think I got the young jade, my wife. The baggage was damnably in love with a young fellow they call Bellmour, they say, that's truth on't; and a pretty estate. But, happening to kill a man, he was forced to fly.

Hang him, rogue, 'sbobs, and all the young fellows in the town deserve it. We can never keep our wives and daughters honest for ram-

pant young dogs, and an old fellow cannot put in amongst 'em ,
under being undone, with presenting, and the devil and all. But what
dost think I did? Being damnably in love, I feigned a letter as from the
Hague, wherein was a relation of this same Bellmour's being hanged. I
did it, I did it! She swooned at the news, shut herself up a whole
month in her chamber, but I presented high. She sighed and wept,
and swore she'd never marry: still I presented. She hated, loathed, spat
upon me: still, adod, I presented. Till I presented myself effectually in
church to her, for she at last wisely considered her vows were cancelled
since Bellmour was hanged.

Cruel? We are but even with the brisk rogues, for they take away our
fame, cuckold us, and take away our wives. So, so, my cap, Francis.
This marriage shall be when I've had livery and seisin of her body, and
that shall be presently, rogue, quick. Besides, this Bellmour dares as
well be hanged as come into England. I have, you must know, got his
pardon already. Dos't think 'twas in kindness to him? No, you fool, I
got his pardon myself, that nobody else should have it, so that if he
gets anybody to speak to his Majesty for it, his Majesty cries he has
granted it. But for want of my appearance he's defunct, trussed up,
hanged, Francis. Ay, I learnt it of a great politician of our times. Pox
on him, it cost me five hundred red pounds, though. Here 'tis. My
solicitor brought it me this evening.

(Gives it him)

So, put it into my cabinet, safe, Francis, safe. My gown, quick, quick,
t'other sleeve, man. So now my night-cap. Well, I'll in, throw open
my gown to fright away the women, and jump into her arms.

(Exit SIR FEEBLE)

yare: skillful, brisk **presented**: persisted **seisin**: legal possession

92

JUPITER, BIDDING FAREWELL TO ALCMENE AFTER THEIR NIGHT OF LOVE, CLAIMS A HIGHER PLACE IN HER ESTEEM THAN 'HUSBAND'

(1690) JOHN DRYDEN, Amphitryon, *Act 2, Sc. 1*

By 1690, two years after the accession to the British throne of William and Mary, the atmosphere of Restoration comedy shifted significantly [see I, #97]. Seduction became a bit less than a happy sport, and cuckolding as its inevitable consequence more than a joke. Consequently, in Dryden's *Amphitryon,* the classic tale of the Divine's seduction of a mortal's wife, Jupiter, the cuckolding God, is to be read as more than a divine libertine. He is something both more grand and more deadly.

Sexually, he is, in the lower sense of the word, divine; but over and above his lust, his sexual vanity rises to the level of the ultimate conqueror's desire to win not only bodies, but hearts and minds. He has, the night before, assumed the appearance of Alcmene's husband Amphitryon, and in that guise, was granted Alcmene's entire love as she would legitimately offer it to her husband. In the morning, he is troubled: was his victory no more than the husband's? Was he assumed to be no more than a husband? She must assure him, he insists, that in the throes of their passion she thought of him as a lover as distinct from a mere husband, so that—and this is the crux of his character—he would be adored only for his prowess, just as a conqueror of a people wins allegiance through his conqueror's prowess alone, rather than through mere title or legitimacy of succession. It is an echo of the self-aggrandizement of the Heroic Play's protagonist.

On the other hand, he feels the constraints of an ordinary politician worried about being caught *in flagrante delicto:* douse the torches, he commands his pages, lest he's discovered before full morning's light in "the secret I would hide." And yet, over and above his succumbing to supreme vanity on the one hand, and gulping uneasily at discovery on the other, there is still a grandeur in his concept of the difference between a husband's and a lover's love. It is a distinction that makes the difference between, so to speak, the divine and the mortal lover: "love refined." "The being happy is not half the joy;/ The manner of the happiness is all." To find "the thousand thousand niceties in love" takes, according to the testimony of the God of All, a surpassing understanding of the aesthetics of sensuality. He has a point, of course.

JUPITER
(to the Pages) Those torches are offensive. Stand aloof.
(to her) For, though they bless me with thy heavenly sight,
They may disclose the secret I would hide.
The Thebans must not know I have been here.
Detracting crowds would blame me that I robbed
These happy moments from my public charge,
To consecrate to thy desired embrace;
And I could wish no witness but thyself,
For thou thyself art all I wish to please.
Alcmena, I must go.
Behold the ruddy streaks o'er yonder hill.
Those are the blushes of the breaking morn
That kindle daylight to this nether world.
Let me not live but thou art all enjoyment!
So charming and so sweet, that not a night,
But whole eternity, were well employed,
To love thy each perfection as it ought.

(Kissing her)
How I could dwell for ever on those lips!
O, I could kiss 'em pale with eagerness!
So soft, by heaven, and such a juicy sweet,

That ripened peaches have not half the flavour.
But yet one scruple pains me at my parting.
I love so nicely, that I cannot bear
To owe the sweets of love which I have tasted
To the submissive duty of a wife.
Tell me, and soothe my passion ere I go,
That in the kindest moments of the night,
When you gave up yourself to love and me,
You thought not of a husband, but a lover.
I would owe nothing to a name so dull
As husband is, but to a lover all.
I ask now because my tenderness
Surpasses that of husbands for their wives.
O, that you loved like me! There you would find
A thousand, thousand niceties in love.
The common love of sex to sex is brutal;
But love refined will fancy to itself
Millions of gentle cares and sweet disquiets.
The being happy is not half the joy;
The manner of the happiness is all!
In me, my charming mistress, you behold
A lover that disdains a lawful title,
Such as of monarchs to successive thrones.
The generous lover holds by force of arms
And claims his crown by conquest.
No, no; that very name of wife and marriage
Is poison to the dearest sweets of love.
To please my niceness, you must separate
The lover from his mortal foe, the husband.
Give to the yawning husband your cold virtue,
But all your vigorous warmth, your melting sighs,
Your amorous murmurs, be your lover's part.
There's mystery of love in all I say.
Farewell; and when you see your husband next
Think of your lover then.

93

JUPITER, OUT OF THE MACHINE, MAKES ALL THINGS CLEAR

(1690) JOHN DRYDEN, Amphitryon, *Act 5, Sc. 1*

Very much in the tradition of Euripides' Apollo, who wreaks havoc in the tragedy of Ion and then, in a smiling voice, makes all things OK when he appears at play's end out of the machine, Jupiter essays the same trick [see II, #92]. The havoc in *Amphitryon* has been considerable. Not only two versions of the servant Sosia meeting face to face [see I, #97] and two of Amphitryon to the confusion of the mortal versions of each, but Alcmena and Amphitryon fall one into mad jealousy of his identical rival, the other into unassuageable grief at love's apparent betrayal.

Oddly, it is not a different Jupiter, a more godlike Jupiter, who appears high over the stage in a crane as though dipped from heaven. It is the same divine vanity, and the same envy of Amphitryon's human happiness that glimmer through his lofty speech of explanation and benediction. It's an interesting battle he fights to maintain his judicious authority over the plot's reconciliations, at the same time expressing infinite regret at surrendering his mortal love to Alcmena's mortal mate. As for the substantial disgrace visited on Amphitryon, it is quickly and easily transformed into his "boast," since being cuckolded by Jupiter, according to the laws of Heaven, is "sanctified from vice" by virtue of the beneficent deity's culpabilities being automatically transformed into blessings.

Finally, after the whimsicalities introduced into this traditional myth, a nod to tradition's pieties. Hercules, according to that myth, was born out of the night's union between Jupiter and Alcmena, and so this ill-fitting intrusion of mythic enormity is crowbarred into the much smaller-scaled domesticity of this rendering of the old story, but with gross inaccuracy. Hercules did not die after winning "peace to his labors;" his death was an excruciating one in the folds of Nessus' poisoned shirt, as powerfully told in Sophocles' *Women of Trachis* [see II, #18].

The actor performing Jupiter's epilogue is best advised to surmount all these contradictions of person and tone by, in a godlike way, overlooking them.

(A peal of thunder. After which Jupiter appears in a machine)

JUPITER
Look up, Amphitryon, and behold above
Th'impostor god, the rival of thy love.
In thy own shape see Jupiter appear,
And let that sight secure thy jealous fear.
Disgrace and infamy are turned to boast.
No fame in Jove's concurrence can be lost:
What he enjoys he sanctifies from vice,
And, by partaking, stamps into a price.
'Tis I who ought to murmur at my fate—
Forced by my love my godhead to translate,
When on no other terms I could possess,
But by thy form, thy features, and thy dress.
To thee were given the blessings that I sought,
Which else not all the bribes of heaven had bought.
Then take into thy arms thy envied love,
And, in his own despite, triumph o'er Jove.
From this auspicious night shall rise an heir,
Great, like his sire, and like his mother, fair—
Wrongs to redress, and tyrants to disseize—
Born for a world that wants a Hercules.
Monsters and monster-men he shall engage,
And toil and struggle through an impious age.
Peace to his labours shall at length succeed;
And murmuring men, unwilling to be freed,
Shall be compelled to happiness—by need.

(Jupiter is carried back to heaven)

secure thy jealous fear: banish your suspicions on your wife **no fame... lost**: having Jupiter (Jove) as your rival, and the lover of your wife, is no blemish to your reputation **by partaking... price**: by sharing it with you, elevates it into something of great value **translate**: transform **disseize**: oust, expel

94

FONDLEWIFE, WHILE WARNING HIS WIFE OF ADULTERY, IS MELTED BY HER TEARS

(1693) WILLIAM CONGREVE, The Old Bachelor, *Act 4, passage excerpted from Scs. 2, 3, 4*

According to the rules of Restoration comedy, old Fondlewife is doomed to cuckoldom. He's a "zealot," i.e., a Puritan "addicted to jealousy, but more to fondness," and just as he is "jealous without a cause, he's as often satisfied without reason." His situation is consequently dire: his young and vigorous wife Laetitia has sent a letter to Vainlove (so surfeited a libertine that he can afford to pass her invitation on to his friend Bellmore) arranging for him to come in disguise on the night Fondlewife is to go abroad. But Fondlewife frets: away for the night, his wife put in the safekeeping of Tribulation, a zealot as "precise and peevish" as Fondlewife himself—is that sufficient safeguard? But still. He prognosticates the Old Hebrew way of *pilpul,* "on the one hand, on the other hand," and concludes that reinforcement of wifeliness is in order.

Laetitia, hearing the familiar accents of her husband's sermon, fearing that jealous pangs are moving him not only to sermonize but to remain at home on guard, resorts to the surest way of dissolving fond Fondlewife's resolve: tears. He's undone by them, drowns suspicion in puling drivel, and hurries off.

Jealous but tender, suspicious but vulnerable, impotent but longing, Fondlewife is doomed.

FONDLEWIFE
Good lack, good lack!—I protest 'tis a very sufficient vexation, for a man to have a handsome wife, but when the man is an insufficient husband, 'tis then, indeed, like the vanity of taking a fine house, and yet be forced to let lodgings to help pay the rent—a very apt comparison. Go and bid my cocky come out to me. I will give her some instructions, I will reason with her, before I go.

(Exit BARNABY)

And, in the mean time, I will reason with—myself.—Tell me, Isaac, why art thee jealous? why art thee distrustful of the wife of thy bosom?—because she is young and vigorous, and I am old and impotent. Then, why didst thee marry, Isaac?—because she was beautiful and tempting, and because I was obstinate and doting, so that my inclination was, and is still, greater than my power. And will not that which tempted thee, also tempt others, who will tempt her, Isaac?—I fear it much. But does not thy wife love thee, nay, dote upon thee?—yes—Why then!—Ay,—but to say truth, she's fonder of me than she has reason to be; and in the way of trade, we still suspect the smoothest dealers of the deepest designs—and that she has some designs deeper than thou canst reach, th'hast experimented, Isaac—but, mum.

(Enter LETITIA.)

Wife, have you thoroughly considered how detestable, how heinous, and how crying a sin, the sin of adultery is? have you weighed it, I say? for it is a very weighty sin; and although it may lie heavy upon thee, yet thy husband must also bear his part; for thy iniquity will fall upon his head. *(Aside.)* I profess she has an alluring eye; I am doubtful whether I shall trust her, even with Tribulation himself.—*(Aloud.)* I say, have you considered what it is to cuckold your husband? Nay, look you now if she does not weep !—'Tis the fondest fool!—Nay, Cocky, Cocky, nay, dear Cocky, don't cry, I was but in jest, I was not i'feck. *(Aside.)* Good lack! good lack! she would melt a heart of oak.—I profess I can hold no longer.—*(Aloud.)* Nay, dear Cocky—I'feck you'll break my heart—I'feck you will. See, you have made me weep—made poor Nykin weep!—Nay, come kiss, buss poor Nykin—and I won't leave thee—I'll lose all first. Won't you kiss Nykin? Kiss, kiss, i' feck I' do. What, not love Cocky! I profess I love thee better than five hundred pounds;—and so thou shalt say, for I'll leave it to stay with thee. Then I will go, I won't be dealous.—Poor Cocky, kiss Nykin, kiss Nykin; ee! ee! ee!—Here will be the good man anon, to talk to Cocky, and teach her how a wife ought to behave herself. That's my good dear!—Come, kiss Nykin once more, and then get you in—so—get you in. Bye! bye! Bye, Cocky! Bye, Cocky! bye! bye!

lack: luck **mum**: hush **fondest**: stupidest **I was not i'feck**: I didn't mean it

95

COUPLER THE MATCHMAKER DREAMS UP A
SCHEME TO GET ONE BROTHER WEALTHILY
WIVED AT THE EXPENSE OF THE OTHER
(1696) JOHN VANBRUGH, The Relapse, *Act 1, Sc. 3*

Coupler, by trade a matchmaker and by inclination a friend to
intrigue, is taken by Young Fashion's plight: elder brother Lord
Foppington, inheriting all, is with cruel indifference leaving younger
brother Fashion penniless. Coupler, anticipating similar treatment
from niggardly Foppington, has a scheme in hand—recited here—to
pass on to Young Fashion the good fortune he's prepared for his elder
brother. The switch will do wonders for the fortunes of both.

Within the mode of familiar libertinism in Restoration stage comedy, there is a mode which does not peep through as regularly as it
does in its fiction and verse, but on occasion, as in the character of
Coupler, it surfaces unblushingly: the mode of flamboyant queerdom.
Coupler, fat as Falstaff and somewhat long in the tooth (he rests,
breathless, on stair landings before venturing the next flight) is warm
and eager for embrace, however incidental and instantaneous, with
"young hot dogs." He brushes, touches, and busses them with no
regard for their revulsion; he likes it, grabs it, and basks in it.
Decidedly different from the fop, with no hint of emulating the "fashion" but if anything deliberately and insouciantly affronting it, he is a
sui generis queen transplantable to our own moment as is. He is, in a
sense, also mother to the young hot lusties, knows their foibles,
accepts their failings with a knowing shrug, and moves agreeably into
the mode of aid. With calculation. Here his calculation is for money;
the sexual innuendo is only his signature ploy.

COUPLER

When you begin to rot, sirrah, you'll go off like a pippin; one winter will send you to the devil. What mischief brings you home again? Ha! you young lascivious rogue, you. Let me put my hand in your bosom, sirrah. Nay, prithee now, don't be so coy. Hast thou then been a year in Italy, and brought home a fool at last? By my conscience, the young fellows of this age profit no more by their going abroad than they do by their going to church. Sirrah, sirrah, if you are not hanged before you come to my years, you'll know a cock from a hen. But, come, I'm still a friend to thy person, though I have a contempt of thy understanding; and therefore I would willingly know thy condition, that I may see whether thou stand'st in need of my assistance: for widows swarm, my boy, the town's infected with 'em. And you stand in need of anybody's assistance, that will help you to cut your elder brother's throat, without the risk of being hanged for him. Egad, sirrah, I could help thee to do him most as good a turn, without the danger of being burned in the hand for't. Pox o' thy soul! give me thy warm body, sirrah. I shall have a substantial title to it when I tell thee my project. Thus lies the scene.—Well, sir, you must know I have done you the kindness to make up match for your brother. The lady is a great heiress; fifteen hundred pound a year, and a great bag of money; the match is concluded, the writings are drawn, and the pipkin's to be cracked in a fortnight. Now you must know, stripling (with respect to your mother), your brother's the son of a whore. He has given bond of a thousand pounds for helping him to this fortune, and has promised me as much more in ready money upon the day of marriage, which, I understand by a friend, he ne'er designs to pay me. If therefore you will be a generous young dog, and secure me five thousand pounds, I'll be a covetous old rogue, and help you to the lady.

This plump partridge, that I tell you of, lives in the country, fifty miles off, with her honored parents, in a lonely old house which nobody comes near; she never goes abroad, nor sees company at home. To prevent all misfortunes, she has her breeding within doors; the parson of the parish teaches her to play upon the bass-viol, the clerk to sing, her nurse to dress, and her father to dance. In short, nobody can give you admittance there but I; nor can I do it any other way than by making you pass for your brother. Thy brother's face not one of the family ever saw, the whole business has been managed by me, and all the letters go through my hands. The last that was writ to Sir Tunbelly Clumsey (for that's the old gentleman's name), was to tell him, his lordship would be down in a fortnight to consummate. Now, you shall go away immediately, pretend you writ that letter only to have the romantic pleasure of surprising your mistress; fall desperately in love, as soon as you see her; make that your plea for marrying her immediately, and, when the fatigue of the wedding-night's over, you shall send me a winging purse of gold, you dog you.

Ah, you young hot lusty thief, let me muzzle you!—

(Kissing)

Sirrah, let me muzzle you. Well, I'll warrant thou hast not a farthing of money in thy pocket now, no, one may see it in thy face. Must I advance then?—Well, sirrah, be at my lodgings in half an hour, and I'll see what may be done; we'll sign, and seal, and eat a pullet, and when I have given thee some farther instructions, thou shaft hoist sail and be gone.

(Kissing)

T'other buss, and so adieu. Ah, you young warm dog you, what a delicious night will the bride have.

burned in the hand for't: minor felons were branded in the hand **pipkin**: vessel or cask; hence, slang for *maidenhead* **stripling**: an adolescent **farthing**: worth one fourth of a penny

Comedy

XVIII CENTURY ENGLISH

96

SABLE THE UNDERTAKER REHEARSES HIS REGULAR MOURNERS FOR THE COMING FUNERAL

(1701) RICHARD STEELE, The Funeral, *Act 1, Sc. 1*

Sable is not privy to the fact that old Lord Brumpton, whose funeral he is to manage, is not dead at all, but recovered from his faint, alive, and set to spend the rest of the play discovering who were the hypocrites and who the honest folk grieving over his loss. But the coffin is ready, the funeral is to commence, Sable is to be its chief master of ceremonies, and he comes to the house of the young widow Brumpton to prepare.

Sable has considerable dark wisdom. He has, as he says, the deepest learning, Experience, and it has been won from a sure perspective: observing men and women during their episodes of mourning, during which interval "the poor dead are delivered to my custody, to be embalmed, slashed, cut and dragged about not to do them honor, but to satisfy the vanity and interest of their survivors." But he has no complaint against this false show, nor against all the shows he detects in the world on that model, but thrives, to the degree he does, on exploiting the world's shams.

But he does it on the cheap, and the cheapness begins with his assembling paid mourners off the street for the funeral. It's their job to wear long faces and decorate the path of the corpse's procession from its bedroom to the hearse waiting at the door, and beyond. And it's a ragtag parade of mourners he assembles, some of whom are doing double duty, digging up old corpses in the graveyard to make room for new ones; whisking dead young ladies off the midwife's table to their homes "to be buried like a maid;" running go-between with the apothecaries and doctors who help keep Sable's business steady and brisk.

The mourners assembled, he begins with a parade of the seedy, assigning them prominence along the path according to the degree of misery their faces project, rearranges expressions to suit, rails at the delinquents who failed to properly perform their assigned atrocities, instructs them again to wipe off the sneer, and as they leave, watches each for a "constant countenance" of eloquent dumbness. "Pretty well," he concludes as they file out, not altogether reassured.

SABLE

Well come you that are to be mourners in this house put on your sad looks, and walk by me that I may sort you: Ha you! a little more upon the dismal;

(Forming their Countenances)

This fellow has a good mortal look—place him near the corps: That wanscoat face must be o'top of the stairs, that fellow's almost in a fright (that looks as if he were full of some strange misery) at the entrance of the hall—So—but I'll fix you all my self—Lets have no laughing now on any provocation:

(Makes faces.)

Look yonder that hale well-looking puppy! You ungrateful scoundrel; Did not I pity you, take you out of a great man's service, and show you the pleasure of receiving wages? Did not I give you ten, then fifteen, now twenty shillings a week, to be sorrowful and the more I give you, I think, the glader you are?

I wonder Goody *Trash* you could not be more punctual; when I told you I wanted you, and your two daughters to be three virgins to-night to stand in white about my Lady *Katherine Grissel's* body, and you know you were privately to bring her home from the man-mid-wifes, where she dy'd in child-birth to be buried like a maid; But there is nothing minded: Well I have put of that till to-morrow; go and get your bag of brick-dust and your whiting. Go and sell to the cook-maids; know who has surfeited about town: bring me no bad news none of your recoverys again; And you Mr. Blockhead I warrant you have not call'd at Mr. *Pestles* the apothecary: Will that fellow never pay

me? I stand bound for all the poison in that starving murderers shop:
He serves me just as Dr. *Quibus* did, who promis'd to write a treatise
against water-gruel, a damn'd healthy slop, that has done me more
injury than all the faculty: Look you now you're all upon the sneer, let
me have none but downright stupid countenances—I've a good mind
to turn you all off and take people out of the play-house; but hang 'em
they are as ignorant of their parts as you are of yours, they never act but
when they speak; when the chief indication of the mind is in the gesture, or indeed in case of sorrow in no gesture, except you were to act a
widow, or so—But yours you Dolts, is all in dumb show; dumb show?
I mean expressive eloquent show: as who can see such an horrid ugly
phiz as that fellow's, and not be shock'd, offended, and kill'd of all joy
while he beholds it? But we must not loiter—ye stupid rogues whom I
have pick'd out of all the rubbish of mankind, and fed for your eminent worthlessness attend and know, that I speake you this moment
stiff and immutable to all sense of noise, mirth, or laughter:

> *(Makes mouths at 'em as they pass by him to bring 'em*
> *to a constant countenance.)*

So they are pretty well—pretty well—

wanscoat: wainscot, wooden **brick-dust and whiting**: the components of their
funeral makeup **murderers**: murderer's **water-gruel**: a kind of cereal **phiz**: face

97

PUZZLE THE ATTORNEY EXPLAINS THE PROFIT FOR LAWYERS OF PROFESSIONAL OBFUSCATION AND TAUTOLOGY

(1701) RICHARD STEELE, The Funeral, *Act 1, Sc. 2*

Only three hours since the presumed death of Lord Brumpton [see II, #96], his young delighted widow has sent for Puzzle the Lawyer to read the will whose contents she already knows and revels in. By persistent young charm and studious solicitation, she's caused old Lord Brumpton's son to be disinherited, and herself to be sole legatee. Puzzle's had a hand in this miracle; not out of allegiance to the widow, but out of an almost disinterested allegiance to his own profession's code. He's brought along his nephew Tom, his own heir and new apprentice, to learn the lawyer's canon from this transaction. By way of schoolroom lesson, he articulates its three fundamental principles for him to learn as Gospel: 1) a true lawyer, in a situation in which a client trusts, cheats; 2) a true lawyer converts every man's will into his own fortune; 3) a true lawyer uses no language in legal deeds but gibberish and tautology, and to add confusion to incomprehension, aims to make the deed's parchment as long and wide as the land for which it is apportioning ownership.

Puzzle is his profession's master, confirming his mastery in every word and gesture. In spelling out the profession's principles, he's downright and absolute. In illustrating his points by tossing out and pulling back the immeasurable length of parchment holding the will, he's as smooth and deft as a stage magician. In exemplifying his rules of lawerly conduct, not a note of moral opprobrium creeps in; the moral and the professional abhor one another.

In *The Funeral,* Steele works in a vein developed more fully by the later great 18th century satire of Pope, Swift, and Fielding, setting more gentle claws than theirs into his quarry—widows, lawyers, undertakers, and most particularly, the hypocrisy of mourning. The play is subtitled *Grief-a-la-Mode.*

PUZZLE

Open the bag good Tom; now Tom thou art my nephew, my dear sister *Kate's* only son, and my heir, therefore I will conceal from thee on no occasion, any thing; For I would enter thee into business as soon as possible: Know then child that the lord of this house was one of your men of honour, and sense, who lose the latter in the former, and are apt to take all men to be like themselves; Now this gentleman entirely trusted me, and I made the only use a man of business can of a trust, I cheated him; for I, imperceptibly, before his face made his whole estate liable to an hundred *per annum* for my self, for good services *&c.* As for legacies they are good or not, as I please, for let me tell you, a man must take pen, ink and paper, sit down by an old fellow, and pretend to take directions, but a true lawyer never makes any man's will but his own, and as the priest of old among us got near the dying man, and gave all to the church, so now the lawyer gives all to the law. Ay. Priests then cheated the nation by doing their offices in an unknown language, but ours is a way much surer, for we cheat in no language at all, but loll in our own coaches, eloquent in gibberish, and learned in juggle—Pull out the parchment; there's the deed, I made it as long as I could—Well I hope to see the day, when the indenture shall be the exact measure of the land that passes by it—For 'tis a discouragement to the gown—that every ignorant rogue of an heir should in a word or two understand his father's meaning, and hold ten acres of land, by half an acre of parchment—Nay I hope to see the time when what there is indeed some progress made in shall be wholly affected, and by the improvement of the noble art of tautology every inn in *Holborn* an Inn of Court—Let others think of logick rhetorick and I know not what impertinence but mind thou tautology—What's the first excellence in a lawyer—Tautology? What the second? Tautology? What the third? Tautology, as an old pleader said of action: but turn to the deed;

(Pulls out an immeasurable Parchment.)

For the will is of no force if I please, for he was not capable of making one after the former—as I manag'd it—But there needs no further perusal—My lord, by this instrument, disinherits his son utterly— Gives all to my lady—and moreover, grants the wards of two fortune—wards to her—*Id est,* to be sold by her; which is the subject of my business to her ladyship, who methinks a little overdoes the affair of grief, in letting me wait thus long on such welcome articles.

tautalogy: pointless repetition **Inn of Court**: in London, where the legal profession is housed **Ward**: control and use of the land of a deceased

98

SIR JEALOUS TRAFFIC, DEVOTED TO SPANISH CUSTOM, CONFINES HIS DAUGHTER TO SPANISH HONOR'S CONSTRAINTS

(1709) SUSANNAH CENTLIVRE, The Busybody, *Act 2, Sc. 2*

Sir Jealous Traffic, "a merchant that had lived some time in Spain, a great admirer of Spanish customs," has the single moral advantage over his Restoration kind—the jealous old fool doomed to being cheated or cuckolded by the ingenuity of the young. His desire is neither for sex nor money, but for virtue. It's the very nature of his notion of virtue that English comedy, unlike its tragedy, detests: Spanish Catholic, like English Puritan, repression of pleasure in all its forms. Lynx-eyed, he guards his daughter's virginity and piety, but necessarily he has to resort to the Spanish custom of the equally lynx-eyed duenna to supplement his care. And there is the loophole of which comedy takes full advantage: the duenna is less likely to be lynx than secret accomplice.

Patch is here the English version of duenna; Sir Jealous Traffic's trust in her is absolute, and his repeated discoveries of his daughter's gestures toward liberty are invariably accompanied by Patch's protestations that she has done everything in her power to restrain her headstrong charge. Sir Traffic upbraids his daughter and commends her English duenna, as he does here, having discovered his daughter once again breaking violently out of restraint: she has exposed herself on the balcony to get a bit of fresh air. His rage is equal to his fear. Failure to prevent the unthinkable has bottomless consequences not only for the sinner but for the guardian against the sin.

> *(Enter SIR JEALOUS and ISABINDA with PATCH following)*

SIR JEALOUS
What, in the balcony again, notwithstanding my positive commands to the contrary!—Why don't you write a bill on your forehead, to show passengers there's something to be let—Is your constitution so hot, mistress, that it wants cooling, ha? Apply the virtuous Spanish rules, banish your taste, and thoughts of flesh, feed upon roots, and quench your thirst with water. 'Tis your high-fed, lusty, rambling, rampant ladies—that are troubled with the vapours: 'tis your ratafia, persico, cinnamon, citron, and spirit of clary cause such swi-mm-ing in the brain, that carries many a whore full tide to the doctor. But you are not to be bred this way; no galloping abroad, no receiving visits at home; for in our loose country, the women are as dangerous as the men.

I'll make her to know, Patch, that you are her Duenna. Oh! That incomparable custom of Spain! Why there's no depending upon old women in my country—for they are as wanton at eighty, as a girl of eighteen; and a man may as safely trust to Asgill's translation as to his great grandmother's not marrying again. Dare to ridicule the cautious conduct of that wise nation, and I'll have you locked up this fortnight without a peep-hole.

And who the devil taught you the art of reasoning? I assure you, they must have a greater faith than I pretend to, that can think any woman innocent who requires liberty. Therefore, Patch, to your charge I give her; lock her up 'till I come back from 'Change: I shall have some sauntering coxcomb, with nothing but a red coat and feather, think by leaping into her arms, to leap into my estate.—But I'll prevent them; she shall be only Babinetto's.

(Exit, with PATCH)

I believe this wench is very true to my interest; I am happy I met with her, if I can but keep my daughter from being blown upon till Signior Babinetto arrives; who shall marry her as soon as he comes, and carry her to Spain as soon as he has married her; she has a pregnant wit, and I'd no more have her an English wife than the grand signior's mistress.

ratafia: a multiflavored cordial **persico**, Sp: peach cordial **clary**: sage liqueur John **Asgill** in 1700 claimed that the rules of English law proved that the redeemed need not die but will be "translated from hence into that external life without passing through death" **Change**: the financial and business exchange

99

THE MERCHANT SEALAND BOLDLY COUNTERS SIR JOHN'S CLAIMS OF ARISTOCRACY'S PRIVILEGED MORALITY
(1722) RICHARD STEELE, *The Conscious Lovers*, Act 4, Sc. 2

In the early 18th century, a reverse class snobbery—of which Steele was a harbinger—began its triumphant ascent. It had been possible even for the Elizabethans to justify a middle class man's being called a gentleman, but not possible for him to fling it in the face of an aristocrat that his claim was the morally superior one.

The merchant Sealand's daughter is being solicited by Sir John Bevil for marriage with his son, Bevil Junior. In their interview, Sir

John exhibits distinct—to his mind, flattering—condescension toward the merchant, since he is offering title for mere money. The merchants of the nation had already won sufficient wealth and power to buy titles, or rescue titles, for money, and so Sealand will have none of the Lord's polite haughtiness. Bluntly and cruelly, he cuts to the chase, and argues:

(1) There's "geneology and descent" in his family too, in the royal line of fighting cocks the family has been raising for generations.

(2) Lineage is neither here nor there in the face of Sir John's son's morals, which will add neither "honor nor credit" to a decent citizen's family.

(3) Young aristocrats assume the iniquitous traditional class privilege of keeping a mistress "because 'tis their opinion they may do it."

(4) Mere "cits" have "grown into the world this last century," and the landed gentry, lazy by habit and inept in industry, no longer have the privilege of calling "trade" or "industry" dishonorable.

(5) Sealand's daughter, as valuable to him as Sir John's "boasted" son to him, will not be given up to the keeper of a mistress who will "soil with his wife for a month perhaps," and then leave her "grazing," out to pasture.

Neither Sealand nor Sir John have reason to know that the "mistress" Bevil Junior is "keeping" is in fact a noble character whom he, a man of feeling, has rescued from want, and though they love, are frozen in the delicacy of their mutual sensibility [see I, #121]. Neither they nor the two fathers know yet the plot's revelation, that the destitute lady is the long-lost daughter of Sealand himself. The scene in which Sealand and Indiana, the forlorn lady, discover their relation is an exercise *in extremis* of sentimental recognitions, and was a main model to emulate for later bourgeois drama and melodrama.

SEALAND

Genealogy and descent! Sir, there has been in our family a very large one. There was Galfrid, the father of Edward, the father of Ptolomy, the father of Crassus, the father of Earl Richard, the father of Henry the marquis, the father of Duke John—

Yes, sir. I have heard my father name 'em all, and more. Yes, sir, he kept 'em all. He was the greatest cocker in all England. He said Duke John won him many battles and never lost one. But, Sir John, value yourself as you please upon your ancient house; I am to talk freely of everything you are pleased to put into your bill of rates on this occasion. Yet, sir, I have made no objections to your son's family. 'Tis his morals that I doubt.

Sir John, the honor of a gentleman is liable to be tainted by as small a matter as the credit of a trader; we are talking of a marriage and in such a case the father of a young woman will not think it an addition to the honor or credit of her lover that he is a keeper of a mistress. Let him apply to any woman else and have as many mistresses as he pleases—

Your son, you say, is a discreet and sober gentleman—Sir, I never saw a man that wenched soberly and discreetly that ever left it off. The decency observed in the practice hides even from the sinner the iniquity of it. They pursue it, not that their appetites hurry them away, but, I warrant you, because 'tis their opinion they may do it.

As much a cit as you take me for, I know the town and the world; and give me leave to say that we merchants are a species of gentry that have grown into the world this last century and are as honorable and almost as useful as you landed folks that have always thought yourselves so much above us, for your trading, forsooth, is extended no farther than a load of hay or a fat ox. You are pleasant people, indeed, because you are bred up to be lazy; therefore, I warrant you, industry is dishonorable.

Look you, Sir John, comparisons are odious and more particularly so on occasions of this kind when we are projecting races that are to be made out of both sides of the comparisons. I am a man exercised and experienced in chances and disasters. I lost in my earlier years a very fine wife and with her a poor little infant; this makes me, perhaps, over cautious to preserve the second bounty of providence to me and be as careful as I can of this child. You'll pardon me, my poor girl, sir, is as valuable to me as your boasted son to you.

There is nothing but this strange lady here, this *incognita,* that can be objected to him. Here and there a man falls in love with an artful creature and gives up all the motives of life to that one passion. Very wise men have been so enslaved; and when a man marries with one of them upon his hands, whether moved from the demand of the world or slighter reasons, such a husband soils with his wife for a month perhaps; then, "Good b'w'y', madam!" The show's over. Ah! John Dryden points out such a husband to a hair where he says, "And while abroad so prodigal the dolt is, Poor spouse at home as ragged as a colt is."

Now, in plain terms, sir, I shall not care to have my poor girl turned a-grazing, and that must be the case when your son—and so forth.

cocker: cockfighter **cit**: citizen, as opposed to aristocracy (78-79) misquoted from Dryden's prologue to Southerne's *Disappointment*

100
PEACHUM CONSIDERS WHICH OF HIS HENCHMEN HE WILL BETRAY TODAY FOR EXECUTION
(1728) JOHN GAY, The Beggar's Opera, *Act 1, Sc. 3*

Peachum's Book of Accounts keeps track of the profit accrued from each of his beggar-thieves on the streets of London. Each day he tallies their worth in a business-like way: is there more profit to be got from their begging and thieving in the near future, or more from "peaching" on them to his friends the police, and so get the reward for them when they're caught and hanged? It's a close calculation, and

Peachum considers multiple factors with the care of the prime minister himself figuring likely profit and loss from bribes and collateral benefits from his constituency.

The comparison is apt. John Gay is satirizing not only the pretensions of Italianate opera and the vogue for the romantic and sentimental, but politics in particular, and in the portrait of Peachum, most particularly Prime Minister Robert Walpole, then known and celebrated for his political sagacity and corruption.

Mrs. Peachum takes exception to the last named on Peachum's current list, Bob Booty, and Peachum explains that Booty is in no immediate danger, only from himself when one of his women betrays him. But there's a cost in leaving the charity of the reward to others: "forty pounds lost to us forever." Peachum is as calculating as a business man, and as necessarily judicious as a politician.

PEACHUM

But 'tis now high time to look about me for a decent execution against next sessions. I hate a lazy rogue, by whom one can get nothing till he is hanged. A register of the gang, *(reading)* "Crook-fingered Jack. A year and a half in the service." Let me see how much the stock owes to his industry; one, two, three, four, five gold watches, and seven silver ones.—A mighty clean-handed fellow!—Sixteen snuff-boxes, five of them of true gold. Six dozen of handkerchiefs, four silver-hilted swords, half a dozen of shirts, three tie-periwigs, and a piece of broadcloth.—Considering these are only the fruits of his leisure hours, I don't know a prettier fellow, for no man alive hath a more engaging presence of mind upon the road. "Wat Dreary, alias Brown Will"—an irregular dog, who hath an underhand way of disposing of his goods. I'll try him only for a sessions or two longer upon his good behavior. "Harry Padington "—a poor petty-larceny rascal, without the least genius; that fellow, though he were to live these six months, will never come to the gallows with any credit. "Slippery Sam"—he goes off the next sessions, for the villain hath the impudence to have views of following his trade as a tailor, which he calls an honest employment. "Matt of the Mint"—listed not above a month ago, a promising sturdy fellow, and diligent in his way:

somewhat too bold and hasty, and may raise good contributions on the
public, if he does not cut himself short by murder. "Tom Tipple"—a
guzzling, soaking sot, who is always too drunk to stand himself, or to
make others stand. A cart is absolutely necessary for him. "Robin of
Bagshot, alias Gorgon, alias Bob Bluff, alias Carbuncle, alias Bob
Booty"—I have set his name down in the black list, that's all, my dear;
he spends his life among women, and as soon as his money is gone,
one or other of the ladies will hang him for the reward, and there's
forty pound lost to us forever.

against next sessions: in anticipation of the next session of the criminal court
(38-40) these names are understood by the audience to be associated with Sir
Robert Walpole (1676-1745), British prime minister **cart**: hangman's cart
Robin...Bob Booty: understood by audience to refer to Robert Walpole

101
PEACHUM WARNS AGAINST THE EVIL OF MARRIAGE
(1728) JOHN GAY, The Beggar's Opera, *Act 1, Sc. 4*

The parody of the Whig politician runs deep in *The Beggar's
Opera;* Peachum is portrayed as a Whitehall clone in the back
alleys of London. Note how he deals with a fanciful premise when it
clashes with the real world. The premise is Mrs. Peachum's, who
argues a bit tearfully that if their daughter Polly is in love, she will naturally want to marry her lover, how could she possibly not? Peachum's
response, in both manner and logic, is impeccably true to the sober,
politely-set-forth calculation of a skilled cabinet man. He deals with
facts, not sentiment. He sets out his points on a platter of objective
fact and reason. And the facts and reason speak, then, for themselves.

What's devastating about Gay's critique of moral corruption is not
merely that he turns propriety upside-down; that was the style of the
Restoration rake who played games with paradox to justify his plea-

sures. What is devastating here is that Peachum is incontrovertibly accurate. Never mind the ardor of romantic (or political) ideals; hold to what is real, stay firmly on the ground. Peachum is teaching a so-to-speak political coworker (his wife) the rule of hard thinking. Whatever Mrs. Peachum or Polly may suppose in their tender hearts is the inevitable longing of lovers, these are its governing realities.

Peachum is the careful politician/businessman who talks soberly and honestly to his troops, and with that sober good sense, he keeps them in line.

PEACHUM

You would not be so mad to have the wench marry him! Gamesters and highwaymen are generally very good to their whores, but they are very devils to their wives.

Look ye, wife. A handsome wench in our way of business is as profitable as at the bar of a Temple coffee-house, who looks upon it as her livelihood to grant every liberty, but one. You see I would indulge the girl as far as prudently we can. In anything but marriage! After that, my dear, how shall we be safe? Are we not then in her husband's power? For a husband hath the absolute power over all a wife's secrets but her own. If the girl had the discretion of a court lady, who can have a dozen young fellows at her ear without complying with one, I should not matter it; but Polly is tinder, and a spark will at once set her on a flame. Married! If the wench does not know her own profit, sure she knows her own pleasure better than to make herself a property! My daughter to me should be, like a court lady to a minister of state, a key to the whole gang. Married! if the affair is not already done, I'll terrify her from it, by the example of our neighbors.

But 'tis your duty, my dear, to warn the girl against her ruin, and to instruct her how to make the most of her beauty. I'll go to her this moment, and sift her. In the mean time, wife, rip out the coronets and marks of these dozen of cambric handkerchiefs, for I can dispose of them this afternoon to a chap in the City.

Temple coffee-house: a coffee-house near the inns-of-court **sift**: to question

102

MACHEATH WELCOMES HIS LADIES TO THE TAVERN WITH SONG

(1728) JOHN GAY, The Beggar's Opera, *Act 2, Sc. 4*

Against every principle of safety and self-interest, Polly has married the highwayman Captain Macheath, who her father Peachum, fence for London's thieves, has warned her now has the power to undo them all. Polly has warned Macheath that her father is planning to betray him to the police for reward, but Macheath delays his flight to safety for one more night with his ladies. But two of them, Jenny Diver and Suky Tawdry, have already betrayed him to Peachum, and his fun is interrupted when Peachum and the constables come for his arrest.

Before that fateful moment, Macheath begins the revels with an elaborate welcome and a song. His love for women is *sui generis,* and his marriage to Polly days before has, out of principle, no hold. "A man who loves money might as well be contented with one guinea as I with one woman…I must have women. There's nothing unbends the mind like them." But Macheath gives as well as he gets: he has the *panache* of a lordly host, and his greetings, his "waters," his song, are all offered up with an air. That "air" never leaves him: in style, he's a great-hearted, swaggering highwayman, a style that undermines, as in this scene, the professional watchdog's vigilance.

> **MACHEATH**
> Dear Mrs. Coaxer, you are welcome. You look charmingly to-day. I hope you don't want the repairs of quality, and lay on paint.—Dolly Trull! kiss me, you slut; are you as amorous as ever, hussy? You are always so taken up with stealing hearts, that you don't allow yourself time to steal anything else. Ah Dolly, thou wilt ever be a coquette.—Mrs. Vixen; I'm yours! I always loved a woman of wit and spirit; they make charming mistresses, but plaguy wives.—Betty Doxy! come hither, hussy. Do you drink as hard as ever? You had better stick to good, wholesome beer; for in troth, Betty, strong waters will, in time,

ruin your constitution. You should leave those to your betters.—
What! and my pretty Jenny Diver too! As prim and demure as ever!
There is not any prude, though ever so high bred, hath a more sanctified look, with a more mischievous heart. Ah! thou art a dear artful
hypocrite!—Mrs. Slammekin! as careless and genteel as ever! all you
fine ladies, who know your own beauty, affect an undress.—But see,
here's Suky Tawdry come to contradict what I was saying. Everything
she gets one way, she lays out upon her back. Why, Suky, you must
keep at least a dozen tally-men.—Molly Brazen!

(She kisses him)

That's well done. I love a free-hearted wench. Thou hast a most agreeable assurance, girl, and art as willing as a turtle.—But hark! I hear
music. The harper is at the door. "If music be the food of love, play on."
Ere you seat yourselves, ladies, what think you of a dance? Come in.

Now, the French tune that Mrs. Slammekin was so fond of.

Youth's the season made for joys,
Love is then our duty;
She alone who that employs,
Well deserves her beauty.
Let's be gay,
While we may,
Beauty's a flower despised in decay.

Let us drink and sport to-day,
Ours is not to-morrow.
Love with youth flies swift away,
Age is nought but sorrow.
Dance and sing,
Time's on the wing,
Life never knows the return of spring.

Now pray, ladies, take your places. Here, fellow. Bid the drawer bring
us more wine.

troth: truth **constitution**: complexion **tally-men**: merchants who sell goods on
credit **If music... play on**: the opening line of *Twelfth Night*

103

SIR SIMON, AFTER OVERHEARING HIS WIFE'S SEDUCER'S PLEADING, CONSIDERS THE FATE OF HUSBANDS

(1735) HENRY FIELDING, The Universal Gallant, *Act 5*

Sir Simon Raffler is determined to believe that he is a cuckold. His brother Captain Raffler is determined to believe that he, on the contrary, is not. They're both wrong. They make a wager: they will eavesdrop on an assignation between Lady Raffler and her supposed lover, and put doubt to rest. But so determined is Sir Simon to prove his cuckoldry, that he forges an inviting letter from his wife, places it for discovery, disguises himself in his wife's clothing, and waits in a darkened room for any seducer.

He is not aware that a counterplot is brewing. His wife, a tigress for virtue, mortified by her husband's jealousy and his forged letter, meets with a mutual plotter and in effect stages a scene in which the pretending lover is urging her to avenge her virtue by confirming her husband's suspicions. "Virtue," as Sir Simon overhears, "obliges her to do it." The encounter in fact demonstrates clearly his wife's innocence, her refusal to countenance or even talk of seduction, but Sir Simon hears what he's determined to hear, and supposes, when they leave, that they might have been on the brink of "action." Proof or not, the encounter triggers Sir Simon's nightmares about wifely adultery, and he expands on his delusions of the dangers surrounding him.

Taking a leaf from classical comedy's long tradition, Fielding follows this scene with another recipient of the letter, who arrives to seduce the still-disguised Sir Simon awaiting seduction as his own wife in the darkened room. Since the play itself, as much as Sir Simon, is fixed on cuckoldry and seduction to the exclusion of every other concern in life, Fielding plays an original variation on the theme in this scene. The young arrival, having no taste for actual seduction but only for the reputation of it, longs to be interrupted, but no one comes. Then, terrified when Sir Simon suddenly speaks in his own voice asking bluntly for confirmation of his wife's adultery, he cries out, bringing the rest of the cast charging on stage to reveal everything and finish the plot.

SIR SIMON RAFFLER

Heaven be praised, they are parted this time. I was afraid it would have come to action. Why, if a husband had a hundred thousand eyes, he would have use for them all. A wife is a garrison without walls, while we are running to the defence of one quarter, she is taken at another. But what a rogue is this fellow, who not only attempts to cuckold his friend, but has the impudence to insist on it as a meritorious action! The dog would persuade her that virtue obliges her to it. Why, what a number of ways are there by which a man may be made a cuckold! One goes to work with his purse, and buys my wife; a second brings his title, he is a lord, forsooth, and has a patent to cuckold all mankind. A third shows a garter, a fourth a riband, a fifth a laced coat. One rascal has a smooth face, another a smooth tongue; another makes smooth verses: this sings, that dances; one wheedles, another flatters; one applies to her ambition, another to her avarice, another to her vanity, another to her folly. This tickles her eyes, that her ears, another—in short, all her five senses, and five thousand follies have their addressers. And that she may be safe on no side, here's a rascal comes and applies himself to the very thing that should defend her, and tries to make a bawd of her very virtue. He has the impudence to tell her that she can't be a woman of virtue without cuckolding her husband—Hark! I hear a noise!—The captain, I suppose, or somebody else after my wife.

104

TRAPWIT DIRECTS HIS ACTORS AND EXPLAINS THE PLAY

(1736) HENRY FIELDING, Pasquin, *Act 2, Sc. 1*

Trapwit, who writes only comedy, is naive enough to suppose that Fustian, who writes only tragedy, believes a word of his play or his explanatory panegyric. They're sitting through a rehearsal of Trapwit's play, which he interrupts with helpful explanations of its implied but unsurfacing gems of wit. In the 18th century manner, they, as observers, share the stage with the actors, so that Trapwit is in an excellent position not only to break into the rehearsal, but into the actors' stage space and conduct their movements—as he does here—with abandon.

Fielding is satirizing not just theatre but current politics; the play Trapwit is rehearsing is about the rivalry of the two political parties, the Whigs and the Tories, each represented in Act One by candidates running for office. Each has only one qualification: bribery, one doing it bluntly with cash, the other with goods, offices and contracts to the highest bidders. Their preference in style of bribery is the only distinction between the two parties. The Second Act shows wives and daughters "governing" the man's vote, and in preparation for the Third, Trapwit arranges the two candidates and their followers to do battle—literal battle—on stage.

By 1736, the tradition of the burlesque play satirizing theatre is well established; Fielding's contribution is in his updating of its focus, taking on not only the traditional subjects of its parody, but also the corruption endemic to two-party electoral politics. (The face-off between the Whig and Tory journalist apologists became as much of a brawl as between the politicians themselves.)

TRAPWIT

There ends act the second.

Mr. Fustian, I inculcate a particular moral at the end of every act; and therefore might have put a particular motto before every one, as the author of Caesar in Egypt has done; thus, sir, my first act sweetly sings, Bribe all, bribe all; the second gives you to understand that we are all under petticoat government; and my third will—but you shall see—Enter my Lord Place, Colonel Promise, and several Voters.

Hitherto, Mr. Fustian, the play has gone on in great tranquillity; now you shall see a scene of a more turbulent nature. Come, enter the mob of both sides, and cudgel one another off the stage. Colonel, as your business is not to fight at present, I beg you would go off before the battle comes on; you, and your brother candidate, come into the middle of the stage, you voters range yourselves under your several leaders.

(The Mob attempt to break in)

Pray, gentlemen, keep back; mind, the colonel's going off is the cue for the battle to enter. Now, my Lord, and the Colonel, you are at the head of your parties—but hold, hold, hold, you beef-eater, go you behind my lord, if you please; and you soldier-maker, come you behind the colonel:

Bravely done, my boys, bravely done!

inculcate: to teach persistently and earnestly **the author of Caesar in Egypt**: a possible reference to Handel's *Julius Caesar* (1724) **petticoat government**: (undue) rule or predominance of women at home, or in politics **beefeater**: popular name for Yeoman of the Guard (the King's Guard)

105

FUSTIAN RECITES HIS DEDICATION FOR THE EDIFICATION OF HIS FRIENDS

(1736) HENRY FIELDING, Pasquin, *Act 3, Sc. 1*

After being bored to tears watching Trapwit's rehearsal of his comedy, it is now Fustian's turn to rehearse his tragedy [see II, #104]. Before he does, he tests the waters with his play's dedication. Just as Trapwit's comedy was devoted to exposing the usual bribery in politics, Fustian exposes the usual bribery in poetry by way of the nauseating flattery of its dedications to potential patrons. But once in the vein, Fustian, never for a moment aware of it, outdoes his target.

FUSTIAN
Before the rehearsal begins, gentlemen, I must beg your opinion of my dedication; you know, a dedication is generally a bill drawn for value therein contained; which value is a set of nauseous fulsome compliments, which my soul abhors and scorns; for I mortally hate flattery, and therefore have carefully avoided it. Well, you shall see it.

(Reads)
"My Lord, at a time when nonsense, dulness, lewdness, and all manner of profaneness and immorality are daily practised on the stage, I have prevailed on my modesty to offer to your lordship's protection a piece, which, if it has no merit to recommend it, has at least no demerit to disgrace it; nor do I question at this, when every one else is dull, you will be pleased to find one exception to the number.

"I cannot indeed help assuming to myself some little merit from the applause which the town has so universally conferred upon me.—"

That, you know, may be omitted, if it should meet with any ill-natured opposition; for which reason I shall not print off my dedication till the play is acted.

(Reads)

"I might here indulge myself with a delineation of your lordship's character: but as I abhor the least imputation of flattery, and as I am certain your lordship is the only person in this nation that does not love to hear your praises, I shall be silent—only this give me leave to say, That you have more wit, sense, learning, honour, and humanity, than all mankind put together; and your person comprehends in it every thing that is beautiful; your air is every thing that is graceful, your look every thing that is majestic, and your mind is a storehouse where every virtue and every perfection are lodged; to pass by your generosity, which is so great, so glorious, so diffusive, that like the sun it eclipses and makes stars of all your other virtues—I could say more—"

"But shall commit a violence upon myself, and conclude with assuring your lordship, that I am, my lord, your lordship's most obedient, most devoted, most obsequious, and most obliged humble servant."

There you see it, sir, concise, and not fulsome. No, sir, I'll let no more flattery go out of my shop.

Sir, flattery is so cheap, and every man of quality keeps so many flatterers about him, that egad, our trade is quite spoiled; but if I am not paid for this dedication, the next I write will be a satirical one; if they won't pay me for opening my mouth, I'll make them pay me for shutting it. But since you have been so kind, gentlemen, to like my dedication, I'll venture to let you see my prologue.

106

FUSTIAN CATALOGUES THE MISERIES OF THE PLAYWRIGHT

(1736) HENRY FIELDING, Pasquin, *Act 4, Sc. 1*

Fustian touches accurately on all the miseries a failed playwright lives through "before he comes to his third night," that is, his benefit night—should his play last that long—when he gets paid from house receipts [see II, #104, 105]. First, inspiration flies; then after many months' wait, either rejection or, possibly worse, acceptance; then, the copying out of all the parts; then rehearsal with complaining actors and "plaguy" calls for revision; finally, the misery of his play's reception. He tells all this to the critic Sneerwell, who doesn't bother to console.

But Fustian is beyond consolation. His plight is so familiar to him, so a matter of course, that it invites neither violent anger nor self-pity. It's a toothache that never goes away, and so he shrugs and lives with it. Of only one thing is he secretly certain: in truth, he deserves praise, homage and genuflection.

> **FUSTIAN**
> These little things, Mr. Sneerwell, will sometimes happen. Indeed, a poet undergoes a great deal before he comes to his third night; first with the muses, who are humourous ladies, and must be attended; for if they take it into their head at any time to go abroad and leave you, you will pump your brain in vain: then, sir, with the master of a playhouse to get it acted, whom you generally follow a quarter of a year before you know whether he will receive it or no; and then, perhaps, he tells you it won't do, and returns it you again, reserving the subject, and perhaps the name, which he brings out in his next pantomime; but if he should receive the play, then you must attend again to get it writ out into parts, and rehearsed. Well, sir, at last, the rehearsals begin; then, sir, begins another scene of trouble with the actors, some

of whom don't like their parts, and all are continually plaguing you with alterations: at length, after having waded through all these difficulties, his play appears on the stage, where one man hisses out of resentment to the author; a second out of dislike to the house; a third out of dislike to the actor; a fourth out of dislike to the play; a fifth for the joke's sake; a sixth to keep all the rest in company. Enemies abuse him, friends give him up, the play is damned, and the author goes to the devil: so ends the farce.

107

KNOWELL NOTES HOW THE GREATEST CORRUPTERS OF CHILDREN ARE THEIR PARENTS

(1751) BEN JONSON, *Everyman in His Humour*, *ad. David Garrick, Act 2, Sc. 2*

Garrick's 18th century adaptations of 16th and 17th century classics are, on examination, not nearly as invasive or distorting as contemporary adaptation. The intent was the same: to make the plays both "relevant" and palatable to contemporary audiences. Now it means removing the play to our own intellectual/cultural backyard; then it meant a few cuts for playability and a bit of moral sanitizing. In Garrick's case, neither was done with a heavy hand; this passage from Jonson's comedy is an excellent case in point; three major cuts for swifter statement, only one of which could conceivably be thought of as in the interest of moral correction. The reason for the difference is simple: the worlds of reference and attitude in the originals were still sufficiently close to need, for the most part, very little retouching.

Knowell is, basically, a hand-me-down from Latin comedy's fathers on the warpath to rein in their rakish sons. But the difference between the traditional figure and Jonson's is notable. Knowell is a moralist who inveighs not so much against "youth's" behavior as against the behavior of the parents who by example and instruction assure their children's corruption. Knowell has read a letter addressed to his son whose author epitomizes for him the kind of "profane and dissolute wretch" who is the model for youthful behavior now, and who, he worries, unknown to him could well be molding his son's behavior. And he compares to this—as comedy's fathers conventionally did— the virtuous behavior of youth in his day. But the bitter satirical thrust of the speech is not against youthful "buffoonery," but against its progenitors, who taught their vices to their children "in their cradles," the children who "sucked in our ill customs with their milk." Jonson's catalogue of "ill customs" in his London was equally apposite to Garrick's. But Knowell concludes with a counter-thought: the influence of consorting with companions "in dung and brothels" might well match, in influence, the "example" of parental corruption.

Knowell's philosophical, judicious manner is somewhat tarnished in the play's subsequent action—when he's racing about chasing after his son, and laying plots for his discovery. Here, however, he remains a man of probity and dignity, intent on solving the mystery of the yawning eternal gap between fathers and sons.

> **KNOWELL**
> I cannot lose the thought yet of this letter
> Sent to my son, nor leave to admire the change
> Of manners and the breeding of our youth
> Within the kingdom since myself was one.
> When I was young, he lived not in the stews,
> Durst [not] have conceived a scorn, and uttered it,
> On a gray head. Age was authority
> Against a buffoon. And a man had then
> A certain reverence paid unto his years
> That had none due unto his life.
> But now we all are fall'n: youth from their fear
> And age from that which bred it, good example.
> Nay, would ourselves were not the first, even parents,

That did destroy the hopes in our own children—
Or they not learned our vices in their cradles
And sucked in our ill customs with their milk.
Ere all their teeth be born, or they can speak,
We make their palates cunning! The first words
We form their tongues with are licentious jests!
Can it call "whore"? cry "bastard"? O, then kiss it,
A witty child! Can't swear? The father's darling!
Give it two plums. Nay, rather than't shall learn
No bawdy song, the mother herself will teach it!
But this is in the infancy;
When it puts on the breeches
It will put off all this. I, it is like,
When it is gone into the bone already.
No, no, this die goes deeper than the coat
Or shirt or skin. It stains unto the liver
And heart in some. And rather than it should not,
Note what we fathers do! Look how we live!
What mistresses we keep! at what expense,
And teach 'em all bad ways to buy affliction!
Well, I thank heaven I never yet was he
That travelled with my son before sixteen
To show him the Venetian courtezans,
Nor read the grammar of cheating I had made
To my sharp boy at twelve, repeating still
The rule, "Get money; still, get money, boy;
No matter by what means."
These are the trade of fathers now! However,
My son, I hope, hath met within my threshold
None of these household precedents, which are strong
And swift, to rape youth to their precipice.
But let the house at home be ne'er so clean—
Swept, or kept sweet from filth,
If he will live abroad with his companions
In dung and brothels, it is worth a fear.
Nor is the danger of conversing less
Than all that I have mentioned of example.

stew: brothel

108

CAPTAIN BOBADILL EXPLAINS HOW, WITH TWENTY MEN TRAINED BY HIMSELF, HE COULD ERADICATE AN ARMY OF FORTY THOUSAND

(1751) BEN JONSON, Everyman in His Humour, *ad. David Garrick, Act 4, Sc. 2*

Captain Bobadill is Jonson's version of the standard character out of Roman comedy, the braggart Captain, traditionally a blustering coward. But the particular energy coming out of Bobadill is more directly from the Italian popular comedy of Jonson's time, *commedia dell'arte,* which exploited the Captain's braggadocio in lengthy "rhotomontades," nonstop disquisitions of warlike exploits that passed beyond the sane (e.g., defeating an army single-handed on the planet Jupiter). It's these that Jonson imitates closely, in effect trying his hand at a conventional *commedia dell'arte* exercise, with no attempt at all at originality.

Though Jonson's exercise is in no way remarkable for originality, it's more than serviceable as "rhotomontade." Bobadill's flight of fancy this time doesn't reach to outer space, but the brag is zany enough. He's with friends, and one of them is quaking at the thought of meeting with a certain Downright, a fellow who's "threatened him with the bastinado." Bobadill reminds him that only this morning he taught him how to defend himself with just such a great club, and he demonstrates by slamming his club against a post. Warmed to his metier, he begins, with a touch of deferential modesty, by offering his credentials as a man of battle: his past engagements, his victories over odds. Odds? And he's moved to higher flights: how he could save half Her Majesty's army expense with 20 men, even against 40,000.

The consequence for Bobadill is what it always is for him: disaster. The very next moment, Downright shows up, and Bobadill, quaking,

takes a beating from Downright's bastinado, and is left with nothing
to cover his vanity before his friends but an explanation: he's always
sworn, after all, to be a man of peace.

> **BOBADILL**
>
> He threatened you with the *bastinado*. Ay, but I think I taught you
> prevention this morning for that. You shall kill him, beyond question,
> if you be so generously minded.
>
> You do not give spirit enough to your motion; you are too tardy, too
> heavy! O, it must be done like lightning—hey!
>
> *(He practices at a post.)*
> 'Tis nothing, an't be not done in a—
>
> *(He lunges)*
> *punto!* I will tell you, sir. They have assaulted me, some three, four,
> five, six of them together, as I have walked alone in divers skirts o'the
> town, where I have driven them before me the whole length of a street
> in the open view of all our gallants, pitying to hurt them, believe me.
> Yet all this lenity will not o'ercome their spleen; they will be doing
> with the pismire, raising a hill a man may spurn abroad with his foot
> at pleasure. By myself I could have slain them all, but I delight not in
> murder. I am loth to bear any other than this *bastinado* for 'em; yet I
> hold it good policy not to go disarmed, for though I be skillful, I may
> be oppressed with multitudes. Indeed, that might be some loss; but
> who respects it? I will tell you, sir, by the way of private and under
> seal, I am a gentleman and live here obscure and to myself; but were I
> known to Her Majesty and the Lords—observe me—I would under-
> take, upon this poor head and life, for the public benefit of the state,
> not only to spare the entire lives of her subjects in general, but to save
> the one—half—nay, three parts—of her yearly charge in holding war,
> and against what enemy soever. And how would I do it, think you?
>
> Why, thus, sir. I would select nineteen more to myself throughout the
> land; gentlemen they should be, of good spirit, strong and able consti-
> tution. I would choose them by instinct, a character that I have, and I

would teach these nineteen the special rules, as your *punto,* your *reverso,* your *stoccata,* your *imbroccata,* your *passada,* your *montanto,* till they could all play very near, or altogether as well as, myself. This done, say the enemy were forty thousand strong, we twenty would come into the field the tenth of March, or thereabouts; and we would challenge twenty of the enemy. They could not in their honor refuse us. Well, we would kill them; challenge twenty more, kill them; twenty more, kill them; twenty more, kill them too; and thus would we kill every man his twenty a day, that's twenty score; twenty score, that's two hundred; two hundred a day, five days a thousand, forty thousand; forty times five, five times forty, two hundred days kills them all up by computation. And this will I venture my poor gentleman-like carcass to perform—provided there be no treason practiced upon us—by fair and discreet manhood—that is, civilly by the sword.

bastinado: a great wooden club ***punto***, It: hit **divers skirts of the town**: different outskirts **lenity**: leniency **pismire**: an ant **under seal**: secretly (25) **three parts**: three quarters ***reverso, stoccata, imbroccata, passada, montanto***, It: moves in fighting with a bastinado

109

DON JOHN, MORTIFIED, FINDS HIMSELF SADDLED WITH A CRYING BABY
(1754) BEAUMONT AND FLETCHER, The Chances, *ad. David Garrick, Act 1, Sc. 5*

Dark. A "night" scene (lights full up on stage, but the audience shares the pretense). Don John hears a cry. A woman's voice. A cry for help. Out of curiosity, out of bravado, he goes nearer. A woman rushes by, puts a bundle in his arms, mumbles protestations, runs off. Don John imagines: What is it? A treasure? To his mortification, he discovers he's holding a tiny baby.

Particularly mortifying for a man of Don John's temperament is to be stuck by chance with a bundle like this. He is, after all, by his own happy assertion and demonstration, a man of determined libertinism, forever on the hunt for a willing wench, forever assuming any woman he meets, whatever her pretensions to virtue and dignity, to be just such a wench.

In cleaning up the play—and Garrick in this case had cleaning up to do—libertine Don John is given a measure of tender feeling, so that after lengthy and self-mocking bemoaning of his ridiculous plight, he takes a look at the wee thing, is moderately touched, and decides: instead of dumping it, he'll take it back to his landlady, and she, God willing! after lengthy "catechism" suspecting him, will take on the care of the thing; but he must hurry before its hunger starts crying aloud, and wins him double mortification.

> **DON JOHN**
> Was ever man so paid for being curious?
> Ever so bobbed for searching out adventures,
> As I am? Did the devil lead me? Must I needs be peeping
> Into men's houses where I had no business,
> And make myself a mischief? 'Tis well carried.
> I must take other men's occasions on me,
> And be I know not whom. Most finely handled!
> What have I got by this now? What's the purchase?
> A piece of pap and caudlework—a child,
> Indeed an infidel. This comes of peeping!
> What a figure do I make now. Good white bread,
> Let's have no bawling wi' ye; 'Sdeath! Have I
> Known wenches thus long, all the ways of wenches,
> Their snares and subtleties? Have I read over
> All their school-learning, studied their quirks and quiddits,
> And am I now bumfiddled with a bastard?
> At my age, too! Fie upon't!—Well, Don John,
> You'll be wiser one day, when you have paid dearly
> For a collection of these butter prints.
> 'Twould not grieve me to keep this gingerbread,
> Were it of my own baking; but to beggar

Myself in caudles, nurses, coral, bells and babies
For other men's iniquities! a little
Troubles me. What shall I do with it now?
Should I be caught here dangling this papspoon,
I shall be sung in ballads; 'prentice boys
Will call me nicknames as I pass the streets.
I can't bear it. No eyes are near; I'll drop it
For the next curious coxcomb. How it smiles upon me!
Ha, you little sugarsop!—'Tis a sweet baby.
'Twere barb'rous to leave it; ten to one would kill it;
Worse sin than his who got it. Well, I'll take it
And keep it as they keep death's head, in rings,
To cry *memento* to me, no more peeping!
Now all the danger is to qualify
The good old gentlewoman at whose house we lodge;
For she will fall upon me with a catechism
Of four hours long. I must endure all,
For I will know this mother. Come, good wonder,
Let you and I be jogging. Your starved treble
Will waken the rude watch else. All that be
Curious nightwalkers, may they find my fee!

bobbed: struck **infidel**: i.e. not yet baptized **caudlework**: thin gruel **quiddits**: essential features **butter print**: a child **keep it... no more peeping**: keep the baby as they keep images of death to remind me of mortality **qualify**: to appease **watch**: nightwatch

110
SIR ANTHONY ABSOLUTE, IN A VIOLENT PASSION, DEMANDS HIS SON MARRY AS HE COMMANDS, OR ELSE
(1775) RICHARD BRINSLEY SHERIDAN, The Rivals, *Act 2, Sc. 1*

Sir Anthony has fixed principles, some of which he's expressed before this scene: ladies should not learn how to read, ladies should have no voice but obedience in the matter of a husband, sons should have no voice at all. He and Mrs. Malaprop have agreed to marry her niece to Sir Anthony's son, and both niece and son are hindering. Sir Anthony confronts his son with patience.

In his own opinion Sir Anthony is a mild man; still obstinacy rouses his anger. A word, a whisper, a look is obstinacy enough for Sir Anthony, and he rises then to his classically comic dimension: the ultimate wrathful father. And in comedy's long tradition of wrathful fathers, surfacing again in this, one of 18th century's greatest comedies, Sir Anthony becomes not only the type's absolute limit but probably its most absolute comic triumph. Because Sir Anthony's measure is not restricted merely to wrath; he's also the epitome of other characteristics: apoplectic lustiness as well as apoplectic anger. Full of beans still, he remembers and applauds the vigor and lust of youth and wants the evidence of his own visibly transferred in his son. And with the same vigor, he imagines Authority's unrestricted power to stamp his son's obedience into perfect servility. He hurls opinion, he drowns contradiction, he plants his foot over the world's face. His plea of patience and forbearance is true: rare obstructions to his will are baffling; they alone rouse him from his inherent gentleness. His strength lies in his knowing nothing about himself. He hasn't a clue as to his own nature, which gives him the unblushing freedom to be himself.

SIR ANTHONY

Hark'ee Jack; I have heard you for some time with patience—I have
been cool—quite cool; but take care—you know I am compliance
itself—when I am not thwarted; no one more easily led—when I have
my own way; but don't put me in a frenzy. Sir, I won't hear a word—
not a word! not one word! so give me your promise by a nod—and I'll
tell you what, Jack—I mean, you dog—if you don't, by—

Z—ds! sirrah! the lady shall be as ugly as I choose: she shall have a
hump on each shoulder; she shall be as crooked as the Crescent; her
one eye shall roll like the bull's in Cox's Museum; she shall have a skin
like a mummy, and the beard of a Jew—she shall be all this, sirrah!—
yet I will make you ogle her all day, and sit up all night to write
sonnets on her beauty. None of your sneering, puppy! no grinning,
jackanapes! I know you are laughing in your sleeve; I know you'll grin
when I am gone, sirrah! None of your passion, sir! none of your violence, if you please. It won't do with me, I promise you.

I know you are in a passion in your heart; I know you are, you hypo-
critical young dog! but it won't do. You will fly out! can't you be cool,
like me? What the devil good can passion do! Passion is of no service,
you impudent, insolent, overbearing reprobate! There, you sneer
again!—don't provoke me!—but you rely upon the mildness of my
temper—you do, you dog! you play upon the meekness of my dispo-
sition! Yet take care—the patience of a saint may be overcome at
last!—but mark! I give you six hours and a half to consider of this: if
you then agree, without any condition, to do everything on earth that
I choose, why—confound you! I may in time forgive you. If not, z—
ds! don't enter the same hemisphere with me! don't dare to breathe the
same air, or use the same light with me; but get an atmosphere and a
sun of your own! I'll strip you of your commission; I'll lodge a five-
and-threepence in the hands of trustees, and you shall live on the
interest: I'll disown you, I'll disinherit you, I'll unget you! and d—n
me! if ever I call you Jack again!

(Exit Sir Anthony)

---

one eye... Museum: a mechanical bull exhibited in 1773-74 in Spring Gardens
jackanapes: ape **five-and-threepence**: a quarter-guinea

111

SIR PETER TRIES TO FATHOM WHY HIS WIFE, ALWAYS IN THE WRONG, QUARRELS WITH HIM

(1777) RICHARD BRINSLEY SHERIDAN, *The School for Scandal*, *Act 1, Sc. 2*

In Sir Peter's plight in marriage with Lady Teazle, Sheridan reaches back almost a century to one of the tenets of Restoration comedy: that marriage begins in rapture and settles quickly into bondage. Back then it was a tedium from which escape to a mistress or a lover was mandatory; in the latter 18th century, when sentimentality had upped the level of propriety, the plight was thought of as considerably less escapable, and so less, in itself, comic. What makes it once again available for comedy are new ingredients to which marriage now could owe its embroilments. One is the attainment of greater independence, in spirit and in fact, by the wife. Manners among the fashionable no longer tolerate the husband's open disregard of her and open derision of her plight. At least among the fashionable, manners look with far more friendly eyes on the wife's severance of social ties from the husband. It is possible, even tolerable, even praised, for the wife to live in altogether different daily worlds from the husband. And so at least socially, women share with sanction the advantage that men had alone a century earlier. Another is "Feeling" which, in the newer fashion, solemnly commits the heart to living half in the Other—a radical departure from the Restoration when the ideal of living, even for lovers, was entirely for the self [see monologue 100, Volume I]. The rhetoric of love borrowed from Romances back in the 17th century, understood then as merely polite discourse for seduction, had over the century been refurbished for the uses of sentiment which spoke directly and piously from the heart, internalizing the old rhetoric, presumed now to be speaking heart's truth. Heart's love didn't necessarily weep blood any more, but certainly self-pitying tears.

Sir Peter, in other words, has lost the option of being cavalier about his wife's foibles, and she has gained the option of being cavalier about his sentiment. In discourse, in opinion, in activity, his claim as husband over her discourse, her opinion, her activity, is gone; but he's stuck with his old-fashioned notions of that claim, and muffled by his sentiment of love which, once he utters it, loses him a last possible shred of advantage. His accurate summary of his plight ends not in a hard but bravely won conclusion, but in total, hopeless bewilderment.

SIR PETER

When an old bachelor marries a young wife, what is he to expect? 'Tis now six months since Lady Teazle made me the happiest of men—and I have been the most miserable dog ever since. We tifted a little going to church, and fairly quarreled before the bells had done ringing. I was more than once nearly choked with gall during the honeymoon, and had lost all comfort in life before my friends had done wishing me joy. Yet I chose with caution—a girl bred wholly in the country, who never knew luxury beyond one silk gown nor dissipation above the annual gala of a race ball. Yet she now plays her part in all the extravagant fopperies of the fashion and the town with as ready a grace as if she never had seen a bush or a grass-plot out of Grosvenor Square! I am sneered at by all my acquaintance and paragraphed in the newspapers. She dissipates my fortune and contradicts all my humors; yet the worst of it is, I doubt I love her, or I should never bear all this. However, I'll never be weak enough to own it. Aye; and what is very extraordinary, in all our disputes she is always in the wrong.

tifted: in a petty quarrel **Grosvenor Square** is in the center of London **doubt**: suspect, believe

112

CENSOR IS CENSORIOUS AGAINST MRS. VOLUBLE'S DISCOURSE
(1779) FRANCIS BURNEY, *The Witlings, Act 1, Sc. 1*

The Witlings opens with a remarkable scene for British comedy in the 18th century: a stageful of ladies sew away in a realistically set hat shop, the activity of the milliners and the action of the play jostling and atmospherically intermingling with one another as the scene progresses. Censor, a character sour in manner (but later in the play discovered to have both heart and reason) has been, in his censorious mind, abused by his friend Beaufort, who made an appointment with him in surroundings such as these. The triviality, in his opinion, of the shop's and its shoppers' world is irritation enough, but the almost mindless volubility of one of its patrons, Mrs. Voluble, drives him to distraction. He has, then, two motives and two responses to his annoying plight. The first is that Beaufort has abused his liberty of choice by settling him among "this valuable collection of dainties;" but the second, the more serious abuse, is that his liberty, trapped by the voluble lady, is altogether taken from him. "The method [mindless talking] she takes for her own relief proves [her fellow creatures'] bane." It's "a disease of all others the most pernicious," since the governing principle of Censor's conduct is the inviolable liberty of the self. Censor speaks for a new social and moral determinant—society's obligation to leave a man, even though he is in its midst, unconditionally free. The principle speaks to, or demands, a society of easily available comforts and enormously wide latitudes of forbearance, as England's comfortable classes were beginning to know their situation to be.

CENSOR

Why how now, Beaufort? is not a man's person his own property? do you conclude that, because you take the liberty to expose your own to a ridiculous and unmanly situation, you may use the same freedom with your friend's?

I take no manner of delight in tapes and ribbons. I leave you, therefore, to the unmolested contemplation of this valuable collection of dainties: and I doubt not but you will be equally charmed and edified by the various curiosities you will behold, and the sagacious observations you will hear. Sir, I heartily wish you well entertained.

Sha'n't go! With what weapons will you stay me? Will you tie me to your little finger with a piece of ribbon, like a lady's sparrow? or will you enthrall me in a net of Brussels lace? Will you raise a fortification of caps? Or barricade me with furbelows? Will you fire at me a broadside of pompons? or will you stop my retreat with a fan?

My good friend. Consider that there is some little difference in our situations. I, for which I bless my stars! am a *free* man, and therefore may be allowed to have an opinion of my own, to act with consistency, and to be guided by the light of Reason: you, for which I most heartily pity you, are a lover, and, consequently, can have no pretensions to similar privileges. With you, therefore, the practice of patience, the toleration of impertinence, and the study of nonsense, are become duties indispensable; and where can you find more ample occasion to display these acquirements, than in this region of foppery, extravagance, and folly?

Do you imagine, that, I *seek* Occasion? Have I not eyes? and can I open them without becoming a spectator of dissipation, idleness, luxury, and disorder? Have I not ears? and can I use them without becoming an auditor of malevolence, envy, futility, and detraction? O Beaufort, take me where I can *avoid* occasion of railing, and then, indeed, I will confess my obligation to you!

Madam!—What, what?—The pleasure of seeing me at your house, when I've called upon Mr. Dabbler? Mr. Dabbler?—O, yes, I recollect.—Why, Beaufort, did you bring me hither to be food to this magpie? This Mrs. Voluble? She's a fool, a prating, intolerable fool.

Dabbler lodges at her house, and whoever passes through her hall to visit him, she claims for her acquaintance. She will consume more words in an hour than ten men will in a year; she is infected with a rage for talking, yet has nothing to say, which is a disease of all others the most pernicious to her fellow creatures, since the method she takes for her own relief proves their bane. Her tongue is as restless as scandal, and, like that, feeds upon nothing, yet attacks and tortures everything; and it vies, in rapidity of motion, with the circulation of the blood in a frog's foot.

Upon my honor, Beaufort, if you don't draw this woman off, I shall decamp.

furbelow: flounces on a woman's gown

113
DABBLER THE POET IS LOST IN THE THROES OF COMPOSITION
(1779) FRANCIS BURNEY, *The Witlings, Act 3, Sc. 1*

Dabbler lives in the upstairs apartment of Mrs. Voluble's [see II, #112] boarding house. She takes great pride in boarding a poet, as much as he takes in being one. He's been abused earlier in the day at the literary club meeting at which he found small opportunity to recite and little praise. Now at his desk, he has a single intent: to dash through a poem to startle the literary club, if not the world.

Playwright Burney, as he crawls from word to word, finding, losing, amending, discarding, is painfully accurate in her depiction of a poet who knows when his effort is awful but can't for the life of him stumble on anything that's good.

Frustration mounts; interruption sends him into frenzy; but it gives him excuse to remember his inept efforts of a moment before as perfect but lost.

New intent: to reach, somehow, gratification very quickly—not writing the new, but reading the old. It's a spurious, but a quick and relaxing fix. While he reads, afflatus grows as he imagines what eluded him today: tomorrow's salon success. Another interruption! But recollecting Mrs. Voluble's guaranteed receptivity, he offers to read a piece to her. And settling to begin, he reads the title, certain of Mrs. Voluble's praise, a step perhaps toward later glory.

(Dabbler is discovered writing.)

DABBLER

The pensive maid, with saddest sorrow sad,—no hang it, that won't do!—*saddest sad* will never do! With—with—*mildest*—ay that's it! *The pensive maid, with mildest sorrow sad,*—I should like, now, to hear a man mend that line! I shall never get another equal to it.—Let's see,—mad, bad, lad, Dad,—curse it, there's never a rhyme will do!—Where's the *Art of Poetry?*—O, here,—now we shall have it; *(Reads.)* Add,—hold, that will do at once,—*with mildest sorrow sad, shed crystal tears, and sigh to sigh did add.* Admirable! admirable by all that's good! Now let's try the first stanza,

(Reads.)

Ye gentle nymphs, whose hearts are prone to love,
Ah, hear my song, and ah! my song approve;
And ye, ye glorious, mighty sons of fame,
Ye mighty warriors—

How's this, two *mightys?*—hang it, that won't do!—let's see,—ye *glorious* warriors,—no, there's *glorious* before,—O curse it, now I've got it all to do over again! just as I thought I had finished it!—ye *fighting,*—no,—ye *towering,* no;—ye,—ye—ye—I have it, by Apollo!—

(Enter Betty.)

(starting up in a rage) Now curse me if this is not too much! What do you mean by interrupting me at my studies? how often have I given orders not to be disturbed?

Tell me nothing!—get out of the room directly!—and take care you never break in upon me again,—no, not if the house be on fire!—Go, I say!

(alone) What a provoking intrusion! just as I had worked myself into the true spirit of poetry!—I sha'n't recover my ideas this half hour. 'Tis a most barbarous thing that a man's retirement cannot be sacred.

(Sits down to write.)

Ye *fighting*,—no, that was not it;—ye—ye—ye—O curse it, *(Stamping.)* if I have not forgot all I was going to say! That unfeeling, impenetrable fool has lost me more ideas than would have made a fresh man's reputation. I'd rather have given a hundred guineas than have seen her. I protest, I was upon the point of making as good a poem as any in the language,—my numbers flowed,—my thoughts were ready,—my words glided,—but now, all is gone!—all gone and evaporated! *(Claps his hand to his forehead.)* Here's nothing left! nothing in the world!—What shall I do to compose myself? Suppose I read?—why where the Deuce are all the things gone?

(Looking over his papers.)

O, here,—I wonder how my epigram will read today,—I think I'll show it to Censor,—he has seen nothing like it of late;—I'll pass it off for some dead poet's, or he'll never do it justice;—let's see, suppose Pope?—No, it's too smart for Pope,—Pope never wrote anything like it!—well then, suppose—

(Enter Mrs. Voluble.)

O curse it, another interruption! Pray, Mrs. Voluble, please leave me alone,—I am extremely busy; *(Aside.)* Yet, she's a mighty good sort of woman,—I've a great mind to read her that song:—no, this will be better. Mrs. Voluble, do you think you can keep a secret? Well, then, I'll read you a little thing I've just been composing, and you shall tell me your opinion of it. *(Reads.)*

On a Young Lady Blinded by Lightning.

Comedy

XIX CENTURY GERMAN/SCANDINAVIAN

114

STRAAMAND, THE VILLAGE PASTOR, DEFENDS HIS "BARNYARD FOWL'S" LIFE AGAINST THE POET FALK'S "SOARING EAGLE"

(1862) HENRIK IBSEN, Love's Comedy, *tr. M. Zelenak and L. Katz, Act 3*

The poet Falk seriously upsets the life of Mrs. Halm's guests who plot marriages, job advancements and profitable friendships during their summer at her boarding house. Deeply affected by Falk's lofty jabs at the prosaically low is Pastor Straamand, the proud father of an even dozen children and an example for his moderately moral and moderately pious middle-class congregants. Unlike Falk, though, he's a man of courtesy and self-restraint, and when he finds himself alone with Falk, he takes the opportunity to defend himself, with kindness and a certain pride, against Falk's attacks on the compromised life.

Straamand, like many of Ibsen's secondary characters, underscores Ibsen's own ambivalence toward his professed moral idealism. The strength of their defense against his apparent beliefs tempers, and in some plays altogether neutralizes, the soaring ideals of characters like Brand, Gregers Werle, the awakened Nora and certainly Falk. In Falk's instance in fact Ibsen so thoroughly deflates poetic mission itself that—miraculously, in Ibsen's canon—it credits the ostensible apologists for lives of committed mediocrity as the play's persuasive victors. Straamand argues that the ordinary, the mediocre, even the backsliding is wholly sufficient support and sustenance for full, rewarding, loving lives. (His argument is to be further articulated with devastating impact on Falkian rapture in the play's final confrontation [see II, #115]).

STRAAMAND

Tell me, Falk, when did I promise allegiance to this ideal you're so fond of preaching? I'm a married man, the father of a family, with twelve little ones to feed, I have chapels to look after, a large parish, and a huge flock of spiritual sheep. Do you suppose I have any time to spare for ideals?

There was a time when I was young too, and no less brave and fearless than you. But I had to earn my bread, and the years went by. Those years harden the soul, just as they do the hands. I went up north to a home in a quiet spot beyond the mountains, and my life was bounded by the four corners of my parish. My *home,* Mr. Falk! Do you know what a home is? A home is a place where there is always room for friends, but where only two people—if they're enemies—are in a very small prison; where one's thoughts can flow freely, like children in the open air; where one can grow old without noticing that the years have passed; and where life always has a background of happy memories, like the line of blue hills above the forest outside my house.

I'm waxing poetic over things you can only laugh at! God has made us very differently. I know I lack much of what you have, but I've won much that you've lost. Well, some of us are born eagles, made to soar into the sky—and others are born barnyard fowls.

I daresay, I am a barnyard fowl, but I have a brood of chicks under my wings, and you have none. And I can fight hard for those that belong to me if necessary. I know very well that you think me stupid—perhaps even worse than stupid—too greedy for the goods of this world. Well, I don't think that's worth our quarreling about.

I'll grant that I'm as greedy and stupid and dull as you think me; but I'm greedy for the sake of the children God has given me, and I've grown stupid in fighting against hunger, and dull from living in loneliness, away from companions of the mind such as you. But for every youthful dream I lost, God gave me a gift of wonderful beauty, and I accepted His gifts with a thankful heart. It's for those gifts that I endured, and for them that I found comfort in God's word. They're *my* field of flowers—my children. But this afternoon, you poisoned

the joy I took in them with your mockery. You said that what I
though was happiness was only a fool's paradise—that what I believed,
was only ridiculous. Now I beg you, give me back my peace of mind.
You destroyed it with a word. Give me a fresh verdict. Think again,
and speak the truth fully and frankly, so that I can hold my head up
once more.

I see, for you, there's no word that can turn brass into gold. Then I
beg you to remember the words spoken just now by a man who pretends to follow nothing but the light of truth: He said, "There's such a
thing as retribution, and no one can escape it." But who would want
to expose you? Who would care enough to bother?

115

GULSTAD, WHO OFFERS ORDINARY MARRIAGE, CONTENDS WITH FALK'S PASSIONATE OFFER OF THE EXTRAORDINARY

(1862) HENRIK IBSEN, Love's Comedy, *tr. M. Zelenak and L. Katz, Act 3*

Gulstad, a four-square businessman and veritable pillar of society,
reduces Poet Falk's soaring conceit of love to fantasy [see II,
#114]. They're contending for the hand of Svanhild, who's already
succumbed to Falk's ardor—which is in fact her own—and is determined to marry him. Guldstad lays claim to a moment of their time
to argue the case of the humdrum. His argument is by no means brilliant; he sticks to facts, and lays out accurately the prospect of the
future for the fire of love on the one hand and for an ordinary commitment to passionless marriage on the other. Inadvertently, he turns
the prose of mediocrity into the poetry of desirability; Svanhild
accepts his offer.

The ordinary has its own appealing subtleties, as opposed to the certain banalities of the extraordinary, and Guldstad, and Ibsen, exploit them all. Hidden in the byways of the ordinary are pleasures that are so close to none at all that they're in slight danger of being demolished by time. Therefore they'll last, argues Guldstad, forever. Rapture, on the other hand, fizzles quickly, and leaves a wasteland of disillusion behind it. It's not Guldstad's arguments alone that win Svanhild—who feels as ardent for Viking freedom and its emotional heroics as does Falk—but her recognition, during Guldstadt's brief, that her life-longings were closer to earth than to air, that she could more comfortably settle for the nostalgia rather than the precarious burden of passion's poetry. She shares with Ibsen the sharp separation between the Ideal beyond reach and beautiful, and the Ideal domesticated and lethal. Although that is not the Ibsen generally remembered from *A Doll House,* it is the Ibsen genuinely lurking there, though not so overtly as here, in *Love's Comedy.*

GULSTAD

I suppose you haven't much time, Falk? You leave in a quarter of an hour. But that will be enough time.

(Svanhild starts to move away.)

No, Svanhild, please stay. Till you've answered me. Everything must be made very clear among us. We've all got to take our masks off now. *(with a smile)* I told you yesterday that I was contemplating a play of some sort—a prosaic kind of play—one I intend to live. And I must tell you now: you and I have chosen the same subject.

No, wait, Svanhild, and hear me out. I wouldn't ask any other woman to do it; but I've learned to know you well. You have too fine a nature to be prudish. I've watched you growing up, and I saw all the qualities I most prize in a woman flowering in you. For a long time, I only thought of you in a fatherly way. Now I'm going to ask you—will you be my wife?

No, Falk! It's for her to answer. You ask her too—so that she can make a free choice. The happiness of three lives is at stake—not only mine. Let's have no pretence; it will do you no good. Even though I live what you call a humdrum business life, it's given me a certain shrewdness. Yes, Falk—you love her. I was delighted to watch the beginning of love's young dream; but this violent, impetuous love of yours is just what may very well ruin her happiness.

Suppose you win her now—Suppose she dared to build everything in her life on that one foundation—staked everything she has on that one throw—and suppose that time ate away at that foundation, and the flower of love faded in the gloom of day-to-day existence? Impossible? So I thought once. In the old days, when I was as young as you, I was all on fire for the love of a girl. Then our ways parted. We met again for the first time last evening—all the romance was gone.

I grieved over my loss for years; and all those years she stayed in my memory as the lovely young girl she was the first time we met on a beautiful spring day. And now you're lighting the same dangerous fire—risking the same chance. That's what I say: "Be careful! Pause a moment and take time for thought. You're playing a risky game."

This afternoon, over those tea-cups in this garden, you made your declaration of faith. It was, I believe, that love by itself is strong enough to defy convention, want, sorrow, old age? You may be right. But consider the question in another way. No one in the world can define exactly what <u>love</u> is, or give reason for the delightful belief that bliss is to be found only two-by-two. But <u>marriage</u> is something practical, and doesn't depend only on love. Love chooses the woman, not the wife, and if it turns out afterwards that she's not the right wife— Well, then it's all up with you, because it has all sorts of obligations and duties that have nothing whatever to do with love. It means a taste for domesticity; it means unselfishness and a devotion to duty— and various other things.

Therefore listen to advice that is worth its weight in gold. Every pair of lovers go about at first as though all the riches in the world had dropped into their laps. They want to gallop to the altar; they set up house and go silly with delight, and for a while are drunk with happiness and mutual devotion. But a day of reckoning has to come—and when it does, it means complete bankruptcy. It means the fading of the roses from the bride's cheek, the fading of hope from her heart; the fading of the triumphant courage in the man's breast; the fading of the last spark of the fire that used to glow so fiercely; failure, complete and disastrous.

Look at Straamand—a man who used to be a musician and an artist of considerable skill and taste in his bachelor days. Can you wonder at his having so degenerated since he and his wife began their life together? She was meant to be his mistress; she was never in the least suited to be his wife.

There are two ways of starting a married life. One way is to try to live as though your age will permanently remain nineteen, and that there are no such things as rheumatism and sciatica. You may try to live on the capital of pink cheeks and bright eyes, and on the conviction of two lives beating as one all through your lives, just as they did the day she first said "yes" to you. What's the right name for ideas of that kind? You know very well! Humbug, my friend—humbug!

There's an affection that can accomplish its end just as well as the exuberance of passion; a sense of the happiness of caring for another's comfort, of mutual consideration , of peace in one's hope, of watching that no stone bruises the other's foot in their journey through life; a strength that's glad to shoulder all the burdens that years bring. That is what I can contribute, Svanhild, towards building up a happy life for you. Now give me your answer. Ah, no, think it over well, so that you may not repent it. Make your choice between us calmly and deliberately.

Now I'm going in. Let's have no more misunderstanding. If you can swear to me, by everything you hold sacred, that you'll be such a friend to her all your life long, such a comfort in time of trouble, as I can be, then—

(He turns to Svanhild)

Then, Svanhild, blot out of your mind all recollection of what I've offered. I shall none the less have had my quiet triumph, because you will be happy, and that is all I want.

(to Falk) Oh, by the way—you said something about money. You can
discount that. I'm a man alone, and no one depending on me. All that
is mine shall be yours. You'll be a son to me, and she my daughter. I
have a place of business on the frontier. I'll move out there, and you
can set up house here; and when a year is over, we will meet again.
Now you know me, Falk. Search out your own heart. But don't forget
that the journey you're undertaking is no child's play, no mere enjoyment or luxury. So for God's sake—make your choice, you too!

116

PEER GYNT PEELS AN ONION WHICH SUMS UP HIS LIFE

(1867) HENRIK IBSEN, Peer Gynt, *tr. Wm. Archer,* Act 5, Sc. 5

Having begun life as a liar, a dreamer, a backslider and compro-
miser, Peer Gynt goes off to America, and with such
indispensable qualifications blossoms into a slave-trader and a captain
of business enterprise whose ambition it is to conquer all the world's
markets, or as Peer puts it, "To be a Caesar of all the world by means
of gold." [see I, #127] But his true lifelong ambition, of which this
striving is a reflection, is to become the "Gyntian Self," or as we say
now, "Me." His 19th century self-made man's career encompasses
many roles, and when his circular journey through the world brings
him back to its beginnings in the forests of the North ("Go roundabout," counseled the prescient Boyg when as a young man he was
lost in these same woods), once more bereft of everything, crawling
through the forest on all fours and in danger of starving, he stumbles
on a funeral. There he hears a eulogy for a dead peasant who lived his
hard life fighting against fortune but who, according to the Priest,
achieved thereby a true greatness "because he was himself." Peer

bethinks himself: how have all his past selves added up to a true "Gyntian" self. Sitting in a patch of onions, he lifts one, peels it, counting off his multiple selves.

He begins with the last: shpwrecked, and barely escaped with his life (when the Devil floated past, and reassured him that the hero doesn't die till the end of the Fifth Act); before that, the querulous Passenger aboard the ship that capsized. Then he jumbles the sequence, and remembers his life in random order: the gold prospector in America; the fur trapper in Hudson Bay; the episode of "the Crown" in the Cairo madhouse when he was anointed King of the lunatics, the greatest worshiper of "self;" his brief sojourn as an archaeologist in North Africa; his days disguised as a Mohammedan prophet, with the worshipful Anitra as his follower; his successful days as a "gentleman" in America, clouded by the "black streaks" in his recollection of his missionary zeal for the natives, and trading in slaves at the same time. With this recollection, the onion falls apart.

"Nature is witty," he shrugs, when he's left with a handful of peelings and no core. Ibsen's delectable fantasy of the career of this non-self Gyntian Self subverts with irony, good humor and cold judgment the upward-and-onward strivings of the earlier 19th century model of "self" in Goethe's *Faust*. By mid-century, that model declines to the level of Peer Gynt the slave-trader, the pursuer of world markets, the devious journeyer "roundabout"—Faust dimly reflected, shriveled and with clay feet. The Gyntian Self reflects too the no less bankrupt moral aspirations of the Christian-merchant Thorowgoods who spouted their dogma of pious conquest in the 18th century [see II, #52]. Ibsen's onion that falls apart and reveals nothing at its core becomes a sustaining critique of the enterprising Westerner, rediscovered many times in Western literature for the next century and a half.

(Peer Gynt is creeping among the undergrowth, gathering wild onions.)

PEER

Well, this is one standpoint. Where is the next?
One should try all things and choose the best.
Well, I have done so,—beginning from Caesar,
And downwards as far as to Nebuchadnezzar.
So I've had, after all, to go through Bible history;—
The old boy has come back to his mother again.
After all it is written; Of the earth art thou come.—
The main thing in life is to fill one's belly.
Fill it with onions? That's not much good;—
I must take to cunning, and set out snares.
There's water in the beck here; I shan't suffer thirst;
And I count as the first 'mong the beasts after all.
When my time comes to die—as most likely it will,—
I shall crawl in under a wind-fallen tree;
Like the bear, I will heap up a leaf-mound above me,
And I'll scratch in big print on the bark of the tree:
Here rests Peer Gynt, that decent soul,
Kaiser o'er all of the other beasts.—
Kaiser?

(Laughs inwardly.)

Why, you old soothsayer's-dupe!
No Kaiser are you; you are nought but an onion.
I'm going to peel you now, my good Peer!
You won't escape either by begging or howling.

(Takes an onion and strips off one coat after another.)

There lies the outermost layer, all torn;
That's the shipwrecked man on the jolly-boat's keel.
Here's the passenger layer, scanty and thin;—
And yet in its taste there's a tang of Peer Gynt.
Next underneath is the gold-digger ego ;
The juice is all gone—if it ever had any,
This coarse-grained layer with the hardened skin

Is the peltry hunter by Hudson's Bay.
The next one looks like a crown;—oh, thanks!
We'll throw it away without more ado.
Here's the archaeologist, short but sturdy,
And here is the Prophet, juicy and fresh.
He stinks, as the Scripture has it, of lies,
Enough to bring the water to an honest man's eyes.
This layer that rolls itself softly together
Is the gentleman, living in ease and good cheer.
The next one seems sick. There are black streaks upon it;—
Black symbolizes both parsons and niggers.

           (Pulls off several layers at once)
What an enormous number of swathings !
Is not the kernel soon coming to light ?

           (Pulls the whole onion to pieces.)
I'm blest if it is! To the innermost centre,
It's nothing but swathings—each smaller and smaller.—
Nature is witty!
           (Throws the fragments away.)
The devil take brooding!
If one goes about thinking, one's apt to stumble.

Nebuchadnezzar: a legendary Babylonian king (604?-561? BC), conqueror of Jerusalem **beck**: a brook **jolly boat**: a life boat hoisted at the side of a sailing ship for handy use

XIX/XX CENTURY ENGLISH Comedy

117

SIR ROBERT CHILTERN CONFESSES TO THE YOUTHFUL CRIME THAT HAS GIVEN HIM HIS WEALTH AND POSITION

(1895) OSCAR WILDE, An Ideal Husband, *Act 2*

The secret is out, and it could mean ruin. The unscrupulous Mrs. Cheveley has found out the details of Sir Robert's long-concealed lapse of eighteen years ago, the insider-trading ploy that made his fortune, and plans to blackmail him into lending his name to an even more dishonorable financial scheme now. Sir Robert is in the midst of confessing the whole matter to a very worldly, very Wildean Lord Goring. But he's not only confessing, he's defending his actions, intent on earning Lord Goring's sympathetic understanding, if not his wholehearted approval. But the more justification he offers, the more he finds it's uphill work convincing a man of even Lord Goring's tolerance. In making his difficult case—there's no getting around its criminality—Sir Robert is finally led into confessing his genuine— and equally questionable—life-credo, but one, he suggests, which is hardly unusual among the stupefyingly successful. It's hardly, he recognizes, defense, but hopes it is mitigating. For in his argument, he's not aiming at subterfuge; Lord Robert, like other of Wilde's self-confessing, self-revealing characters, and unlike Ibsen's pillars of society, has no difficulty recognizing his own inherent hypocrisy; his private integrity lies in his now frankly confronting it and now spelling it out.

What makes the matter particularly scorching for Sir Robert is that since that definitive and shameful moment in his career, he's won and actually lived up to not only the reputation of an ideal husband but of the ideal man of political and financial propriety. The sham of his career, though, is unraveling now, and he's fighting hard to find a way out from under disaster. The presentation of his defense before Lord Goring is only rehearsal, only trial balloon, only step one, but each unfolding assertion carries with it the unspoken query: Is it convincing, is it enough, can I be redeemed?

SIR ROBERT
I did not sell myself for money. I bought success at a great price. That is all. Baron Arnheim was a man of a most subtle and refined intellect. A man of culture, charm and distinction. One of the most intellectual men I ever met. One night after dinner at Lord Radley's the Baron began talking about success in modern life as something that one could reduce to an absolutely definite science. With that wonderfully fascinating quiet voice of his he expounded to us the most terrible of all philosophies, the philosophy of power, preached to us the most marvellous of all gospels, the gospel of gold. I think he saw the effect he had produced on me, for some days afterwards he wrote and asked me to come and see him. He was living then in Park Lane, in the house Lord Woolcomb has now. I remember so well how, with a strange smile on his pale, curved lips, he led me through his wonderful picture gallery, showed me his tapestries, his enamels, his jewels, his carved ivories, made me wonder at the strange loveliness of the luxury in which he lived ; and then told me that luxury was nothing but a background, a painted scene in a play, and that power, power over other men, power over the world, was the one thing worth having, the one supreme pleasure worth knowing, the one joy one never tired of, and that in our century only the rich possessed it.

Wealth has given me enormous power. It gave me at the outset of my life freedom, and freedom is everything. You have never been poor, and never known what ambition is. You cannot understand what a wonderful chance the Baron gave me. Such a chance as few men get. When I was going away he said to me that if I ever could give him any private information of real value he would make me a very rich man. I was dazed at the prospect he held out to me, and my ambition and my desire for power were at that time boundless. Six weeks later certain private documents passed through my hands.

Do you really think, Arthur, that it is weakness that yields to temptation? I tell you that there are terrible temptations that it requires strength, strength and courage, to yield to. To stake all one's life on a single moment, to risk everything on one throw, whether the stake be power or pleasure, I care not—there is no weakness in that. There is a horrible, a terrible courage. I had that courage. I sat down the same afternoon and wrote Baron Arnheim the letter this woman now holds. He made three-quarters of a million over the transaction. I received from the Baron 110,000. That money gave me exactly what I wanted, power over others. I went into the House immediately. The Baron advised me in finance from time to time. Before five years I had almost trebled my fortune. Since then everything that I have touched has turned out a success. In all things connected with money I have had a luck so extraordinary that sometimes it has made me almost afraid. I remember having read somewhere, in some strange book, that when the gods wish to punish us they answer our prayers.

118

JULIUS CAESAR READS THE RIDDLE OF THE SPHINX
(1899) BERNARD SHAW, Caesar and Cleopatra, *Act 1*

After defeating Pompey's forces in Egypt, Caesar held undisputed Roman power in the East. It was then that he encountered Cleopatra, and before returning to Rome, dallied with her, as legend has it, in Alexandria for nine months. (It was to be only six months later when he was assassinated by the republican conspiracy in Rome.)

Shaw begins his reinvention of Caesar at the moment of his arrival in Egypt's capital, Alexandria, and devises a remarkable figure of almost unlimited sagacity, judicious temper, military genius (which he had), and political vision—he presaged a just and peaceful world under omnipotent Roman rule. But probably most remarkable of all is Shaw's invention of this encounter between a Sphinx who sits eternally motionless and a conquering Caesar who wanders the world, and yet both inherently invested with the same genius. "We are no strangers," he informs her, "to one another."

The equation Shaw devises is that between the man of action who surpasses ordinary levels of practical understanding and ambition, and the Sphinx whose vision, mystical and transcendent, is the secret source as well of Caesar's genius. In him, as in Shaw himself, the pragmatist and the mystic are one, and the ingredients of that being are, as in the composition of the Sphinx, "part brute, part woman, part God." At that level of concordance, the rationality, the appetites and the pursuits of the male give place to instinct, intuition and an all-encompassing insight.

Caesar, greeting his counterpart and his original, is humbled, overwhelmed, but still—his intellect neither humbled nor overwhelmed—accomplishes an almost mystical assessment, in his "reading," of the Sphinx, and consequently a similarly transcendant assessment of himself, one which considerably surpasses his more or less confirmed historical reality. It is essentially Shaw's portrait of the genius in history, the counterpart of his later portrait of the saint in history, neither, as he renders them, within the compass of normal human grasp or endurance.

THE MAN

Hail, Sphinx: salutation from Julius Caesar! I have wandered in many lands, seeking the lost regions from which my birth into this world exiled me, and the company of creatures such as I myself. I have found flocks and pastures, men and cities, but no other Caesar, no air native to me, no man kindred to me, none who can do my day's deed, and think my night's thought. In the little world yonder, Sphinx, my place is as high as yours in this great desert; only I wander, and you sit still; I conquer, and you endure; I work and wonder, you watch and wait; I look up and am dazzled, look down and am darkened, look around and am puzzled; whilst your eyes never turn from looking out—out of the world—to the lost region—the home from which we have strayed. Sphinx, you and I, strangers to the race of men, are no strangers to one another: have I not been conscious of you and of this place since I was born? Rome is a madman's dream: this is my Reality. These starry lamps of yours I have seen from afar in Gaul, in Britain, in Spain, in Thessaly, signalling great secrets to some eternal sentinel below, whose post I never could find. And here at last is their sentinel—an image of the constant and immortal part of my life, silent, full of thoughts, alone in the silver desert. Sphinx, Sphinx: I have climbed mountains at night to hear in the distance the stealthy footfall of the winds that chase your sands in forbidden play—our invisible children, O Sphinx, laughing in whispers. My way hither was the way of destiny: for I am he of whose genius you are the symbol: part brute, part woman, and part God—nothing of man in me at all. Have I read your riddle, Sphinx?

Gaul: a Roman province conquered largely by Caesar, including today's France, Belgium, and parts of Italy, Germany and Switzerland **Britain**: Caesar conquered today's England and Wales as the Roman province of Britannia **Thessaly**: a province in northern Greece

119

SHAW, THROUGH THE MOUTH OF YOUNG AUBREY, MOURNS THE UNHINGING OF WESTERN CIVILIZATION'S VALUES FOLLOWING THE FIRST WORLD WAR
(1932) BERNARD SHAW, Too True To Be Good, *Act 3*

The legend goes that when *Too True to Be Good,* one of Shaw's late (neglected) plays was in rehearsal at the Malvern Festival, the director suggested to him that a speech was needed to conclude the play. Shaw, so the legend has it, composed it right then, handed it to the director, and it was given to the young Preacher Aubrey—whose

Preacher father, the Elder, "vanishes into the recesses of St. Pauls [cathedral], leaving his son to preach in solitude." And so Aubrey bears the burden of confronting what none of the cast of 1920s disenchanted characters, "too absurd to be believed in; yet they are not fictions," bother to confront: the gods that failed. Shaw, out of the mouth of the babe Aubrey, preaches his lonely sermon:

"I am Ecclesiastes. But I have no Bible, no creed: the war has shot both out of my hands." After the first World War, Shaw faced the debilitating fact that along with its unprecedented destruction of life and property, it had "rent a hole" in the "impossible idealisms" of the pre-war period. Then, they were life-sustaining; now they were insupportable, and his lament is that, like the young, he too is without "creed," and to have no truth to preach and no struggle to sustain is beyond bearing. His bewilderment, his inability to find the clothing for "the souls that go in rags now," produces, if not resolution, a soul's lamentation of Biblical proportions, and perhaps the greatest speech Shaw ever wrote.

> **AUBREY**
>
> *(rising)* If I may be allowed to improve the occasion for a moment——it is clear to me that though we seem to be dispersing quietly to do very ordinary things: Sweetie and the Sergeant to get married
>
> > *(the Sergeant hastily steals down from his grotto, beckoning to Sweetie to follow him. They both escape along the beach)*
>
> the colonel to his wife, his watercolors, and his K.C.B.
>
> > *(the colonel hurries away noiselessly in the opposite direction)*
>
> Napoleon Alexander Trotsky Meek to his job of repatriating the expedition
>
> > *(Meek takes to flight up the path through the gap)*
>
> Mops, like Saint Teresa, to found an unladylike sisterhood with her mother as cook-housekeeper

(Mrs Mopply hastily follows the sergeant, dragging with her the patient, who is listening to Aubrey with signs of becoming rapt in his discourse)

yet they are all, like my father here, falling, falling, falling endlessly and hopelessly through a void in which they can find no footing.

(The Elder vanishes into the recesses of St Pauls, leaving his son to preach in solitude).

There is something fantastic about them, something unreal and perverse, something profoundly unsatisfactory. They are too absurd to be believed in; yet they are not fictions: the newspapers are full of them: what storyteller, however reckless a liar, would dare to invent figures so improbable as men and women with their minds stripped naked? Naked bodies no longer shock us: But the horror of the naked mind is still more than we can bear. You may throw away the outer garments of your souls: the manners, the morals, the decencies. Swear; use dirty words; drink cocktails; kiss and caress and cuddle until girls who are like roses at eighteen are like battered demireps at twenty-two:

But how are we to bear this dreadful new nakedness: the nakedness of the souls who until now have always disguised themselves from one another in beautiful impossible idealisms to enable them to bear one another's company. The iron lightning of war has burnt great rents in these angelic veils, just as it has smashed great holes in our cathedral roofs and torn great gashes in our hillsides. Our souls go in rags now; and the young are spying through the holes and getting glimpses of the reality that was hidden. And they are not horrified: they exult in having found us out:

But when they have stripped themselves and us utterly naked, will they be able to bear the spectacle?—When the old woman had the mask struck from her soul and reveled in it instead of dying of it—I shrank from the revelation as from a wind bringing from the unknown regions of the future a breath which may be a breath of life, but of a life too keen for me to bear, and therefore for me a blast of death. I stand midway between youth and age like a man who has missed his train: too late for the last and too early for the next. What am I to do? What am I? A soldier who has lost his nerve, a thief who at his first great theft has found honesty the best policy and restored his booty to its owner. Nature never intended me for soldiering or thieving: I am by nature and destiny a preacher. I am the new Ecclesiastes. But I have no Bible, no creed: the war has shot both out of my hands. The war has been a fiery forcing house in which we have grown with a rush like flowers in late spring following a terrible winter. And with what result? This: that we have outgrown our religion, outgrown our political system, outgrown our own strength of mind and character. The fatal word NOT has been miraculously inserted into all our creeds:

But what next? Is NO enough? For a boy, yes: for a man, never. Are we any the less obsessed with a belief when we are denying it than when we were affirming it? No: I must have affirmations to preach. Without them the young will not listen to me; for even the young grow tired of denials. The negative-monger falls before the soldiers, the men of action, the fighters, strong in the old uncompromising affirmations which give them status, duties, certainty of consequences; so that the pugnacious spirit of man in them can reach out and strike deathblows with steadfastly closed minds. Their way is straight and sure; but it is the way of death; and the preacher must preach the way of life. Oh, if I could only find it!

> *(A white sea fog swirls up from the beach to his feet, rising and thickening around him).*

I am ignorant: I have lost my nerve and am intimidated: all I know is that I must find the way of life, for myself and all of us, or we shall surely perish. And meanwhile my gift has possession of me: I must preach and preach and preach no matter how late the hour and how short the day, no matter whether I have nothing to say—

*(The fog has enveloped him; the gap with its grottoes is
lost to sight; the ponderous stones are wisps of shifting
white cloud; there is left only fog: impenetrable fog; but
the incorrigible preacher will not be denied his perora-
tion, which, could we only hear it distinctly, would
probably run—)*

—or whether in some Pentecostal flame of revelation the Spirit will
descend on me and inspire me with a message the sound whereof shall
go out unto all lands and realize for us at last the Kingdom and the
Power and the Glory for ever and ever. Amen.

K.C.B.: Knight Commander of the Bath, a knightly order established by George I
in 1725 **demirep**: short for demi-reputation, a fallen woman

GLOSSARY

Aphrodite: Greek mythology — goddess of love, daughter of Zeus

Apollo: Greek mythology — god of the sun, healing, music, prophecy, patron of the Oracle at Delphi, son of Zeus

Ares: Greek mythology — god of war, husband of Aphrodite

Argive: poetic epithet for Greek or Grecian

Artemis: Greek mythology — virgin goddess of the hunt, also identified with the Moon, twin sister of Apollo

Ate: Greek mythology — Avenger, goddess of rage and mischief, daughter of Eris (Strife) and Zeus; she personifies infatuation, with guilt its cause and evil its consequence

Athena Pallas: Greek mythology — a warrior goddess of Wisdom, the Arts and Sciences, daughter of Zeus, patroness of Athens

Bacchus: Roman equivalent of Dionysus

Charon: Greek mythology — with his boat, he takes the souls of the dead across the river Lethe/Styx to Hades

Cypris: see *Aphrodite*

Delphi: a town in northern Greece, site of the famous oracular shrine of Apollo (see *Pytho*)

Demeter: Greek mythology — goddess of agriculture, sister of Zeus, mother of Persephone

Dionysus: Greek mythology — god of wine, patron of drama in Athens, son of Zeus

Elysium: the equivalent of Heaven in Greek mythology

Erynyes: see *Furies*

Furies: Greek mythology — spirits of Divine Vengeance, especially transgressions that touch on the basis of human society. They punish violations of filial duty, the claims of kinship, rites of hospitality, murder, perjury, and the like; eventually reconciled by Athena to Athenian law

Hades: Greek mythology — god of the Underworld where the souls of the dead are kept, brother of Zeus; also used as a name for the Underworld

Hecate: Greek mythology — a confusing divinity, identified with the Moon, Artemis and Persephone, and invoked by sorcerers; she is the great sender of visions, of madness, and of sudden terror; Medea was her witch-priestess before falling in love with Jason

Helios: Apollo

Hera: Greek mythology — sister and wife of Zeus

Hermes: Greek mythology — messenger of the gods, guide of souls departing to Hades

Hymen: Greek mythology — god of marriage

Ilion: Troy

Ilium: Troy

Jove: see *Jupiter*

Jupiter: Roman mythology — chief deity (equivalent of Zeus)

Lethe: Greek mythology — the river in Hades from which the souls of the dead drank and became oblivious of their past lives; then they were carried across by Charon in his boat

Neptune: Roman mythology — god of the sea

Orpheus: Greek mythology — a Thracian philosopher, poet and musician, won permission by his music to bring his wife back to earth from Hades

Pallas: Athena

Persephone: Greek mythology — wife of Hades, queen of the underworld, daughter of Demeter

Phoebus: Apollo

Phrygian: of Phrygia, an ancient country in Asia Minor, one of whose cities was Troy

Pluto: Roman equivalent of Hades

Poseidon: Greek mythology — god of the sea, brother of Zeus and Hades

Pytho: ancient name for Delphi, Apollo's seat of prophecy, which was conducted by the prophetess Pythia (a girl or woman) seated on a tripod over the Oracle proper, which was a cleft in the ground in the innermost sanctuary from which rose cold vapors that had the power of inducing the ecstasy that gave rise to the priestess's prophetic vision. Her responses were ambiguous, but though always true, gave rise to misinterpretation.

Styx: see *Lethe*

Tartarus: Greek mythology — the infernal depths of Hades

Zeus: Greek mythology — chief of the gods, master of the lightning bolt